TECHNOLOGY,
DEVELOPMENT,
AND DEMOCRACY

SUNY series in Global Politics
James N. Rosenau, editor

*A complete listing of books in this series
can be found at the end of this volume.*

TECHNOLOGY, DEVELOPMENT, AND DEMOCRACY

International Conflict and Cooperation
in the Information Age

EDITED BY

Juliann Emmons Allison

STATE UNIVERSITY OF NEW YORK PRESS

Published by
State University of New York Press, Albany

© 2002 State University of New York

For information, address State University of New York Press,
90 State Street, Suite 700, Albany, NY 12207

Production by Cathleen Collins
Marketing by Michael Campochiaro

Library of Congress Cataloging in Publication Data

Technology, development, and democracy : international conflict and cooperation in
the information age / edited by Juliann Emmons Allison.
    p. cm. — (SUNY series in global politics)
    Includes bibliographical references and index.
    ISBN 0-7914-5213-1 (alk. paper) — ISBN 0-7914-5214-X (pbk. alk. paper)
    1. Information society. 2. Information society—Political aspects.
3. Globalization. I. Allison, Juliann Emmons, 1965- II. Series.

HM851.T45 2002
303.48'33—dc21

                            2001031123

10 9 8 7 6 5 4 3 2 1

Contents

Figures

Tables

Preface

*T*echnology, Development, and Democracy: International Conflict and Cooperation in the Information Age *originated one hot, humid summer afternoon just over five years ago in a discussion that I had with Glenn Oclassen, then a graduate student at Binghamton University, on the role of the Internet and other information technologies (ITs) in democratic development. Our conversation that day developed into a collaborative project on the impact of IT and the ongoing communications revolution on the solidification of an international security community of mostly democratic nation-states. The ensuing search for a literature that could provide a rich context for our research revealed a lack of theoretical and empirical scholarly development with respect to the very real connections among technology, advanced communications, political development, democratization, and the processes of international conflict and cooperation. This volume responds to that lacuna by bringing some of the most renowned scholars and newest voices in the fields of communications, comparative politics, and international relations together to comment on contemporary innovations in ITs as sources of change or continuity in international politics, and the relationship between IT and the incidence of conflict versus cooperation among nations.*

Acknowledgments

Many people have assisted me in completing this project. Foremost among them is Glenn Oclassen, who has long since moved out of academia and into the private sector where he is now Senior Director of Business Development for the e-learning company Headlight, Inc.. Glenn deserves credit especially for cultivating an interest in the project among publishers and making contact with seminal contributors, including Christopher Kedzie and Frank Webster. John LeMothe was also important to the formative stages of this project by providing valuable guidance with respect to the processes of academic publishing. Thanks are due as well to my friend and mentor, Sheldon Kamienecki, for his unerring advice on relating to contributors and generally managing the editing process as the project developed. I am also deeply indebted to Janni Aragon, who has grown during the course of this project from admittedly the best research assistant I've ever had, into a trusted friend and collaborator who has provided invaluable editorial assistance.

Of course, others have assisted at various stages in the project, including my colleagues at the University of California, Riverside—Shaun Bowler, Eric Davis, Andy Kydd, and Chris Laursen; friends and scholars in the fields of comparative politics, international relations, political theory, and research methods—Brooke Ackerley, Ann Florini, Jennifer Nagler, and John Pippen; and my research assistants—Jaron Lofquist, Miguel Pesantes, and Janni Aragon. I would also like to acknowledge a chance conversation with John Cioffi, then a graduate student at the University of California, Berkeley, who is knowledgeable not only about comparative judicial politics, but also about information markets. I thank the contributors to this volume, all of whom responded willingly, and often also promptly, to my own comments and suggestions as well as to those of an astute group of anonymous reviewers. Finally, I would like to note that I have received institutional support for this project from the University of California, Riverside, Academic Senate and College of Humanities, Arts, and Social Sciences.

This book is dedicated to my children, Quentin, Reiley, and Parker, whose births punctuated the course of this project, giving me time and reason to consider its deeper purpose: the promise of international cooperation and lasting peace rooted in coming to understand the underlying connectedness of all peoples.

PART ONE

Introduction

CHAPTER ONE

Information and International Politics

An Overview

JULIANN EMMONS ALLISON

> About the NATO thing, you know I feel they should come here and protect us. I wish somebody could. I don't even know how many people get killed anymore. You just see them in the memoriam pages of newspapers. I really don't want to end up raped, with no parts of body like the massacred ones.
> —E-mail from Adona, age 16[1]

> Today we have sunny and warm weather in Belgrade. . . . Last night's raid was civilized and decent—it all ended at midnight, so we could go to sleep in our beds, not in shelters. . . . But this very moment the sirens are going off.
> —E-mail from a man in Belgrade[2]

At the time of this writing, the civil war in Yugoslavia is already being touted as the first "cyberwar" (Pollock and Peterson 1999), or more accurately, *netwar*—the term Arquilla and Ronfeldt (1996) use to designate conflicts short of war that may involve civilians as well as military personnel. In this case, the civilian response to NATO bombing has included a Serbian electronic counterattack in the form of spam messages[3] to Western journalists, decision-makers, and economic leaders among others, particularly in the United States, in addition to the thousands of E-mail messages, most of them from grateful Kosovars, detailing life at ground zero.

The centrality of E-mail to the conduct of Yugoslavia's civil war only extends the growing role of the Internet—essentially a computer communications network with no hub, no switching station, and no governing authority—in international affairs, from a source of mostly officially sanctioned information, to a venue for the creation of knowledge steeped as much in political diatribe and innuendo as fact (MacFarquhar 1999). That is, the Internet not only provides erstwhile surfers with up-to-the-minute stories, including sound, pictures, and opportunities to interact with one another and with experts on a developing international crisis at conventional news sites, but also enables anyone with access to a computer, a modem, and a telephone line to influence international affairs directly.[4]

The Internet and related information technologies (ITs) have thus increased the capacity of individuals to generate and manipulate knowledge, and to communicate ideas and values quickly, irrespective of geographic distance. With 2.2 billion E-mail messages, compared to just 293 million pieces of first-class mail, each day, the United States has already, according to some observers, become an E-mail nation (Skarloff 1999). Arguably, this astounding increase in electronic communications has not only improved interpersonal relationships and deepened family values (Harrow 2000), but also empowered the general public to intrude upon national policy-making processes (Neuman 1996).

What does this mean for the future of international politics? The contributors to *Technology, Development, and Democracy. International Conflict and Cooperation in the Information Age* respond by providing a select range of theoretical perspectives and empirical analyses for understanding the impact of the communications revolution on international security, the world political economy, human rights, and gender relations. Despite differences in their approaches, each contributor addresses two key debates: (1) contemporary innovations in ITs as sources of change or continuity in international politics; and (2) the consequent incidence of conflict versus cooperation among nations. The resulting discussion suggests that ITs may hold no greater prospects for economic and political development than previous technological advances (Stover 1984). Yet the Internet and related ITs, arguably, *do* portend significant advances for democracy, the democratization process, and international peace.[5]

The remainder of this chapter is intended as an overview of the theoretical literature linking IT to both economic and political development and international peace, and as an orientation to the chapters contained in the volume. This overview is divided into two parts. The first part consists of a discussion of IT and change, which highlights the volume's theoretical contributions, particularly authors' comments on issues of the economic, social, political development of nations in the Third World. The second part of the chapter focuses on the theoretical relationship between ITs, interpersonal and international communications, and peace. Given this theoretical backdrop, the section develops contributors' empirical assessment of these arguments as a basis for claiming that, in general, there are clear reasons to expect that IT will foster significant, positive changes in international politics, including peace.

Information Technology and Change in International Politics

Technological advancement is commonly associated with economic growth and political development. This general relationship is particularly prevalent among development economists and regime theorists, the latter being International Relations scholars whose work suggests that technological change, in combination with the increasing economic interdependence that characterizes contemporary international politics, will both increase domestic demands for better standards of living, and overwhelm established patterns of international interaction. As a consequence of these simultaneous pressures on the domestic-international system, new international norms, organizations, and regimes will emerge. This "simple economic process model" would suggest that the impact of ITs would likely be the gradual adaptation of nations to new volumes and new forms of transnational economic activity (Keohane and Nye 2001, 35).

The Neutral Response

This logic is representative of *neutral* responses to the question: Will innovation in ITs, such as the Internet, serve as forces for change or continuity in international politics? The neutral approach is best represented in this volume by Steele and Stein, who concur with economists and others that the current communications revolution exists within political and economic structures that channel the flow of information (Keohane and Nye 2001; see also De Long 1998). Steele and Stein's review of the history of internationally significant technological changes, including steamships, railroads and automobiles, telegraphy, and radio and telephones is sufficient to demonstrate that ITs do not necessarily portend a new international politics in which high-tech communications "make of the entire globe, and of the human family, a single consciousness" (McLuhan 1964, 67). Steele and Stein argue, more specifically, that innovations in the tools we use to communicate, from telegraph (point-to-point communication) to broadcasting (one-to-many communication) and, finally, to the Internet (mixed point-to-point and one-to-many communications), have reflected and magnified, rather than driven, international politics, and will continue to do so.

This balanced view of international politics in the information age is often checked by those who discount earlier telegraph and broadcast technologies—including radio, television, and satellite—relative to the Internet, as the harbingers of revolutions in interpersonal and international communications.

Today's IT, which exits as a "combination of computers, satellites, telephones, radio, television, and other electronics information technology"
arguably "provides more effective and efficient interaction" now than any
single technological advance did previously (Stover 1984, 2). As the emblem
of this IT, the Internet facilitates the inexpensive and rapid processing and
transmitting of information. As a result, the significance of nation-states,
multinational corporations, and other large, bureaucratic organizations is
waning relative to that of individuals and the nongovernmental and "network" organizations so effective at penetrating national borders and mobi-
lizing domestic constituencies (Keohane and Nye 2001, 218). It is by so
vastly increasing the opportunities for communication among people and
cultures that IT is changing international politics (Frederick 1993; Keohane
and Nye 2001). According to Davis (1999);

> the ubiquity of computers and computer networks will produce a
> 100 millionfold increase in the information available world-wide
> compared with the precomputer era. That's a far greater information
> leap than the one that followed the invention of the printing press,
> and [ought] to have similarly revolutionary consequences. (R14)

The Positive Response

Arguably, the quantity, and often also quality, of information readily available
on-line both enables national and international leaders to make more informed
decisions, and empowers individuals and, by extension, groups within society
to influence national governments and international organizations and institutions more effectively. IT thereby engenders more representative governance.
Thus it would seem obvious that the ongoing communications revolution
must be a basis for unprecedented *positive* change in the processes and outcomes of international politics. And indeed, a rich and diverse body of literature on the sources of international cooperation suggests that IT is likely to
facilitate more pacific international relations by (1) increasing the amount of
contact among individuals and nations (Stein 1993); (2) improving the quality of interpersonal and diplomatic communication (see, e.g., Holsti 1977);
(3) extending economic interdependence (see most recently Gowa 1999);
and (4) deepening the democratic processes that permit the pacific inclina-
tions of individual citizens to influence their nations' strategic decisions (see
Weart 1998 for a recent review of this literature).

Steele and Stein (in this volume) provide a general discussion of the arguments just summarized, while other contributors provide more specific, theoretical arguments in favor of IT as a positive force in international relations.
Foremost among these is Rosenau and Johnson's postinternational analysis of

the impact of IT on international politics. Rosenau and Johnson emphasize the role of the Internet and related technologies in the widespread mobilization of subnational groups demanding recognition, status, and some degree of independence from the nation-states to which they were once loyal (Rosenau 1990). Perhaps the most important consequence of this transformation in international politics is the breakdown of the nation-state—in some issue areas, such as environmental protection and human rights—accompanied by more interactions and much higher levels of communication among individuals and groups. Rosenau and Johnson thus argue that the greatest change associated with the communications revolution is occurring in the development of individuals' technological skills and imaginations. It follows that IT may be associated with wide-scale improvements in international politics insofar as individuals and groups use the information and technologies available to them to integrate and organize themselves to demand more just social, political, and economic governing institutions.

Rosenau and Johnson's perspective is representative of more generally pluralist arguments that IT is reshaping international politics in fundamentally positive ways. Pluralist examinations of the impact of IT on international organizing recognize that the myriad foreign policy decisions that constitute international politics are increasingly made under the auspices of international institutions, or under the influence of intergovernmental and nongovernmental organizations (IGOs and NGOs) and multinational corporations (MNCs). Such nonstate entities exist, in part, to bring greater awareness and consideration of specific issues—for instance, human rights (see Richards, in this volume) or the natural environment (see O'Gorman 2000 and Schubert 2000)—to the practices of international institutions, IGOs, and MNCs. It follows that the Internet and other technological means of increasing communication, by enhancing democratic decision making, facilitates organizing among activists at the international and the national, levels.[6] Notably unlike Rosenau and Johnson's approach in this volume, straightforwardly pluralist scholarship does not usually suggest that the resulting democratization of international politics (see Dougherty and Pfaltzgraff 2001) will naturally contribute to the erosion of the nation-state (Evans 1997).

In addition to the postinternational and pluralist approaches already discussed, liberal responses to the impact of IT on international politics— represented by Kedzie, Baum, and Richards, in this volume—are also overwhelmingly positive. In keeping with classical liberalism, Kedzie, Baum, and Richards do regard the individual as theoretically foundational; however, their specific arguments reflect more contemporary liberal emphases on (1) democratic, as opposed to authoritarian, forms of government; (2) international peace rather than conflict; and (3) economic interdependence, cooperation, and free trade over protection. This orientation is reflected most directly in Kedzie's argument that IT is a significant determinant of democratization, while Baum and Richards each address particular instances of how exactly IT impacts the democratic processes of nation-states. More specifically, Baum explains how IT increases public attentiveness to foreign crises and thereby constrains presidential crisis decision making. Richards presents his argument that although IT does not directly improve nations' human rights records, it might nonetheless have such an effect as a basis for democratization.[7]

The Critical Response

In a 1999 essay entitled "Putting People First in the Information Age," then U.S. vice president Albert Gore suggested that "We should not view . . . IT as an end itself, but as a tool that we can use to create economic opportunity, improve our quality of life, and advance our most basic values" (9). This statement reiterates the importance that positive views on the relationship between IT and international politics place on individuals—both alone and collectively. At the same time, it begs the question posed by many *critics* of the information age: What is the capacity of the innovations of IT to empower the least advantaged people within national societies, and the most poorly endowed members of the international community? In other words, the Internet and other advanced technologies may be conceptualized simply as tokens of this latest stage in a long history of progress in the creation and dissemination of knowledge. As such, IT may be unlikely to impact (domestic and/or) international politics without ensuring broader access to it (Luke 1989).

In much of the industrialized West, of course, where telephone lines are standard and children learn to use computers in school, access to the Internet and other ITs is a matter of the ability to purchase a computer. Currently, the falling price of low-end, Internet-ready computers ensures the near ubiquity of the computer in American homes.[8] Moreover, even though computer prices are higher in Europe and elsewhere in the world, the number of Internet users worldwide has increased phenomenally in recent years—to an estimated 147 million. Not surprisingly, half of these users are American (Horwitt 1999, Paquet 1999). Not all of the remainder are Western, though, and it is these people, many of whom live in the nations comprising the Third World that arguably should concern us. Citizens of, and others living in, these developing and often impoverished nations must overcome not only poverty, but also relatively few years of education, low levels of telephone and computer penetration, a primitive network infrastructure—for example, network access lines, Web software and Internet services—and, increasingly, heavy government censorship.[9]

Such concerns regarding the limited access of the class of less-skilled individuals internationally to burgeoning information technologies relative to that of the highly skilled, who reside primarily in the industrialized, and more importantly, capitalist, West, underlies Webster's Marxist critique of the role of IT in international politics (in this volume).[10] According to his class analysis, the Internet and the phenomenon of globalization, more generally, do represent significant changes in the sheer of volume of information available and the speed with which it may be disseminated. Yet precisely because the "Internet, cable television services, portable PCs . . . [so] facilitate and affect how we analyze situations and stay in touch with one other" (80), it is difficult to judge the impact of this change. If the skills required to take advantage of the Internet's promise accrue only to some subset of people, and this is the same group that has always exploited technological innovations, then we should expect, by extension, little change in international political processes and outcomes. Thus, Webster argues that significant change at the level of international politics will require modification of nations' educational systems and other means for preparing young people for high-skilled employment, which will alter the composition and characteristics of the labor force, and so also national politics and foreign policy.

Mazrui and Ostergard's chapter (in this volume) likewise recognizes Marxist concerns that whoever controls the international economic system, which is dominated by the United States and by other Western industrialized nations with a comparative advantage in IT, also controls the world's political systems (Poster 1999). It also more directly complements Webster's chapter by emphasizing the important role education plays in teaching individual members of a society to use computers, the Internet, and other technological keys to capitalizing on the communications revolution. Mazrui and Ostergard, however, are overall more optimistic with respect to education's capacity to restructure labor relations and other aspects of African societies, in particular, in the interest of modernizing in a manner that is culturally independent of the West.[11] They even go so far as to suggest that if managed well, the ongoing diffusion of the information technologies could catalyze a redistribution of international power, perhaps enabling African nations to avoid imitating the West in their collective bid to "catch up." Not that this transformation will be easy. Despite the environmental and other social movements that often herald national reorientations to the international community, most Africans have limited access to radio and television, not to mention the Internet, as the reigning technologies of mass organization. As a result, African governments have been able to integrate the computer and Internet use, but far less successful in finally closing the gap between North and South (Bellman, Tindimubona; and Arias 1993; Cambridge et al. 1996, 48).

In addition to these Marxist analyses, this volume includes a straight-forwardly critical analysis of the relationship between IT and international relations. According to Stienstra (in this volume, 190) critical international relations theory examines the inequalities that exist in international politics in an effort to understand why specific institutions and practices are developed, and for whose benefit they continue to exist. She uses this point of view to argue, in particular, that the Internet embodies not only domestic, but also international, power relations. That is, the institutions and practices of international relations that define and regulate the Internet have developed in response to underlying power relations, which have yet to change (see also Ebo 1998). Consequently, we cannot expect the Internet to provide a venue for equal participation.

International Conflict and Cooperation

Evaluating the impact that IT has had, and is having, on international conflict and cooperation represents what is perhaps *the* way we understand how the communications revolution might transform international politics.[12] The review of approaches to understanding the relationship between IT and international politics provided in the first part of this chapter suggests that the Internet and related ITs are most likely to modify the potential for conflict, or cooperation, rather than to cause either of these phenomena to occur. Indeed, Steele and Stein's review of the international political history of communications (in this volume) suggests convincingly that IT is most likely to "parallel and amplify trends in international relations." They continue to point out, though, that because the current communications revolution is occurring during a period,

> free of major conflict between the great powers . . . a revolution in the nature of relationships among [them] may very well be occurring. But it is not being driven by changes in communications technology. Other recent changes in the international system have increased the incentives for states to choose more pacific strategies. (43)

It is, therefore, important to consider the establishment of the national information infrastructures and corresponding international institutions that manage and coordinate the transnational flow of messages and diplomatic communiqués that undergird instances of both international cooperation and international conflict.

Of course, the role of ITs in matters of war and peace far exceeds the prospect of E-mail from the front lines directly to the folks back home (Arquilla and Rondfelt 1996; Drogin 1999). It also includes, at least (1) the education of populations and leaders that enables nations to make better, even more peaceful, decisions; (2) the transmission of often classified information among national leaders and on the battlefield; and (3) advanced espionage (Drogin 1999; Steele and Stein, in this volume). In addition, it is reasonable to suggest that some—perhaps, less-developed—nations might use the international community's desire to secure electronic communications as leverage to gain access to information and ITs as the price for their cooperation.[13]

International cooperation in this information and technology penetrated era might then be fairly related to increasingly high levels of interdependence and more strident popular demands for greater quality of life. In the West, such demands have included increasing pressure for government deregulation of telephone, commercial television, cable, satellite and Internet services. They have yielded local, national, and international societies that are becoming more and more heavily networked. In other words, the citizens of civil societies—consisting of myriad associations, such as churches and synagogues, schools, labor unions, business and other professional organizations, and volunteers and interest groups—are increasingly able "to reduce their isolation, build far-flung networks within and across national boundaries, and connect and coordinate for collective action" (Arquilla and Ronfeldt 1996, 23).

The nature of, and potential for, conflict under these conditions are the bases for studies of netwar. The expectation is that netwars will be relatively easy to initiate and wage. Participants will be able to build and maintain complex networks at some distance from the front, to move openly and covertly across practically inconsequential territorial borders, and to play on shifting identities and loyalties. Yet it is also possible that citizen-based networks could yield a major new "global peace and disarmament movement" (Arquilla and Ronfeldt 1996, 46, 76; see also Keohane and Nye 1998 and Steele and Stein, in this volume).

Information Technologies and the "Democratic Peace"

Recognizing that international conflict may thus be attributed just as easily as international cooperation to innovations in IT, a select number of scholars have shifted their attention to how nations manage information to achieve specific domestic and international goals. Of course, there are a multiplicity of possible relationships between nations' political and socioeconomic systems on the one hand, and their use of raw information and the regulation of information flows on the other. The most pronounced among these is the general expectation that the compromise-based patterns of conflict resolution key to effective democratic government is a potent basis for arguing that information technologies are indeed likely to foster not only international cooperation, but also peace (Allison and Oclassen 1996; Keohane and Nye 1998; Splichal and Wasko 1993). Kedzie (in this volume) suggests outright that increased international communication, manifest primarily in the Internet, is a boon to democratization and, by extension, peace.

Kedzie's argument builds on a growing body of evidence in support of the "democratic peace," in reference to the observed absence of war between democracies. This empirical finding arguably buttresses Immanuel Kant's prescription for perpetual peace (Reiss 1970). According to contemporary interpretations of Kant's treatise, it is representative government, together with the legal equality of all citizens and a private property, market-oriented economy, which supports individuals' rational opposition to the costs of war as a domestic constraint on the use of force (most recently, Bueno de Mesquita and Lalman 1992; Chan 1993; Dixon 1994; Gowa 1999; Maoz and Russett 1993; Morgan 1993; Ray 1993; and Russett 1993). A derivative democratic institutions argument suggests that "open" domestic institutions make it difficult for the leaders of democracies to gain the widespread support necessary for war (Gowa 1999; Russett 1993). The alternative democratic culture argument suggests instead that leaders of democracies share democratic norms that facilitate mutual accommodation in the avoidance of all but the most restrained conflict (Gowa 1999; Russett 1993; Weart 1998). The establishment of a community of nation-states that share an interest in honoring the ultimate right of its members to protect their citizens' individual liberties, and ensuring conditions of "universal hospitality" among them, creates an additional, international impediment to war (see Gowa 1999 and Reiss 1970).

Kedzie's theoretical contribution to this now predominantly empirical discussion lies in his recognition of the inherent relationship between IT and the practically axiomatic absence of war between democracies. As a result of the ongoing communications revolution, governments have generally become increasingly unable to maintain exclusive power over politics. Likewise, individual citizens have become increasingly free to exchange ideas as well as goods internationally and domestically, thereby facilitating the widespread diffusion of the technologies, ideologies, and behavioral norms considered necessary for a democratic peace.[14] Briefly, the reigning argument is that the importance of communication to democratic political culture and institutions supports the expectation that democracies will strive to develop and sustain similar, intensely communicative international relationships. To the extent that the leaders and citizens of democratic nations achieve communicative successes internally, especially with respect to those methods necessary for policy-making effectiveness and electoral success, they will seek open and reliable means of communication internationally as well (see Pye

1963 and Weart 1998). It follows that, because such communication enables international commerce and collective security (Deutsch et al., 1957; Stopford and Strange 1991), we should expect peace, rather than war, among the world's democracies.

Democracy in the Information Age

> Can democracy, a form of government born in the ancient
> world and designed to bring small numbers of individuals
> with consensual interests together into a self-governing
> community where they might govern themselves directly,
> survive the conditions of modern mass society?
>
> —Benjamin Barber; "Three Scenarios for the
> Future of Technology and Strong Democracy"

The foregoing discussion of the theoretical and practical relationship between the increased communication associated with the Internet and, more generally, the diffusion of ITs begs the question of whether or not IT actually improves communications and so also democracy. Or, alternatively, does IT foster public participation in the political process, particularly popular involvement in the deliberative processes that are needed for true democracy? As is typical of the most accurate response to complex questions, there is no entirely right answer:

> [the] scientistic wisdom suggests that science and technology, by opening up society and creating a market of ideas, foster more open politics. . . . Yet technology coexisted with tyrannical government in Nazi Germany, and was made to expedite the liquidation of the Jews in a fashion that suggests its utility in rendering dictatorship more efficient. (Barber 1998, 1)

According to Barber, however, there are three "prospects" for the future of democracy and technology. What Barber refers to as the "Pangloss" possibility would be the outcome of a complacent projection of current attitudes and trends. That is;

> for all of its technological potential for diversification, the domination of these new technologies by the market . . . assures that to a growing degree, the profit-making entertainment industry in the Anglo-American world will control what is seen, felt, and thought about around the globe. (Barber 1998, 4; see also Resnick 1997)

The "Pandora" alternative would instead be tempered by caution in light of the worst case scenario—that of a dangerous technological determinism of "supercorporations" and "government monopolies" (Barber 1998, 5). Finally, Barber's "Jeffersonian" prospect is a hopeful one, which would discover and implement affirmative uses of IT in the interest of fostering democracy. Yet it is one requiring that

> citizen groups and governments take action in adapting the new technology to their needs . . . [information] technologies can challenge passivity, they can enhance information equality, they can overcome sectarianism and prejudice, and they can facilitate participation in deliberative political processes. (Barber 1998, 6; see also Roper 1997)

Barber argues that actions of this kind would enable contemporary democratic governments to overcome the tyranny of opinion in the greater interest of "rational discourse and citizen education" (1998, 7). Baum (in this volume) effectively argues, in a manner consistent with this position, that the impact of IT on international war will ultimately occur in the area of foreign policy making. More specifically, the results of his examination of competing arguments regarding exactly how the public constrains democratically elected leaders suggests that the sheer amount of information now easily available to Americans has increased their attentiveness to foreign policy, and prompted the kind of popular oversight that could limit the president's use of force. Thus, according to Baum (in this volume, 132), was President Bush constrained to conduct a quick and bloodless war in the Persian Gulf (see also Gottschalk 1988)?

Empirical studies such as Baum's clearly do support the potentially positive role of IT—refering, in this case, to the mass media—in the foreign policy making of democratic nations. Yet it is still possible to argue that when IT is understood to mean the Internet, it is inherently antithetical to the kind of popular discourse that is typically associated with established democratic processes. Democratic forms of government are, for instance, expected to engage "most" of the adult population (see Weart 1998), but the Internet can involve exchanges among only a relatively small number of people in a given nation. Moreover, democratic communication is supposed to be reflective (Flammang 1997; Young 1996), while discussions on-line are characteristically rapid and urgent. Finally, democracy should foster meaningful interaction, something the cacophony associated with the Internet might easily inhibit (Garson 1995). Such concerns prompt investigations—including, in this volume, chapters by Stienstra and Richards—into how the Internet is used, and to what effect.

Stienstra, for instance, anticipates significantly more discord as women take their inherently counter hegemonic movement on-line. That is, women may be able to disguise their gender on-line, but this potential is not rightly regarded as a basis for expecting fewer disparities in gender relationships off-line (Poster 1999; see also Sampaio and Aragon 1997). This observation problematizes the question of how the Internet fosters women's organizing, shifting attention from how women represent themselves on-line to how they organize off-line, particularly in the Third World. In other words, "information technology issues are enmeshed in an ecology of interest group trade-offs, conflict, competition, and compromise" (Garson 1995, 39).

Richards, alternatively, begins a discussion that speaks directly to the relationship among IT, democracy, and violence by pointing out that those who are mostly in need of the Internet and other ITs as a democratic aid, typically have the least access to it, and are therefore practically unable to influence either national governments or international institutions. Richards's specific point of reference here is human rights. In this case, he sadly reports his finding that although the world may seem smaller as a result of IT, and its inhabitants consequently more familiar with one another, the violation of individual citizens' human rights by national governments continues, except in democratic nations. Therein lies reason for optimism.

IT and Choosing Peace

Richards's analysis portends optimism with respect to the relationship between IT and international cooperation because it suggests that enhanced communication under conditions of political openness yields reductions in violence at a very primitive level: the individual citizen and those who govern him or her. Considering any lasting international peace will, ultimately, require the abolition of all forms of violence—that is, not only that which occurs between nation-states, but also that which is inflicted upon individual citizens at the hands of their governments (Forcey 1991; Rock 1989)—this conclusion is particularly heartening. Moreover, it provides a conceptual focal point for the contributions to this volume as a whole. Whether or not the communications revolution yields international cooperation and peace amounts to choice. Average citizens as well as national leaders must *choose* to use IT to coordinate and voice coherent and unceasing demands for both more extensive political participation, and more equitable enjoyment of physical and emotional health, economic well-being, and full self-expression.

A Culture of Peace

Peace understood as a "special and more stable condition [of peace] in which the threat itself of conflict is effectively lacking" (Rock 1989, 2) is said to evolve (Modelski 1990; see also Boyd and Richerson 1985 and Jantz 1980). Theories of cultural evolution, in particular, suggest that individuals possess the capacity to respond to the international community as well as to their more immediate national and/or local communities, and thereby affect changes in them (Boyd and Richerson 1985; Habermas 1972). Human evolution depends, more specifically, on the inheritance of cultural as well as genetic information. People grow and develop in social situations that enable them to learn, or to inherit, nongenetic information, such as dietary preferences and social mores, that they then can pass onto other members of a given society (Boyd and Richerson 1985). In a more technical sense, humans' metabolic processes enable them to create their world, and to communicate it via demonstration, emulation, and other forms of social learning, rather than genetically (Jantz 1980, 174–177; see also Chopra 1992).

Culture is thus the collective outcome of individuals' reactions to the world around them, and their attempts to envision and then develop alternative social orders. Whether or not a culture of peace eventually characterizes the international community must then be a function of what the individual citizens of still disparate and statutory sovereign nations know, and how they come to know what they know. Thus the significance of the current communications revolution for international politics, according to the contributors to this volume, is obvious: within given limits to access and institutionalized barriers to use, IT will spur political participation, deepen democracy, and foster international peace.[15]

Notes

1. CNN In-Depth Reports (1999) contains reports and ongoing E-mail conversations between Finnegan Hamill, a Berkeley high school student and Adona, one of Kosovo's ethnic Albanians.

2. CNN Interactive (1999).

3. "Spam" refers to E-mail messages sent nearly indiscriminately by list to hundreds or thousands of addresses at once.

4. In contrast to the immediate and heavy use of E-mail in the Yugoslavian case, millions of people hit news Websites within minutes of the 5:00 P.M. announcement on December 16, 1998 that the United States and Britain had begun to bomb Iraq; 500 reportedly streamed into chat rooms at CNN's site, where traffic ultimately peaked at 475,000 hits per minute (Kornblum 1998). See also Hu (1999).

5. The general argument is summarized in Allison and Oclassen (1996) and developed more fully in this volume by Kedzie, Richards, and Baum.

6. "Democratic" refers to political decision making that is open to significant levels of public participation and deliberation. That said, and despite

a common tendency to conflate traditional "participatory" democracy with the more recently explicated "deliberative" democracy, note that the former advocates active participation in the democratic political process, while the latter instead emphasizes the design of political institutions and decision-making practices intended to encourage discussion in which all "reasonable" viewpoints are heard (I thank Brooke Ackerley for this clarification).

7. Note that because the contributions by all three of these authors bear on this larger relationship among IT, democracy, and international conflict and cooperation, they are treated more thoroughly in the second part of this chapter.

8. Computer production currently serves two markets: a high end catering to professionals and enthusiasts, and a low end including "everyone else" (Crothers 1999). Low end personal computers may now be purchased for as little as $299, which includes free Internet service for a year as well as system and word-processing software (Kanellos 1999).

9. Horwitt (1999). Consider also Keohane and Nye's argument that the theoretical and practical centrality of the territorial nation-state will survive the revolution in personal communications, in part because "three quarters of the world's population does not own a telephone, much less a modem and computer (Keohane and Nye 1998, 82).

10. See Dougherty and Pfaltzgraff for a concise, up-to-date distinction between classical Marxism—as "an admixture of metaphysics (dialectical materialism), theory of history (economic determinism), economic and social science, political ideology, theory and strategy of revolution, social ethics, and an eschatological moral theology that looks toward secular salvation: the advent of a classless social order of perfect justice, in which conflict ceases and the psychology of a new human being is generated" (Dougherty and Pfaltzgraff 2001, 428)—and contemporary Marxist thought on the legacy of colonialism with respect to the economic, social, and political development of the Third World.

11. Mazrui and Ostergard in this volume define "development" as "modernization minus dependency," and furthermore associate that process with efforts to become more secular, more technologically sophisticated, and more oriented toward the future.

12. This lead-in reflects the centrality of the conflict-cooperation continuum to the academic study of international relations.

13. See, for instance, Mofson (1997), which provides evidence of just this sort of generally strategic behavior on the part of Zimbabwe as a party to the Convention on Trade in Endangered Species (CITES).

14. Huntley (1997). In contrast to those who naively examine the exchange of information and ITs in "the market," De Long argues that "information goods," including specific ITs, have the potential to "defy the

very principle of scarcity and control over commodities that has convinced economists that the market is the single, best system for directing the production and distribution of goods and services" (De Long 1998, 14).

15. This qualified liberal conclusion is intended to capture the concern that in a given nation at a given time in history, the politico-social context in which individuals' technologically assisted interactions occur may well limit the diversity and equality actually experienced via on-line communication (Streck 1997; see Hassner [1997] for a related argument).

References

Allison, Juliann and Glenn A. Oclassen. 1996. "Peace, War and the Internet: Is the "Information Highway" a Force for International Peace?" Paper presented at the annual meeting of the International Studies Association, San Diego, CA, 21–24 April.

Arquilla, John and David Ronfeldt. 1996. *The Advent of Netwar*. Santa Monica: RAND Corporation.

Barber, Benjamin R. 1998. "Three Scenarios for the Future of Technology and Strong Democracy." *Political Science Quarterly* 114 (Winter): 573. URL: http://128.48.120.7/mw/mwcgi?sesid=3927314170&zsl.llcm&cs cs=1&cdisplay(1,11on.txt,abbrev)

Bellman, Beryl, Alex Tindimubona, and Armando Arias Jr. 1993. "Technology Transfer in Global Networking: Capacity Building in Africa and Latin America." *Global Networks: Computers and International Communication*. Ed. Linda M. Harasim, pp. 237–254.

Boyd, Robert and Peter J. Richerson. 1985. *Culture and the Evolutionary Process*. Chicago: University of Chicago Press.

Bueno de Mesquita, Bruce and David Lalman. 1992. *War and Reason: Domestic and International Imperatives*. New Haven: Yale University Press.

Cambridge, Vibert C., James Phillip Jeter, Kuldip R. Rampal; and Cornelius B. Pratt. 1996. *International Afro Mass Media: A Reference Guide*. Westport, CT: Greenwood Press.

Chan, Steve. 1993. "Democracy and War: Some Thoughts on the Future Research Agenda." *International Interactions* 18: 205–213.

Chopra, Deepak. 1992. *Unconditional Life: Discovering the Power to Fulfill Your Dreams*. New York: Bantam.

CNN In-Depth Reports-Conflict in Kosovo. 1999. "E-mails from Kosovo, Part I." URL: http://www.cnn.com/SPECIALS/1998/10/kosovo/email/a-rchive.html.

CNN Interactive. 1999. "Kosovo: The Message Always Gets Through." URL: http://cnn.com/.

Crothers, Brooke. 1999. "Low-cost PCs Forge New Mainstream." CNET News.com's "Personal Technology." 21 January: 1–3. URL: http://www.news.com/News/Item/0,4,31202,00.html.

Davis, Bob. 1999. "Think Big: What Is the Greatest Technological Innovation of the Past 1,000 Years?" *Wall Street Journal,* 11 January.

De Long, Bradford. 1998. "What 'New' Economy?: New Technologies Do Not Necessarily Equate to a New Economy." *Wilson Quarterly* 22: 14–26.

Deutsch, Karl W., Sidney A. Burrell, Robert A. Kann, Maurice Lee Jr., Martin Lichterman, Raymond E. Lindgren, Francis L. Loewenheim, and Richard W. Van Wagenen. 1957. *Political Community in the North Atlantic Area: International Organization in the Light of Historical Experience.* Princeton: Princeton University Press.

Dixon, William J. 1994. Democracy and the Peaceful Settlement of International Conflict." *American Political Science Review* 88: 14–32.

Dougherty, James E. and Robert L. Pfaltzgraff Jr. 2001. *Contending Theories of International Relations: A Comprehensive Survey.* New York: Addison Wesley Longman.

Drogin, Bob. 1999. "On the Internet, Anybody Can Be in the Spy Game." *Los Angeles Times,* 16 May.

Ebo, Bosah. 1998. "Internet or Outernet?" *Cyberghetto or Cybertopia? Race, Class and Gender on the Internet.* Ed. Ebo Bosah, pp. 1–12. Westport, CT: Praeger.

Evans, Peter. 1997. "The Eclipse of the State? Reflections on Stateness in an Era of Globalization." *World Politics* 50: 62–87.

Flammang, Janet A. 1997. *Women's Political Voice: How Women Are Transforming the Practice and Study of Politics.* Philadelphia: Temple University Press.

Forcey, Linda Rennie. 1991. "Women as Peacemakers," *Peace and Change* 16 (October): 331–354.

Frederick, Howard H. 1993. *Global Communication and International Relations.* San Diego: Harcourt.

Garson, G. David. 1995. *Computer Technology and Social Issues.* New York: Idea Group.

Gore, Albert. 1999. "Putting People First in the Information Age." *Masters of the Wired World: Cyberspace Speaks Out.* Ed. Anne Leer, pp. 7–17. London: Pitman Publishing.

Gottschalk, Marie. 1988. "Operation Desert Cloud: The Media and the Gulf War." *Readings in the Politics of American Foreign Policy.* Ed. Jerel A. Rosati, pp. 517–541. Fort Worth: Harcourt.

Gowa, Joanne. 1999. *Ballots and Bullets: The Elusive Democratic Peace.* Princeton: Princeton University Press.

Habermas, Jürgen. 1976. *Communication and the Evolution of Society*. Boston: Beacon.

Harrow, Jeffrey R. 2000. "Don't Think You'll Need the Wireless Web? Think Again" Tech Web News, 18 August. URL: http://www.techweb.com/

Hassner, Pierre. 1997. "Rousseau and the Theory and Practice of International Relations." *The Legacy of Rousseau*. Eds. Clifford Owen and Nathan Tarcov, pp. 200–219. Chicago: University of Chicago Press.

Holsti, K. J. 1977. *International Politics: A Framework for Analysis*, 3rd ed. Englewood Cliffs, NJ: Prentice-Hall.

Horwitt, Elisabeth. 1999. "Global Warming to the 'Net." CNN.com and IDG.com: 1–3.

Hu, Jim. 1999. "News on Portals Drawing Larger Audiences." CNET News.com. 8 December: 1. URL: http://www.news.com/News/Item/Textonly/o,25,29679,00lhtml.

Huntley, Wade L. 1997. "An Unlikely Match? Kant and Feminism in IR Theory." *Millennium* 26: 279–320.

Huth, Paul. 1999. "Another Study of Democracy and International Conflict? Typescript.

Jantz, Erich. 1980. *The Self-Organizing Universe*. New York: Pergamon Press.

Kanellos, Michael. 1999, "PCs Nearly Free, but Questions Loom." URL: http://www.news.com/News/Item/0%2C4%2C33771%2C00.html?sa s.mail 15 March: 1–2. Jantz 1980.

Keohane, Robert O. and Joseph S. Nye Jr. 1998. "Power and Interdependence in the Information Age." *Foreign Affairs* 77 (September/October): 81–94.

Keohane, Robert O. and Joseph S. Nye. 2001. *Power and Interdependence*, 3rd ed. New York: Addison Wesley Longman.

Kornblum, Janet. 1998. "Iraq Air Strikes Consume Net News Sites." URL: http://www.news.com/News/Item/0%2C4%2C30030%2C00.html?s as.mail.

Luke, Timothy. 1989. *Screens of Power: Ideology, Domination, and Resistance in Informational Society*. Chicago: University of Illinois Press.

MacFarquhar, Neil. 1999. "For the First Time in War, E-Mail Plays a Vital Role." *New York Times*. 29 March.

MacMillan, John. 1998. "'The Power of the Pen': Liberalism." *Millennium* 27: 643–668.

Maoz, Zeev and Bruce Russett. 1993. "Normative and Structural Causes of Democratic Peace, 1946–1986." *American Political Science Review* 87: 624–638.

McLuhan, Marshall. 1964. *Understanding Media: The Extensions of Man*. New York: New American Library.

Modelski, George. 1990. "Is World Politics Evolutionary Learning?" *International Organization* 44: 1–24.

Mofson, Phyllis. 1997. "Zimbabwe and CITES: Illustrating the Reciprocal Relationship between the State and the International Regime." *The Internationalization of Environmental Protection*. Eds. Miranda A. Schreurs and Elizabeth Economy, pp. 162–187. Cambridge: Cambridge University Press.

Morgan, T. Clifton. 1993. "Democracy and War: Reflections on the Literature." *International Interactions* 18: 197–203.

Neuman, Johanna. 1996. *Lights, Camera, War*. New York: St. Martin's.

O'Gorman, Mark J. 2000. "Email and NIMBY: The Boon or Boondoggle of Environmental Technology." Typescript.

Paquet, Cheri. 1999. "Report Counts 147 Million Global Net Users." CNN.com 12 February: 1–2.

Pollock, Ellen Joan and Andrea Petersen. 1999. "Serbs Take Offensive In the First Cyberwar, Bombing America." *Wall Street Journal*, 8 April.

Poster, Mark. 1999. "Cyberdemocracy: The Internet and the Public Sphere." *Masters of the Wired World: Cyberspeak Speaks Out*. Ed. Anne Leer, pp. 212–228. London: Pitman Publishing.

Pye, Lucian W. 1963. *Communications and Political Development*. Princeton: Princeton University Press.

Ray, James Lee. 1993. Wars between Democracies: Rare, or Nonexistent?" *International Interactions* 18: 251–276.

Reiss, Hans. 1970. "A Perpetual Peace: A Philosophical Sketch." *Kant's Political Writings*. Trans. H. B. Nisbet, pp. 93–130. Cambridge: Cambridge University Press.

Resnick, David. 1997. "Politics on the Internet: The Normalization of Cyberspace." *New Political Science* 41–42: 47–68.

Rock, Stephen. 1989. *Why Peace Breaks Out: Great Power Rapprochement in Historical Perspective*. Chapel Hill: University of North Carolina Press.

Roper, Juliet. 1997. "New Zealand Political Parties On-line: the WWW as a Tool for Democratization or Political Marketing." *New Political Science* 41–42: 69–84.

Rosenau, James N. 1990. *Turbulence in World Politics: A Theory of Change and Continuity*. Princeton: Princeton University Press.

Russ, Mitchell. 1999. "Why Big Pipes Rock." *U.S. News and World Report* 1 February: 40–41.

Russett, Bruce. 1993. *Grasping the Democratic Peace: Principles for a Post-Cold War World*. Princeton: Princeton University Press.

Stein, Arthur A. 1993. "Governments, Economic Interdependence, and International Cooperation." *Behavior, Society, and International Conflict*.

eds. Philip E. Tetlock, Jo L. Husbands, Robert Jervis, Paul C. Stern, and Charles Tilly, pp. 241–324. New York: Oxford University Press, for the National Research Council of the National Academy of Sciences.

Stover, William James. 1984. *Information Technology in the Third World: Can it Lead to Humane National Development?* Boulder: Westview Press.

Sampaio, Anna and Janni Aragon. 1997. "To Boldly Go (Where No Man Has Gone Before): Women and Politics in Cyberspace." *New Political Science* 41–42: 145–168.

Schubert, Louis. 2000. "The Internet and Environmental Organizing: The Prospect for On-line Democracy." Typescript.

Skarloff, Sara. 1999 "E-mail: Americans Are Connecting On-line Like Never Before and It's Changing the Way we Live, Work and Love." *U.S. News and World Report,* 22 March: 54–62.

Splichal, Slavko and Wasko, Janet. 1993. *Communication and Democracy.* Norwood, CT: Ablex Publishing Corporation.

Stopford, John and Susan Strange. 1991. *Rival States, Rival Firms.* Cambridge: Cambridge University Press.

John Streck. 1997. "Pulling the Plug on Electric Town Meetings: Participatory Democracy and the Reality of the Usenet." *New Political Science* 41–42: 17–46.

Weart, Spencer R. 1998. *Never at War: Why Democracies Will Not Fight One Another.* New Haven: Yale University Press.

Young, Iris Marion, 1996. Difference as a Resource for Democratic Communication. Toronto: Faculty of Law, University of Toronto.

PART TWO

Contending Perspectives

CHAPTER TWO

Communications Revolutions and International Relations

CHERIE STEELE AND ARTHUR STEIN

> Nobody who has paid any attention to the peculiar features
> of our present era will doubt for a moment that we are liv-
> ing at a period of [a] most wonderful transition, which
> tends rapidly to accomplish the great end to which all his-
> tory points the realisation of the unity of mankind. . . . The
> distances which separated the different nations and parts of
> the globe are rapidly vanishing before the achievements of
> modern invention, and we can traverse them with incredible
> ease. . . .
> —The Prince Consort, March 1850

A communications revolution is underway.

Without the vast increase in the power of computers, computer
software, satellites, fiber-optics cables, and high-speed electronic
transfers, markets could not act as one, and economic and other
information—politics, ideas, culture, revolutions, consumer trends—
could not be delivered instantaneously to the more than 200,000
monitors connected into this global communications system. (Kennedy 1993, 50–51)

The personal computer and the internet will, we are told, transform economic, social, and political life, including international relations, by creating
new forms of community and interaction not yet imaginable.[1] "This new civilization, as it challenges the old, will topple bureaucracies, reduce the role of
the nation-state, and give rise to semiautonomous economies in a postimperi-
alist world" (Toffler 1980, 10–11). We are entering the information age.

There is talk of virtual communities and even "the virtual state" (Rosecrance 1996).[2]

This is not the first such revolution that has occasioned such wondrous rhapsody. It is important to recognize that the world has evidenced earlier revolutions in both transportation and communications. Steamships, railroads, automobiles, and airplanes transformed the ability to move people and materials vast distances in ever shorter amounts of time. Telegraphy, radios, and telephones transformed the ability to communicate over immense spaces even faster than people could move.

Each development was thought to herald a new age of international politics. People would be able to travel and interact with others and the result would be more understanding. Thomas Henry Buckle, a prominent British author of the nineteenth century, referring to British-French relations, wrote, "every new railroad which is laid down, and every fresh steamer which crosses the Channel, are additional guarantees for the preservation of that long and unbroken peace which, during forty years, has knit together the fortunes and interests of the two most civilised nations of the earth" (quoted in Blainey 1973, 20).

Four themes underlie this rosy view. First, a continuous component of liberal views on international politics has been the pacific consequences of contact and communication. "The greater the contact, the greater the respect" (quoted in Stein 1993) epitomizes the view that conflict is rooted in miscommunication and misunderstanding and that increasing interaction improves the prospects for cooperation. The Internet is only the current expression of hopes voiced during the last two centuries, hopes that underlay the modern Olympic movement, world's fairs, cultural exchange programs, and so forth.[3]

Second, also reliant on the view that conflict is rooted in misperception, is the idea that improved communications lowers forecasting errors, and reduces or eliminates accidental wars. Communications revolutions, more than ones in transportation, hold special significance because of the central role of information in our understanding of how the world works.[4] A revolution in the theory of games has transformed our understanding of almost all strategic interaction as being about information. Game theory now sees many social realizations as the products of incomplete information. Indeed, in these works, conflict is a product of incomplete information; thus any improvement in the speed and quality of information transmission in theory holds the potential for changing the prospects for conflict.

Third, developments in transportation and communication increase trade and economic interdependence which, in turn, produces international cooperation (Stein 1993). In this way, technological developments lead to peace indirectly rather than directly (see Kedzie, in this volume). Thus, revolutions in transportation and communication bring greater cooperation either by way of increasing contact and understanding or by way of commerce and its pacifying consequences.

The fourth impact of such technological revolutions, which in turn affects international politics, is the impact on the state and on the relationship between ruler and ruled. Better communications can help a ruler both keep tabs on citizens and also can help a ruler build support by controlling what version of events citizens see. Greater control leads to greater stability, by lessening internal conflicts and, in turn, by lessening the possibility of conflict spilling over to surrounding states or of diversionary wars. Furthermore, improved communication between the ruler and the ruled increases the pacifying impact of public opinion on foreign policy. In particular, as trade leads to greater prosperity, the demand for the continuation of such (peaceful) trading relationships grows.

Real improvements in transportation and communications during the nineteenth century did not necessarily fulfill this promise of peace, however. Internal improvements in transportation and communication transformed the prospects for state power, improving the relative power position of those states most able to take advantage of the technology. The prospects for war and peace changed as relative positions shifted. Furthermore, technology that so clearly could be used to lower the costs of trade and increase profits could also be used to improve military power. Communications technology, excellent for transmitting orders for goods across oceans, could also improve the coordination of military maneuvers over long distances; vessels that transported people and goods could also transport soldiers and weapons. Toward the end of the century, states that had industrialized and grown richer, in part due to communications and transportation improvements, expanded. As they pursued both wealth and military power made possible with the new technology,[5] their expansion posed new threats and intensified rivalries in the period leading up to World War I. And the speed of such communications and transportation technologies made possible the rapid mobilization of troops and the quick exchange of diplomatic messages immediately preceding World War I, which severely limited the opportunities for a diplomatic solution to the crisis.

Relative Returns and International Political Transformation

In a quite general framework (drawn from Steele 1995), broad technological change is the key determinant of changes in the prospects for war or peace (see also Webster, in this volume). States are assumed to be interested both in security and welfare but find the prospects for those affected by the nature of technology. Technological changes that disproportionately increase the returns to states from war-making result in a more belligerent world. Conversely, technological changes that predominantly increase the returns to states from commerce and exchange result in a less belligerent world. The rise of territorial states or trading states is a result of technological change. Major changes in the nature of international politics and the international system come from technological revolutions. However, technological changes that increase the returns from both military and trading strategies may improve the relative position of technologically advanced states but do not, in themselves, transform the system from a conflictual one to a peaceful one, or vice versa.

This argument is much broader than the current analytic debate about the relative dominance of offensive and defensive weapons. The security literature contains the argument that technology would change the prospects for war by changing the balance between defensive and offensive weapons. A world in which offensive weapons are dominant is one that is more prone to war, one in which defensive weapons are dominant is less prone to war. But this narrows the focus solely to the prospects for successful warfare and ignores the reasons for waging war.

The purposes as well as the prospects for war matter. Given the nature of technology, additional territory is more or less valuable and more or less readily controlled. Thus, the utility of military expansion is a product of more than the existence of offense dominance. Similarly, the prospects for a trading state strategy result from more than the perceived superiority of defensive weapons.

The impact of technological change is multifaceted and entails changes in the relative rates of return for different state strategies that in turn determine the prospects for world peace and stability. Assessing the impact of a revolution in communications then entails whether it produces or augments a major shift in the ratio of returns to militaristic versus pacific international strategies.

The First Communications Revolution

The history of communications development is one of continuing technological progress. Each new technology improved the speed, capacity, and reliability of communications, and the costs of communicating declined dramatically over time. Each invention held commercial and personal use. Businesses made early use of these technologies, but individuals also used them for private messages once the costs came down.

In the last two centuries, there have been two clear-cut "revolutions" in modern communications. The first occurred during the nineteenth century with the development of the telegraph (and later the telephone). This type of "point-to-point" communications meant that information could now travel faster than people could, faster than any mode of transportation. The second revolution included the development of real broadcasting, which enabled public and private entities to send out information from one source to many people and places at once (e.g., through television pictures). The second revolution also included the development of satellites (first launched in 1960), which made it possible to cover the entire planet and beam words and pictures from anyplace on earth to any other. We are currently undergoing a possible third modern communications revolution that includes the development of the Internet and networking, linking any number of distant sites in multidirectional communications. This third "revolution" is a mix of point-to-point and broadcasting types of communications, with one new twist: the source for broadcasting information now is not a prohibitively expensive (and easily monitored) television transmitter, but any small personal computer equipped with a modem.

The first modern communications revolution, which occurred in the nineteenth century, meant that information, for the first time in world history, could move faster than people and things.[6] Previously, information was conveyed by people and depended on means of transportation.[7] The first telegraph message in 1832 implied virtually instantaneous communication. It required a vast infrastructure: laying of cable and the development of standard codes and operators. Point to point communication was pushed still further with the first telephone conversation in 1876. More and more varied information could now be communicated and did not necessarily require intermediaries and translation (coding and decoding) at both ends.[8]

The nineteenth century saw the development not only of point-to-point communication but also the very beginning of broadcasting, the transmission of information through airwaves. The radio, developed at the very end of the century[9] was the first communication medium that could be sent broadly, could cross borders without permission, could be heard on moving objects such as ships, and could be heard by anyone with the right equipment. The subsequent invention of television (1927) expanded the range and scope of what could be broadly transmitted over the air without requiring laying cable. Still, radio and television operate on a regional, rather than a global scale.

Each of these developments initially brought wonder and amazement and soon was simply incorporated into people's expectations: "In the early days of cables it seemed miraculous to send a message over thousands of kilometers in a matter of hours. Pulpits, podiums, and editorial pages resounded with paeans of praise for the 'annihilation of time and space'" (Headrick 1991, 73). As Capt. George Squier of the United States Army Signal Corp (itself a military organization created because of the new technology) put it in 1901, "The fastest mail express, or the swiftest ocean ship, are as naught as compared with the velocity of the electrical impulse which practically annihilates any terrestrial dimension" (Headrick 1991, 4).

Like improvements in transportation, communications technologies increase the scope and scale of commercial enterprises. A message that previously would have taken a month could be sent in less than a week once the overland cable from Karachi, Pakistan, to Europe was completed in 1865; the time was further shortened in 1870 with the completion of a Bombay to London cable (Jones 1987, 103). The trans-Atlantic cable was completed in 1866, cutting the time between the ordering and the receipt of goods almost in half. Inventory requirements were reduced, and middlemen were bypassed as orders could be sent directly from wholesalers to manufacturers (Jones 1987, 104–106). Communications technologies not only facilitated growth in international trade and investment, but also made possible central control of multilocational enterprises. In 1900, the House of Rothschild had branches in Frankfurt, Vienna, Paris, and London in daily contact with each other (Kennedy 1993, 50). The communications revolution thus led to a managerial revolution that transformed the nature of productive enterprises.[10]

The telegraph led to the coordination of finance as well as commodity markets. By 1914, every continent was linked to London, and Britain dominated a global financial market, linking banks and stock exchanges, although firms were less directly linked (Schwartz 1994, 157).

Governments have been essential to the spread and use of modern communications innovations. While the earliest cables were laid by single entrepreneurs or by newly formed companies, in 1870 the British government nationalized its domestic telegraph companies. Further private investment in *international* telegraph cable followed, which, in turn, later became heavily subsidized (Headrick 1981, 162). Other Great Powers, too, fostered the development of these technologies and agreed to the creation of international communications networks: "Before quarrels could arise over the control and security of international communications, there had to be telegraph lines connecting countries to one another, and these lines required international agreements" (Headrick 1991, 12).[11] Indeed, "because telegraph messages often had to cross international borders, they required something that few technological innovations had required before: international cooperation" (Mokyr 1990, 124). Initially, these came in the form of bilateral agreements in the 1850s and 1860s, followed by the creation of the International Telegraph Union in 1865. In other words, besides increasing trade and financial interdependence, the communications revolution led to the creation of new international institutions needed to ease transactions. The first interstate telegraph line linked France and Great Britain in 1851: for the next forty years, private cables, mostly controlled by British companies, dominated the telegraph system. Other countries accepted British hegemony over communications and reaped the economic rewards made possible by cheaper, faster, and more reliable communications. It was a period of relative great power peace (Headrick 1991, 6).

The Dark Side

But communications revolutions have been double-edged: they have been used for war and have generated conflict even as they have increased international communications and understanding. The innovations of the nineteenth century became central to modern warfare.

One consequence of the new technologies was that they increased the scale and scope of political and military control: "Large empires went to great lengths to speed the flow of information: the Romans built roads, the Persians and Mongols established relays of horses, the British subsidized mail steamers" (Headrick 1991, 6). As one historian put it, the one new thing about the new imperialism of the end of the nineteenth century was that the imperial states had "secure and rapid means of communicating with their provinces and agents abroad" (Headrick 1991, 50). All European states pursued these efforts to control communications in newly conquered territory. France, for example, moved slowly north in Indochina starting in the 1850s, building telegraph lines as they conquered first Cochin China, then Annam, and finally Tonkin (Headrick 1991, 53).

The managerial revolution made possible by telecommunications also transformed the battlefield (Creveld 1985; McNeill 1982). Information was the key to consolidating and controlling warfare. Armies laid cables as they marched forward in the nineteenth century. Battlefields could be orchestrated by generals in the rear holding large amounts of information: In the words of Fieldmarshel Alfred von Schlieffen, "[The 'Modern Alexander' would direct the battle] from a roomy office where telegraph, telephone, and wireless signaling apparatus are at hand" (Van Creveld 1985, 153). According to one historian, "Effective centralized command depended on new means of transport and communication" (McNeill 1982, 248).[12]

The centrality of communication to national security meant that each communications technology became an arena of Great Power competition and rivalry. Telegraphy initially emerged during a period of relative Great Power peace.[13] States were willing to allow this important medium of communication to be controlled by others (specifically by Britain, which also controlled the seas through which the cables were laid). But as Great Power rivalry reemerged in the latter part of the nineteenth century, competition in telegraph communications was one domain for that rivalry.[14] The possibility of attacks on lines of communication, and the prospect of censorship and espionage, led France and Germany to build their own subsidized cable networks.

Not only did states compete in these technological domains, but these domains became politicized and militarized and played prominent roles in both world wars. States developed agencies specializing in monitoring and decoding others' secret communications. The new information technologies, by separating communication from transportation, created new forms of espionage and warfare (Headrick 1991, 8). In fact, the need to streamline communications in wartime and, more specifically, to handle the enormous number of messages during World War I led to enormous improvements in radio and telephone technology (Landes 1969, 422–423). States also created agencies intended to use modern communications technology for propaganda.[15]

Moreover, governments wanted to be able to keep secret their communications even as these forms of communication increased their ability to spy and gather information. The centrality of communications channels made them weapons of war: victory or defeat could hinge on information and who had it when (Headrick 1991, 138). An asymmetry in the nature and use of communication technology could be the difference between victory and defeat on the battlefield.[16]

Finally, there is the question of the impact of real-time communications on international politics. Whatever the net impact of communications upon interstate rivalries and internal state power, they do reduce the reaction time of governments and increase the pressures on central decision makers.[17] The ability to communicate quickly reduces the role of foreign ambassadors and representatives. One argument, voiced as early as the beginning of this century, was that rapid communications exacerbated international conflict. Tensions anywhere around the globe were instantaneously transmitted and magnified and were more difficult to allay. Instantaneous communications reduce the diplomatic room for maneuver, make it difficult if not impossible to wait for the course of events, and increase the costs and certainly the visibility of the costs of conflict.

One early disaster attributed in part to this impact of electronic communication is the occurrence of World War I: "Diplomats failed to understand the full impact of instantaneous communications without the ameliorating effect of delay" (Headrick 1991, 139 quoting Stephen Kern, *Culture of Time and Space*). A number of examples of the role of new technologies are provided from the crisis days preceding World War I. First, Austria gave Serbia an ultimatum and only forty-eight hours to reply, after having taken almost a month deliberating on how to respond to the Archduke's assassination. When the Serbian foreign minister replied that some ministers were away and more time would be needed, he was told by the Austrian ambassador, "The return of the ministers in the age of railways, telegraph, and telephone in a land of that size could only be a matter of a few hours." Second, when Austria then declared war on Serbia, it was done with a telegram. Finally, the ultimatums issued prior to the outbreak of war stipulated short response times. The German ultimatum to Russia on July 31 had a twelve-hour limit. Great Britain gave Germany only five hours to answer its ultimatum.[18]

In many ways, then, communications became weapons of control and war, and at times even exacerbated conflict. States were willing to spend vast sums both to ensure the secrecy and security of their own communications and to break and decode the communications of their adversaries and competitors. Yet the efforts to control communications as an aspect of international rivalry did not really occur until states had moved away from the trading strategies of the midnineteenth century and the tensions and conflicts of the imperialist period emerged. Once territorial expansion again became a clear goal for the European states,[19] governments became much more active in controlling and developing communications technology.[20] Whereas communications technology had increased profits for financiers, manufacturers, and entrepreneurs during the nineteenth century as it lowered transaction costs, the same technology led to great efficiencies and increasingly effective strategies in ever larger wars in the opening half of the twentieth century.

Communications in the Twentieth Century: The Second Revolution

Satellite technology, and advances in radio, television, and telephones have led to another round of dramatic decreases in the cost of communication, increases in speed, increases in reliability and in the scope of areas that can now be linked instantaneously. Global reach and broadcasting, the ability to reach large numbers of people from one source, are dramatically different from the point-to-point communications of the nineteenth century. Governmental as well as private organizations can reach masses of citizens in their own countries—and across borders. In addition, such advances in technology again stimulated international trade and commerce, and helped lead to the growth of multinational corporations and of foreign direct investment.

Again, however, governments have been quick to recognize advantages in applying improvements in communications to warfare. Satellite technology was funded by the U.S. and Soviet governments, in great part, for security reasons.[21] Instantaneous and reliable communications were developed, which further refined certain types of warfare. These developments included accurate guidance systems for cruise missiles, "smart" laser-guided bombs such as those used in the Gulf War, and vastly improved command and control systems with which to coordinate forces and which, in turn, also become the target of war (e.g., that the United States targeted in Iraq during the Gulf War). As in the earlier communications revolution, there is both a light and a dark side to the application of these technologies.

Similar to earlier advances in communications, improvements in the twentieth century have continued to lower the cost of communicating and to broaden the speed and scope of transactions. Communications technologies provide more, and more current, information that makes possible a "more informed" judgment, both for security issues and economic issues. Our very language, the phrase "more informed," implies the superiority of decisions made with more information. Improvements in communications lower the costs of trade and investment. They may actually lower the likelihood of accidental wars,[22] due to increased access to more accurate information on both the capabilities and intentions of rivals.[23] Nothing, however, in more rapid and speedy information and communication makes it inherently a force for cooperation or conflict.[24] In fact, broadcasting itself was utilized by expansionist and authoritarian regimes, which took advantage of such advances in communications to spread propaganda more effectively, allowing them both to solidify their power and to whip up nationalist support for possible expansion.[25] The danger of rapid information in a crisis situation has already been discussed in the case of World War I. More recently, rapid communications also increased pressure during the Cuban Missile Crisis.[26] Both the ability to gather complete information and to process such information fully may be limited in this type of crisis. And more rapid—though accurate—information can actually lead to war: the preemptive Israeli strike that started the 1967 Six-Day War followed observations of Egyptian troop mobilizations.

We have enjoyed a half century with little Great Power wars since 1945, although it has not been a period completely devoid of conflict. The question is, Are we likely to see these trends continue or are we likely to see a repeat of the nineteenth century, when states turned from cooperation to conflict, and began to compete even in the domain of communications? Other changes in the international system suggest that there is some reason for optimism. There is less of a focus today on an expansion of territory as a goal for states (see Steele 1995). This removes at least one cause of war. Institutions and norms have been established to help prevent the repetition of costly Great Power wars, especially in a nuclear age. This also diminishes the likelihood of conflict. Institutions and norms established to encourage cooperation and improve returns on trading and investment strategies also help mitigate conflict, including such institutions as the General Agreement on Tariffs and Trade, the World Trade Organization, and the International Monetary Fund. Access to accurate, rapid information makes these institutions more effective, helps spread cooperative norms, and, as already suggested, leads to greater levels of interdependence as the benefits of trading strategies increase. Communications innovations have magnified and intensified the post-World War II shifts toward an interdependent world. It is important, however, to examine the dark side of communications technology more fully before becoming too sanguine. In the last century, communications technologies, initially helping to lower the costs of trade and to increase interdependence, were utilized by states at the end of the century to consolidate their power, control their populations, control information and thus gain a powerful propaganda tool, and to gain access to secret information about rivals in order to follow more successful predatory policies. Such uses for communications technology continue to be possible.

Communications and the Power of the State

One piece of conventional wisdom is that communications technologies empower people and reduce the power of the state. This vision of communications goes back to the last century and is even associated with earlier technologies. Thomas Carlyle, writing in 1836 about the implications of the invention in the 1450s of the printing press, said, "He who first shortened the labor of copyists with the device of moveable types was disbanding hired armies and cashiering most kings and senates, and creating a whole new democratic world" (Neuman 1996, 8).

If Carlyle's judgment was premature, it is certainly widely argued today. People, and their most immediate representatives in a communications age, the media, can obtain information quickly and directly and no longer need to rely on governments.[27] Moreover, the decentralization implied by communications technologies means that it is more difficult for the state to exercise central control. Thus, the current argument is that communications technologies are transforming the relationships between people, between rulers and their citizens, and between rulers. One author describes the purveyors of such arguments, "utopian techno-revolutionaries" (Surman 1996).

The result is that governments cannot lie and act with their otherwise characteristic impunity. The nuclear disaster at Chernobyl, for example, was "swiftly photographed by a French commercial satellite, and transmitted all over the world—including within the Soviet Union itself" (Kennedy 1993, 53). The result was that governments had to respond since their populations had independent sources of information. Neither Western nations nor the Soviet Union could cover it up.[28] The consequences for the use of military force are potentially profound. Domestic populations can see their country's soldiers fighting across the globe on their TV screens. Foreign interventions become more difficult to sustain in an age of global television. Governments in the information age will be forced to be truthful and pursue only popular policies, the argument goes. The availability of real-time information directly accessible by individuals generates these pressures. The impact of instantaneous nongovernmentally controlled global communications has now reached an extreme as we now see public officials tune in to Cable News Network (CNN) and obtain their information at the exact same moment and from the same source as their publics.[29] This argument is directly equivalent to the one made about capital mobility: in an age in which capital can instantaneously flow anywhere, governments have no choice but to pursue good economic policies.[30]

Citizens have direct access to foreign views and governments have no monopoly on the information their citizens receive. Radio, telephone, telegraph—and television, fax machines, and now cellular phones—are difficult (at best) for governments to control. Governments, individuals, or international organizations can link subnational groups together, provide monetary support, coordinate political movements, and spread ideas or emerging norms. In this case, communications are seen to have helped undermine authoritarian regimes, such as the South African apartheid regime, as communications helped interested parties organize internal resistance, rally foreign economic pressure, and spread norms of political representation.

Thus, it is now argued that the communications revolution not only constrains but can topple governments. Sermons and messages of the Ayatollah Khomeini were widely distributed on audiotape as were copies of their transcripts and this is seen as central to the Iranian revolution that brought down the shah (Rosenau 1990). As the well-connected Arab journalist, Mohamed Heikal, put it, "What was happening was a revolution for democracy, against autocracy, led by theocracy, made possible by xerocracy" (Heikal 1981, 139).

Similarly, the communications revolution, we are told, brought down Communist rule in the former Soviet Union and East Germany and the authoritarian rule of Ferdinand Marcos in the Philippines (Ganley 1991; Shane 1994; Sonenshine 1990, 29).[31] It became clear to citizens in the East that Communist regimes could not match Western standards of living that then led to deep dissatisfaction; it became clear government information could not be trusted that then led to increased cynicism; it became clear ideas were spreading and the regime was unstable that led to the rapid spread of change once it began (Skolnikoff 1993, 96–97).[32] Even where it did not bring down the regime, as in China, the communications revolution challenged the state. The Chinese government's suppression of students in Tiananmen Square was communicated by radio, television, and fax messages back into China (Kennedy 1993, 52).[33] In short, external sources of information can undercut a regime. Indeed, governments make use of this by directly appealing to the citizens of foreign adversaries. Broadcasting information (and cultural programming) abroad has been a widely used tactic during this century.

Governments, fearful of the new technologies, have tried to retain control. In the nineteenth century, all kinds of governments made use of the new technologies: "Governments of every sort [of] autocracies like Russia, democracies like the United States, colonial regimes like India, even non-Western states like Turkey and Japan all seized upon it [the telegraph] as a means of enhancing their power and improving their efficiency. Only China stood back, seeing in the telegraph an alien intruder" (Headrick 1991, 46). Governments came to recognize that organizations mediate between machines and society and that these could be governmental ones: "These organizations . . . in effect control the flow of interactions between technology and society by purchasing, investing, subsidizing, patenting, sharing or withholding secrets, and many other means" (Headrick 1991, 9). In many countries, these organizations were organs of the state. In the twentieth century, states recognized the importance of broadcast as well as point-to-point communications. They found that the scope of their power was increased by broadcast technologies such as radio and television. In most countries these were state-owned and dominated. Not surprisingly, the most totalitarian regimes, exercising the most control of their citizenry, are twentieth-century phenomena and make extensive use of the new technologies (see Taylor 1990).[34]

In wartime, all states, totalitarian and democratic alike, have heightened the extent of control. Britain licensed shortwave radio sets and monitored owners during World War I. Japan simply banned such sets entirely (Taylor 1990, 211).[35] More recently, Communist regimes have held out for different technical standards to make communications more difficult.[36] China cracked down on fax machines and cellular phones after Tiananmen Square and controls the Internet, resisting horizontal communications links in an effort not only to limit the spread of reformist ideas, but to maintain control over information and the tools of propaganda (see Skolnikoff 1993, 97–101).

It is not easy, however, to control the content of information given modern day communications and increased transnational links. This loss of control was evident in the fall of the Soviet Union, the end of the apartheid regime in South Africa, and the demonstrations in Tiananmen Square. It is not impossible to retain at least some governmental control over communications (as China continues to do), but it is very costly, and probably impossible to retain total control in an age of satellites. Many governments have tried to do so and failed. The only sure way to control the content of messages is to limit the access to, and availability of, the technology severely; this, of course, means severely limiting the accessibility of a vital economic tool. Governmental control is eroding: in an earlier era, states consolidated their position in part by expanding communications technology while still controlling the content of the information available to citizens and in part by utilizing their monopoly over the presentation of information to manipulate the forces of nationalism.

Governments and the Development of Communications Technology

The difficulty in limiting outside information in order to control domestic forces does not mean that governments no longer support the development of these new technologies for both economic and national security goals, or that they do not reap great advantages from them. They continue to be extensive and early users of advances in communications. In the nineteenth century, governments were at first slow to recognize the military and political consequences of technological developments. But it did not take long for them to see the possibilities and the essential need for incorporating innovative ideas. In the twentieth century, governments are in the forefront of much of the initial research and often subsidize much of the development of communications technology.

Even in open societies in which the media is not controlled, broadcast communication allows political leaders to address citizens directly without an intermediary. It allows them direct appeals and increases their relative power. Moreover, even open democratic governments that do not directly control the media have found that the media can be quite constrained and military censorship can be effectively used. This may not always be the case in peacetime, but governments have been able to control information in wartime. The British government, for example, was able to get the kind of media coverage it wanted during the Falklands War in 1982, and coalition forces were able to confine the media during the Gulf conflict (Atkinson 1993, 159–162).[37]

Governments have been central to the development and growth of technologies of mass communication. They have also been at the forefront of the development of new communications technology for warfare. The nature of the two world wars, for example, transformed the U.S. government's relationship with universities as scholarship that was potentially useful to the military began to receive public support and funding.[38] Yet, they have been constrained as well as strengthened by these technologies. For example, the development of communications satellites initially followed a development path similar to that of the telegraph in the nineteenth century. The United States, the hegemon, initially gave avid support to efforts by private enterprise to develop a communications satellite system.[39] The U.S. government supported the creation of INTELSAT (International Telecommunications Satellite Organization), established in 1964 as an international not-for-profit organization to launch and manage communications satellites (McNeil 1990). Other nations at first accepted U.S. hegemony in this area. Over time, however, as with the telegraph, states began to chafe under U.S. control.[40] Unlike in the nineteenth century, however, twentieth-century pressures for unregulated competition won the day. In a world in which territory is less of a concern for Great Powers, and one in which benefits for pursuing economic strategies surpass benefits for military strategies (Steele 1995), support for international organizations and cooperative control over communications has overcome security concerns and efforts to maintain independence. Today over two hundred nations, including China, Vietnam, Iran, Russia and the former Soviet republics are members of either INTELSAT or the newer INMARSAT (International Mobile Satellite Organization), established in 1979. Hegemonic control has been replaced by a multinational organization, lessening the chance of conflict because smaller states are (at least somewhat) less vulnerable to superpower whims.[41] The number of countries that share access to communications satellites will continue to grow in the future; hegemonic monopolistic control is limited. Increasing these ties will lead to continued pressure for intergovernmental cooperation, which has been a prerequisite to the cross-border flow of information and the wiring of the world.

A Third Communications Revolution at the End of the Millennium?

Recent developments, such as the Internet and the World Wide Web, are again leading to prophecies of revolution.[42] It has all been said before. As with other advances in communications, the technology itself can be used for commercial or military ends. The improvements in the speed of communication can lower the costs of trade and investment, or can broaden the speed and scope of military action. Such improvements can improve information for customers and for commercial rivals, or for military allies and enemies. More accurate information can help prevent misunderstandings, or the increased speed and flow of information can create pressured or crisis situations that may increase cognitive errors.

The claims for the new technology are similar to the claims in earlier communications revolutions, particularly to the changes in the twentieth century. Specifically, networking and the Internet have a similar effect on government control as broadcasting (as opposed to point-to-point communications): transnational ties improve just as governmental control over their own citizens weakens. The wired world, it is claimed, will provide community, democracy, empowerment, wealth, and peace. There is talk of cyberocracy and cyberology and the cybercratic state (Ronfeldt 1991).[43]

The technology of the information age certainly improves transnational communications, yet governments continue to try to gather information both about rival states and their own citizens. Gathering information and maintaining control over it is still seen as a core security interest. Still, the newest improvements in information technology are occurring in a time of limited Great Power war and high levels of interdependence. Domestic demands for the pursuit of prosperity are increasing, accompanied by increased pressure to deregulate communications and allow for the free flow of information, which comes from both corporate and financial institutions as well as from private citizens. Transnational ties between individuals, corporations, and groups continue to increase. The end result is that governments do try to retain as much control over information as possible—but it is becoming more difficult and more costly to do so.

Ironically, the Internet itself is a product of U.S. defense concerns. It began during the Cold War as a network created by ARPA (Advanced Research Projects Agency) of the Defense Department (called "ARPANET"). Its structure, in which packets of information can travel via a multiplicity of routes and reroute around bottlenecks, was designed to ensure uninterrupted routing of data even in a nuclear war. Now that very structure makes Internet control by governments more difficult (Lewis 1996): intentionally created bottlenecks or roadblocks are as easily overcome as unintended ones.[44]

Also ironically, the initial reaction of many computer literate U.S. citizens to the arrival of computer networks in the late 1980s was that they were a retrograde and regressive force.[45] Today the very networks that make surveillance and central control possible are once again being lauded for the personal freedom they provide and for the new communities they make possible. But there are some opportunities for government to reassert control. The fact that they have limited incentives to do so, or that they show little willingness to pay the opportunity costs associated with doing so (in terms of lost commercial benefits), does not mean that they cannot do so.

In most societies, including democratic ones, the desire to control Internet communications stems neither from a concern about political opposition nor from a perceived need for emergency surveillance but from a concern with the dissemination of certain kinds of information.[46] Governments are being pressed to regulate and prevent certain information from being gathered and spread. Most typically, the concern is over pornography,[47] but other issues have also arisen.[48] A loss of control over security issues and defense technologies is also seen as a vital concern.

Democratic governments, again including the United States, want to be able to exercise control and surveillance of information. The U.S. government has been extraordinarily active in limiting the ability of private actors to encrypt their communications and has pressed for a "key recovery" plan so that it might be able to decrypt messages when necessary (Clausing 1997). In 1993, the U.S. State Department ruled that a graduate student in mathematics could not publish his encryption program nor discuss it at any open meeting that might be attended by foreigners unless he registered as an international weapons dealer.[49] Governments continue to insist that all nongovernmental information should be open to governmental surveillance.

An array of states, autocratic to democratic, are linking their societies to the Web but many are continuing to exercise substantial constraints.[50] Vietnam and Saudi Arabia permit access only through a single government-controlled gateway. Singapore treats the Net as a broadcast medium and requires content providers to register with the state.[51] China requires users and providers to register with authorities. The Chinese telecommunications minister stated in June 1995, "as a sovereign state, China will exercise control on the information" entering China. "By linking with the Internet, we do not mean the absolute freedom of information." China's official Xinhua News Agency stated that individuals and organizations are not "allowed to engage in activities at the expense of state security and secrets" and "they are also forbidden to produce, retrieve, duplicate, or spread information that may hinder public order." The fear persists that influential forces from outside state borders may undermine authoritarian regimes.

Governments' capabilities for monitoring both people and objects from a distance are also continually improving in all states. Again, improved capabilities in themselves can be used either for benign or more pernicious goals. There has been pressure to protect privacy rights and to block the dissemination of information about people's Web activity, something that is easily monitored and of great commercial value. New technology can even be used to monitor the physical whereabouts of individuals.[52] While this is nominally to help people is distress, the notion that the government can track anyone's exact whereabouts through his or her (mobile) telephone uncomfortably reminds us that Big Brother Is Watching.

Internationally, there are also some forces working against pressures toward transnational links and deregulated communications. There are concerns, for example, about U.S. dominance in information technologies. Countries are choosing to hook up to the Net but are maintaining controls and negotiating the terms of their integration into the global communications networks. As was the case with earlier technology (e.g., the telegraph or communications satellites), smaller governments do not want to be dependent on a hegemonic power's good will for access to communications.

Finally, the U.S. military establishment (and presumably others as well) are planning for war in the information age. There are studies of information war, cyberwar, and netwar.[53] RAND has already undertaken, at Defense Department request, cyberwar simulation exercises. As before, the latest communications technology has wartime consequences and can be used for military advantage (Arquilla and Ronfeldt 1993). The new information technologies can be used by advanced states like the United States to disrupt both an enemy's decision-making process and its ability to carry out military actions effectively—but increased reliance on such technologies create new vulnerabilities as well.

Still, the system does not seem to be headed toward rivalry and conflict. The end of this century does not appear to be a repeat of the prior one, at least as far as Great Power tensions are concerned. Despite the active involvement of the military establishment in the development and application of communications technology, and despite the often strenuous efforts by some states to use such technology to control information and their citizens, on balance, states appear to be utilizing the new communications technologies more to increase cooperation and interdependence than to expand at the expense of others. Although military applications for these technologies continue to be developed, the benefits of cooperation currently appear to outweigh the benefits of predation. This will not last if other factors in the system emerge to increase conflict: communications technology alone cannot lead to peace. The newest technology increases the speed and scope of both economic and military communications; it is useful for both. Transnational links may be increasing but governments are still able to assert control over the access to technology, should they decide it is in their interest. But the balance today looks to be in favor of continued pacific strategies, at least for now.

Conclusion

Revolutions in communication underlie both international cooperation and international conflict. They increase the returns to both. They increase the amount of independent information available to citizens but also increase the power of the state.[54]

The dual impact of communications on international relations was recognized by Charles Bright, a leading expert on submarine telegraphy. He recognized the fact that rapid communications produced ruptures that could have been avoided with more time to think, but they also prevented ruptures by rapidly learning the interests and concerns of other governments. His conclusion, "But, on the whole, experience distinctly pronounces in favour of the pacific effects of telegraphy" (Headrick 1991, 75). Ironically, he was writing in 1898. Would he have struck the same balance were he writing two decades later?

The international political history of communications is that they parallel and amplify trends in international relations. The

> telegraph, appearing in an era of peace, was long thought to be peaceful by nature; it did not become an object of dissension until the turn of the century, when nations turned antagonistic for other

reasons. The radio, in contrast, was born into a world of jittery jingoism and started life as a weapon in the commercial and military rivalries of the great powers. (Headrick 1991, 117)

Conflict between the Great Powers spilled over into telecommunications, as "conflicts over cable networks were a metaphor for the clash between an old and satiated empire and an upstart rival" (Headrick 1991, 177). During the earlier nineteenth century, when states pursued trading strategies and wealth, communications led to greater interdependence and cooperation. At the end of the nineteenth century and into the twentieth, as states again pursued expansionary policies and territory, communications improved warfighting capabilities and led to massive, bloody, Great Power conflicts.

The central feature of the information revolution occurring in the 1990s is that it comes during a period free of major conflict between the Great Powers. Indeed, it is precisely this peace that has allowed such technologies to become so widely available so quickly. This communications revolution, like the ones before it, will lead to increased communication and higher volumes of information flow and will become integrated into the fabric of daily life, especially in the rich advanced postindustrial nations of the world. It will facilitate commerce and contact and make possible new ways of producing, new ways of organizing, and new ways of communicating and living. It will lead to more cooperative institutions necessary to manage increased interdependence and communication.

But states will continue jealously to guard their prerogatives and will find new ways to use the technology to control even as they are constrained by it and need to react to it. Moreover, the nature of competition will manifest itself in communications as well. Peaceful commercial competition will see states engage in practices to assure domestic information firms and domestically located systems. And should political rivalries rearise among the Great Powers, communications technology will be an arena of conflict like others.

A revolution in the nature of relationships among the Great Powers may very well be occurring. But it is not being driven by changes in communications technology. Other recent changes in the international system have increased the incentives for states to choose more pacific strategies. By themselves, changes in communication only heighten and magnify the dynamic implications of other technological changes.[55]

Notes

1. One author even suggests that the Internet will constitute "the fifth internationale" of the Labor movement (Waterman 1996). The author's paper

talks of "new social movements . . . creating a new kind of internationalism, or global solidarity, this being in large part a 'communication internationalism.'"

2. "A popular and somewhat shallow interpretation of these trends . . . is that the economic consequences of globalization can only be beneficial" (Kennedy 1993, 52).

3. We characterize the liberal argument that increased contact and communication leads to increased cooperation as "sociological liberalism" (Stein 1993). The quotation at the beginning of the article, from the Prince Consort, comes from a speech preceding the opening of an international exhibition. The modern exponent of the pacific impact of communication was Karl Deutsch. The obvious retort is that familiarity can breed contempt as well.

4. Information has emerged at the heart of our understanding of physical, biological, and social phenomena. There are some who argue that a new paradigm has emerged in physics in which "physical systems are viewed as . . . processing information" (Wright 1988, 62, quoting a 1984 article). Similarly, the genetics revolution in modern biology transforms our view of human nature, and genes are now conceptualized as encoding information. Biology textbooks in the 1950s used to begin with definitions of life. They no longer do. Virtually every textbook definition of life could apply to a computer virus.

5. Completion of submarine cables in the 1870s, along with such innovations as curb transmissions (a second pulse following the first to improve quality) and duplex telegraphy (enabling messages to be sent in opposite directions at the same time) all helped increase the speed of communications while lowering the cost. This lowered transaction costs for trade and also allowed for tighter centralized control of distant colonies. Whereas a couple of dozen telegraph messages were sent between India and Britain in 1870, two million were sent in 1895. Britain had monopolized underwater cables early on, but as competitive tensions increased between the Great Powers late in the century, Germany and France, fearful of relying on British good will, laid their own cables in the 1890s (v.i.). This era also saw the birth of radio. The first patent for wireless telegraphy was taken out in 1896; Marconi's first customer was the British War Office for use in the Boer War (Headrick 1991, 118).

6. Dr. H. H. Crippen, on board the SS *Montrose*, was quoted as saying about the wireless, "What a marvelous invention it is! How privileged we are to be alive in an age of such scientific miracles!" He was arrested for murder when the ship arrived in New York because of a wireless message sent by Scotland Yard to the ship's captain (Vansittart 1984, 213).

7. The use of semaphores, smoke signals, and pigeons constitute the minor exceptions.

8. All of the communications inventions were really a series of inventions. They combined separate technological innovations and required improvements to be reliable (Mokyr 1990, 123).

9. The first patent for wireless telegraphy was taken out in 1896; the first documented wireless broadcast was Christmas Eve 1906 when Reginald Fessenden broadcast from Brant Rock, MA (McNeil 1990, 726).

10. During this period the modern corporation emerged. Economic historians document the centrality and importance of this development (Yates 1989).

11. Stein (1993) makes a similar point about the implications of trade for international cooperation. Whether trade does or does not increase cooperation among states, trade itself reflects the prior agreements of states to facilitate and allow exchanges among their nationals.

12. By the second half of the twentieth century a White House Situation Room could be in direct contact with forces in the field and battlefield decisions could be made by political commanders. President Truman exercised a degree of control that his field commander in Korea, General MacArthur, found intolerable. President Johnson found it easier to control air strikes over Vietnam than to govern the nation (Buchan 1972, 173).

13. Nonetheless the period was not totally devoid of conflicts involving various Great Powers, including the Crimean War (1854–1856), the Franco-Austrian War of 1859, and the Wars of German Unification in the 1860s.

14. Nation-states saw the strategic uses of cables in small wars at the end of the century. The United States, for example, cut cables to prevent communication between Spain and the Philippines in 1898. The United States also censored the cables it did allow to continue operating (Headrick 1991, 82–83). Even Great Britain, which controlled most of the world's cables, decided to subsidize "strategic cables" (ones that only passed through British controlled territory or water) so that vital communication with critical areas would not have to go via cables not controlled by Britain. Britain's communication superiority was instrumental, though not decisive, in its ability to get the French to back down during the Fashoda crisis. Britain had communications with the area; France did not. British messages were shown to the French and used to deceive them (Headrick 1991, 84–85).

15. There is abundant literature devoted to both topics; however this is not the place to reproduce that material. For a broad historical overview of propaganda see Taylor (1990).

16. Perhaps the best example, "one of the greatest blunders in military history," is provided by Russian decisions in the Battle of Tannenberg in the early days of World War I. Earlier, Russian czar Nicholas I, fearful of the consequences of widespread telegraphy, turned down a contract with Samuel F. B.

Morse, the inventor. As a result, Russian telegraph lines were so rudimentary that the Russian military used the radio to transmit orders (Neuman 1996). Finally, a momentous decision was made in the field by Russian general Samsonov, who ordered that radio messages be transmitted in plain language and not in code. The Germans listened in and the Russian suffered a massive defeat in East Prussia in mid-August 1914, with one hundred thousand men taken prisoner (Headrick 1991, 155–156).

17. At this point, the argument intersects with the modern literature on crisis decision making and on the consequences of short response times for the quality of decisions.

18. The short response time was in part due either to the issuing party's interest in waging war (in which case the ultimatum itself constitutes a relic of an earlier day and age) or by the requisites of offensive military plans with strict timetables.

19. See Steele (1995) for a more extensive discussion of the link between technology and changing goals.

20. For example, use of the telegraph by governments earlier in the nineteenth century focused on consular matters, travel plans, requests for information, ceremonial matters, and the like. The Foreign Office began to use the telegraph more and more for security issues after the turn of the century. There were roughly 200 messages a year between Washington and London between 1866 and 1910. Exchanges increased to about 550 a year from 1910 to 1914, 15,000 per year from 1914 to 1919, and between 500 and 1300 per year in the 1920s and early 1930s (Headrick 1991, 74; see also Webster, in this volume).

21. Once the Soviets put up two satellites in 1957 (*Sputnik* I and II), followed by the first man in space (Yuri Gagarin in April 1961), the United States feared it was facing a technology gap in the Cold War (as well as a propaganda gap). The United States committed to the space program; communications satellites followed.

22. It is not clear how many truly accidental wars actually occur.

23. The Hot Line between Moscow and Washington, for example, lessens the chance of a nuclear accident.

24. This point mirrors that of the impact of misperception on international politics: misperception can cause otherwise avoidable conflict but need not and can lead to otherwise unattainable cooperation (Stein 1990).

25. For an elaboration of this argument, see Gordon (1974).

26. For a general discussion on impaired cognitive function in crises, particularly dealing with the effects of time pressure, see George (1980, 25–55). For a discussion on the occurrence of crises due to limited information, see Powell (1987, 717–735.) For a discussion on the limited effects of misperception on war, see Stein (1990, 55–86).

27. This argument presumes either that there are no state monopolies of information or that the ability of communications to permeate national boundaries is such as to make all government communications monopolies inherently contestable.

28. More recently, an Israeli newspaper "just went to Moscow and bought Russian spy satellite photographs of new Scud missile cases in Syria. Then [it] hired a private U. S. expert on satellite photos to analyze the pictures. Then . . . [it] published the package as a scoop, without ever quoting a government official" (Friedman 1997).

29. Neuman (1996) tells the story of Ambassador Strobe Talbott on the phone with an official at the Russian Foreign Ministry. Both were watching events unfold on CNN even as they were negotiating about them.

30. Montesquieu argued back in the eighteenth century that bills of exchange allow commerce to "elude violence, and maintain itself everywhere," and as a result "rulers have been compelled to govern with greater wisdom than they themselves might have intended" (quoted in Hirschman 1977, 72). Stein (1993) characterizes such arguments as "financial liberalism."

31. A similar argument is made about hierarchical organizations, that the new communications technologies will liberate people in the workforce (Fukuyama 1995, 23–24).

32. Control over communications is vital in bringing about change. Eugenia Bogdan of Romanian television announced, a few days after the fall of Nicolae Ceausescu, "If television falls, the revolution falls" (Skolnikoff 1993, 272).

33. Discussions about communication revolutions sometimes imply that all communications are good and progressive. Experience with the Internet and other communications technologies is that they are readily adapted and used not just by progressive forces but by reactionary ones. People have discovered that right-wing kooks and leftist revolutionaries have gone on-line with great facility.

34. This was, of course, the basis of Orwell's vision in 1984. Perhaps, not surprisingly in a time quite different than the one in which he wrote, Orwell's argument has been turned on its head (Huber 1994).

35. The nature of censorship is intimately linked to the nature of technology and to the kinds of fears of foreign influence. Within a century after the invention of the printing press, the Papacy had barred the works of more than five hundred authors. The Nazis censored jazz as a degenerate form of music. The United States Supreme Court exempted motion pictures from free speech protection, treated them as purely a business, and upheld the constitutionality of state censorship laws. Most recently, countries have excluded movies for a variety of cultural offenses.

36. Just as Russia adopted different railroad gauges to make movement across the border more difficult, the Soviet Union adopted a different VCR standard to make it difficult to play foreign tapes on domestically produced VCRs.

37. Both militaries had learned lessons from the U.S. experience with media coverage of the Vietnam War.

38. In the United States an array of scientific fields with potential military applications were subsidized, including mathematics (useful for cryptography) as well as the study of mass communications (Simpson 1994).

39. The first communications satellite to relay data, voice, and television, Telstar, was launched in 1962. National Aeronautic and Space Administration (NASA), a governmental agency, provided the launch, although a private corporation (AT&T) owned the satellite. A few months later, Congress authorized creation of COMSAT (Communications Satellite Corporation) as a private corporation.

40. The Soviets created "Intersputnik," the Europeans worked on a European-wide system called "Symphonie," and tensions increased over demands for limited geostationary orbits and limited space in the frequency spectrum (Skonikoff 1972, 58).

41. The newest generation of satellites, both for data and cellular telephones, will be placed in lower orbits than previously, in part solving the problem of competition for limited geosynchronous orbits. Even the launch monopoly of superpowers has been challenged since 1979: the European Space Agency (ESA) can launch satellites with the Ariane rocket; China and India have launching capabilities, while Japan and others have their own satellites.

42. Transnational links for both individuals and groups can be expected to continue to grow in pure numbers in the near future: access to the Internet from private households has grown from 50 million households in 1996 to around 150 million in 2000; corporate use, has grown even more dramatically (Evans 1998).

43. "Anyone with a modem is potentially a global pamphleteer" (Markoff, 1995, A).

44. An Internet axiom, attributed to the engineer John Gilmore, states, "The Internet interprets censorship as damage and routes around it" (Lewis 1996).

43. Techies had lauded the personal computer revolution, for it allowed for the decentralization of computer power. Within corporations, for example, the personal computer meant freedom from the control of management information systems departments. Throughout corporations, there were guerrillas sneaking in personal computers defying the attempts of central computing to rationalize and systematize. Professionals with a computer on

their desk were freed from central control. When IBM introduced networks, the move to wire and hook everyone up was seen by many as the empire striking back. Other divisions would again be dependent on the management information systems people. Their files and their programs would again be elsewhere subject to others' whims and control. Communications can be monitored.

46. The United States and Germany presented alternative visions of Internet regulation in 1997 (Giussani 1997).

47. Even the United States passed the Communications Decency Act to control such Internet content.

48. In France, Holocaust-denying propaganda is illegal, whereas the spread of anti-Semitic propaganda is a crime in Germany. Both statutes have been used against Internet providers as well as against other media (Human Rights Watch 1996).

49. The mathematician took the government to court and prevailed (Flynn 1997).

50. Information on the 'net can reach users by one of many pathways, avoiding bottlenecks. But governments can control the gateway to the Internet, much as they used to own or at least control access to the cable in the nineteenth century. For the time being, at least, access to the Internet is easier for governments to control than access to broadcast information has been (which can cross borders without governmental permission). Once access to the Internet in general is available, however, the government cannot easily control the content of the information accessible.

51. Singapore also filters CNN broadcasts and bans private ownership of direct-broadcast television dishes (Sanger 1997).

52. The Global Positioning System (GPS), which uses geosynchronous satellites to pinpoint locations within twenty yards, was first used by the American military to help soldiers find their way in the Iraqi desert. The Russians have a similar system (the Global Navigation Satellite System, or GLONASS). Two-way messaging (using a small transmitter or pager) utilizes the Remote Determination Satellite Service (RDSS). The Federal Communications Commission has recently required that cellular and personal communications systems be able to provide a caller's number and, by the year 2001, locate a user to within 125 meters two-thirds of the time (Stutzman and Dietrich 1998).

53. In the aftermath of the Gulf War, "more than 120 countries [were] reported to be developing 'information warfare techniques'" (Shenon 1996, A22).

54. "They [communications] have both increased the power of governments and decreased their freedom of action" (Buchan 1972, 174).

55. During the last two centuries, revolutions in communications and transportation have proceeded alongside revolutions in the nature of warfare. Many attribute the advent of nuclear weapons as portending a transformation in the nature of warfare (Jervis 1989; Steele 1995).

References

Arquilla, John J. and David F. Ronfeldt. 1993. "Cyber War Is Coming." *Comparative Strategy* 12: 141–165.

Atkinson, Rick. 1993. *Crusade: The Untold Story of the Persian Gulf War.* New York: Houghton.

Blainey, G. 1973. *The Causes of War.* New York: Free Press.

Buchan, Alastair. 1972. "Technology and World Politics." *The Aberystwyth Papers: International Politics, 1919–1969.* Ed. Brian Porter, pp. 161–82. London: Oxford.

Bury, J. B. [1932.] 1955. *The Idea of Progress: An Inquiry into its Origin and Growth.* New York: Dover Publications.

Clausing, Jeri. 1997. "FBI, Security Chiefs Ask Senate for Keys to All Encrypted Data." *New York Times,* 10 July.

Creveld, Martin van. 1985. *Command in War.* Cambridge: Harvard University Press.

Evans, John V. 1998. "New Satellites for Personal Communications." *Scientific American* 278, no. 4: 70–77.

Flynn, Laurie J. 1997. "Ruling Frees Professor to Teach Cryptography." *New York Times,* 27 August.

Friedman, Thomas L. 1997. "www.mideast.com.war." *New York Times,* 18 September.

Fukuyama, Francis. 1995. *Trust: The Social Virtues and the Creation of Prosperity.* New York: Free Press.

Ganley, Gladys D. 1991. "Power to the People via Personal Electronic Media." *Washington Quarterly* 5–22.

George, Alexander L. 1980. *Presidential Decisionmaking in Foreign Policy: The Effective Use of Information and Advice.* Boulder: Westview Press.

Giussani, Bruno. 1997. "U.S. and German Internet Plans Compete for Dominance in Europe." *New York Times,* 8 July.

Gordon, Michael R. 1974. "Domestic Conflict and the Origins of the First World War: The British and the German Cases." *Journal of Modern History* 46: 191–226.

Headrick, Daniel R. 1981. *The Tools of Empire: Technology and European Imperialism in the Nineteenth Century.* New York: Oxford University Press.

Headrick, Daniel R. 1991. *The Invisible Weapon: Telecommunications and International Politics 1851–1945*. New York: Oxford University Press.

Heikal, Mohamed. 1981. *Iran: The Untold Story*. New York: Pantheon.

Hirschman, Albert O. 1977. *The Passions and the Interests: Political Arguments for Capitalism Before its Triumph*. Princeton: Princeton University Press.

Huber, Peter W. 1994. *Orwell's Revenge: The 1984 Palimpsest*. New York: Free Press.

Human Rights Watch. 1996. "Silencing the Net: The Threat to Freedom of Expression On-line."

Jervis, Robert. 1989. *The Meaning of the Nuclear Revolution: Statecraft and the Prospect of Armageddon*. Ithaca, NY.: Cornell University Press.

Jones, Charles A. 1987. *International Business in the Nineteenth Century: The Rise and Fall of a Cosmopolitan Bourgeoisie*. New York: New York University Press.

Kennedy, Paul. 1993. *Preparing for the Twentieth-First Century*. New York: Random .

Kern, Stephen. 1983. *The Culture of Time and Space 1880–1918*. Cambridge, MA: Harvard University Press.

Landes, David. 1969. *The Unbound Prometheus: Technological Change and Industrial Development in Western Europe from 1750 to the Present*. Cambridge: Cambridge University Press.

Lewis, Peter H. 1996. "The Internet's Very Nature Defies Censorship by Government or Individual." *New York Times*, 15 January.

McNeil, Ian, ed. 1990. *An Encyclopedia of the History of Technology*. London: Routledge.

McNeill, William H. 1982. *The Pursuit of Power: Technology, Armed Force, and Society since A. D. 1000*. Chicago: University of Chicago Press.

Markoff, John. 1995. "If Medium Is the Message, the Message Is the Web." *New York Times*, 20 November.

Mendels, Pamela. 1996. "Worldwide, Internet Restrictions are Growing." *New York Times*, 10 September.

Mokyr, Joel. 1990. *The Lever of Riches: Technological Creativity and Economic Progress*. New York: Oxford University Press.

Neuman, Johanna. 1996. *Lights, Camera, War: Is Media Technology Driving International Politics?* New York: St. Martin's.

Powell, Robert. 1987. "Crisis Bargaining, Escalation, and MAD." *American Political Science Review* 81: 717–735.

Ronfeldt, David F. 1991. "Cyberocracy, Cyberspace, and Cyberology: Political Effects of the Information Revolution," P-7745. RAND.

Rosecrance, Richard. 1996. "The Rise of the Virtual State." *Foreign Affairs* 75: 45–61.

Rosenau, James N. 1990. *Turbulence in World Politics: A Theory of Change and Continuity.* Princeton: Princeton University Press.

Sanger, David E. 1997. "China's Balancing Act: Complex and Delicate." *New York Times*, 2 January.

Schwartz, Herman. 1994. *States versus Markets: History, Geography, and the Development of the International Political Economy.* New York: St. Martin's.

Shane, Scott. 1994. *Dismantling Utopia: How Information Ended the Soviet Union.* Chicago: Ivan Dee.

Shenon, Philip, 1996. "Report Warns of Security Threats Posed by Computer Hackers," *New York Times*, 23 May.

Simpson, Christopher. 1994. *Science of Coercion: Communication Research and Psychological Warfare, 1945–1960.* New York: Oxford University Press.

Skolnikoff, Eugene B. 1972. *The International Imperatives of Technology: Technological Development and the International Political System.* Berkeley: University of California Press.

Skolnikoff, Eugene B. 1993. *The Elusive Transformation: Science, Technology, and the Evolution of International Politics.* Princeton: Princeton University Press.

Sonenshine, Tara. 1990. "The Revolution Has Been Televised." *Washington Post National Weekly Edition*, 8–14 October.

Steele, Cherie J. 1995. *"Altered States: Innovation, Power and the Evolution of the International System."* Ph.D. diss., University of California at Los Angeles.

———. "Trading Up and Trading Down: The Impact of Technological Change on the International System." Manuscript.

Stein, Arthur A. 1990. *Why Nations Cooperate: Circumstance and Choice in International Relations.* Ithaca, NY: Cornell University Press.

———. 1993. "Governments, Economic Interdependence, and International Cooperation." *Behavior, Society, and International Conflict.* Eds. Philip E. Tetlock, Jo L. Husbands, Robert Jervis, Paul C. Stern, and Charles Tilly, pp. 241–324. New York: Oxford University Press, for the National Research Council of the National Academy of Sciences.

Stutzman, Warren L. and Carl B. Dietrich Jr. 1998. "Moving Beyond Wireless Voice Systems." *Scientific American* 278: 92–93.

Surman, Mark. 1996. "Wired Worlds: Utopia, Revolution, and the History of Electronic Highways." Paper presented at INET96, Montreal.

Taylor, Philip M. 1990. *Munitions of the Mind: War Propaganda from the Ancient World to the Nuclear Age.* Northamptonshire, England: Patrick Stephens.

Toffler, Alvin. 1980. *The Third Wave.* New York: Bantam Books.

Van Creveld, Martin. 1985. *Command in War.* Cambridge, MA: Harvard University Press.

Vansittart, Peter. 1984. *Voices, 1870–1914.* London: Jonathan Cape.

Waterman, Peter. 1996. "International Labor Communication by Computer: The Fifth International?" Paper presented at INET96, Montreal.

Wright, Robert. 1988. *Three Scientists and Their Gods: Looking for Meaning in an Age of Information.* New York: Times Books.

Yates, JoAnne. 1989. *Control through Communication: The Rise of System in American Management.* Baltimore: Johns Hopkins University Press.

CHAPTER THREE

Information Technologies and Turbulence in World Politics

JAMES N. ROSENAU AND DAVID JOHNSON

The temptation to become a technological determinist is enormous. It is surely the case that the world, its peoples, societies, economies, and polities, would be very different than they are if the microelectronic revolution had not occurred, if the Internet, the fax machine, global television, the VCR, and numerous other recent technological innovations were not part of the human landscape. More specifically—and to anticipate a central thrust of our argument—without these innovations people would be less skillful and thus an enlarged capacity for challenging traditional authority through collective action is unlikely to have occurred. Inescapably, it would seem, the course of events is thus determined by the extant technologies.

No, such logic is profoundly erroneous. Technologies can provide opportunities and they can set limits, but they do not determine when and where opportunities are seized or when and where limits are operative. People do that, and so do societies, economies, and polities. Powerful as modern information technologies are, they do not deprive humans of their capacity for choice. They can shape the orientations people bring to the choices they need to make, but the shaping processes get filtered through the values and personalities that individuals have acquired from a variety of sources. Clearly, then, to ascribe determinative power to information technologies is to misread the human condition. Like any determinism—geographic, climate, Marxist, or Freudian—technological determinism amounts to a closed system of thought that cannot be negated and is thus often bound to fall short of adequate explanation.

Put more forcefully, information technologies are neutral. They can serve to tyrannize publics as well as to liberate them. They can facilitate the dynamics

55

of globalization as well as those of virulent nationalism. They can mislead policymakers as well as enlighten them. In short, whether the consequences of information technologies are beneficial or deleterious depends on the uses to which they are put by citizens and their leaders (see Steele and Stein, in this volume).

Technology as a Prime Variable

This cautionary note about the limits of technological analysis is not to say, however, that modern information technologies are not among the major, or even the primary, determinants of the course of events. On the contrary, the ensuing discussion presumes that much of global life and the change dynamics that it is undergoing have their roots in the technologies that have greatly increased the flow of information around the world. The analytic task is to identify how information technologies have shaped individual and collective behavior in conjunction with the other transformative dynamics that have rendered the present era so turbulent. Teasing out the precise contribution of the microelectronic revolution to the causal chain is, of course, exceedingly difficult and well beyond what can be undertaken here. But how information technologies interact with other prime sources of change does fall within our competence.

The consequences of the microelectronic revolution are numerous, ranging from its impact on the skills and orientations of individuals to the coherence and mobilizability of societies to the decisiveness and effectiveness of policy-making processes. There are, in other words, a variety of ways in which microelectronic technologies operate as independent variables, more in fact than can possibly be covered in the space and time available (Rosenau 1990, 316–318).[1] Accordingly, we have fallen back on a particular model of world politics as a basis for specifying the key points where information technologies may be prime independent variables. The model is variously known as the "turbulence" or "postinternational" model (Rosenau, 1990), and for present purposes it has the virtue of clustering the many relevant variables under three main headings: a microlevel skill parameter, a macrolevel structural parameter, and a macro-micro-level relational parameter. The model is founded on the proposition that the transformation of these three parameters underlies the dynamics that have infused turbulence into world politics—in part because turbulent conditions feed on themselves and in part because the transformations at work have yet to run their course—and given rise to global conditions that are so different from the past as to justify regarding them as postinternational rather than as merely international. Postinternational theory posits the onset of turbulence as occurring when all three of the parameters enter a condition of high complexity (extensive interactions among numerous, interdependent actors) and high dynamism (extensive variability in the way the actors conduct their affairs). The microelectronic revolution plays an important role in the continuing transformation of each of the three parameters.

Postinternational theory leads us to see a variety of implications for world politics as a result of the turbulence that is apparent in the microelectronic revolution. Information technologies enhance the ability of individuals to organize collectively in order to challenge traditional authorities and to facilitate the formation of common values and interests, and hence, of performance criteria for authorities. Similarly, information technologies enhance the ability of collectivities to evaluate the performance of these new authorities. There are no apparent reasons to believe that the circumstances of high complexity and dynamism posited by postinternational theory will settle down. The skills of people can be expected to continue to expand as the microelectronic revolution yields new technologies, thereby raising ever higher the performance criteria demanded of authorities. Likewise the continuing microelectronic revolution seems likely to sharpen the bifurcation of global structures and to intensify the proliferation of actors in the multicentric world. Finally, the impact of information technologies upon the incidence of conflict and cooperation should no longer be considered only in terms of actors within the state-centric world; the likelihood of conflict between, and cooperation among, globalizing and localizing forces in both the state-centric and multicentric worlds also needs to be traced.

Information

Several prior questions need to be considered before using the turbulence model to assess the impact of the microelectronic revolution on world affairs. Such an assessment requires clarity on what is meant by information and information technologies. In neither case are the meanings self-evident and confusion is best avoided by specifying the nature of the concepts at the outset.

What is information? Raw facts, interpretations of facts, or inferences drawn from observations? Established knowledge or slipshod impressions? Words or pictures? Does a skillful person use information or are the skills a form of information?

We have developed a broad conception of information in response to questions such as these. Here information is conceived to be the observations, interpretations, and understanding that people acquire and exchange with others. Such information can be accurate or distorted, true or false, elaborate or simple, stored or distributed—to mention only a few of the dimensions along which it can be arrayed—but as long as it is susceptible to being communicated in one form or another among people, we consider it to be information. Put differently, information is generated and refined through a three-stage process: it derives from (1) observations that can then be converted into (2) patterns of data which, in turn, can be transformed into (3) knowledge when understandings are drawn from the data patterns. Since observations and understandings are all capable of being communicated, we regard information as being present at any point in this process.

The distinctions between the three information stages are relevant in terms of the way in which communications among people and organizations unfold. Each stage lends itself to different types of technologies and thus is more readily available to different individuals and societies, depending on the kinds of technologies available to them. Data, for example, are easier to classify and store than is the case for knowledge, with the result that communications among people or organizations with more advanced technologies are likely to be more elaborate than is the case for those with more rudimentary technologies. Of course, even the less-advanced technologies allow for the processing of more observations and data patterns—and thus more understanding—than was the case prior to the microelectronic revolution.

It should be noted that the conversion of observations into knowledge need not pass through the second stage of data that have been quantified in order to discern recurring patterns. One can derive from observations what can be called "working knowledge" without being familiar with specific facts. The distinction here is between knowing how things work in general and having specific details about how they operate. It is plausible, perhaps even pervasive, for example, that people know the implications of an upheaval in Pakistan without knowing the name of that country's capital. Accordingly, when we refer henceforth to the "skills" of people we have in mind the level of their working knowledge as well as the level of their factual knowledge. This ability to operate on the basis of "working knowledge" suggests more skillful individuals who can interpret and understand information (i.e., are able to distinguish between relevant and irrelevant facts) rather than merely being able to store and retrieve data patterns or observations.

Information Technologies

Irrespective of how information may be conceived, what are information technologies? Is the hardware of the personal computer on which this chapter was drafted an information technology? Is the software of the word-processing application? Is the hardware and software of the local area network (LAN) that connects the personal computer to the printer? Is the gateway that connects the LAN to the Internet? Are the node servers and transmission networks of the World Wide Web?

All of these are information technologies, but this is far from an exhaustive list. Information technologies include the databases, the data storage tools, the "supercomputers," and the other advanced information-processing facilities used by private sources as well as those available to the public through the Internet. From our broad perspective, moreover, television, fax machines, telephones, and a host of other telecommunications, print, and broadcast media are information technologies.

But a descriptive list is not sufficient to assess the impact of information technologies upon world politics. A conceptualization of their components is also needed. All of the information technologies just noted, as well as many others that could be enumerated, fall into two principal categories: *information-processing* technologies and *communications* technologies that transmit and receive the information. The former are those technologies that store, manipulate, and display information. These include personal computer random-access memory (RAM), World Wide Web graphic browser software, and supercomputers such as those of the National Center for Supercomputing Applications (NCSA) at the University of Illinois, Urbana-Champaign. At the heart of computerized information processors are the electronic switches of the integrated circuit. The "on" and "off" positions of these switches correspond to the binary digits one and zero that are used to represent data in mathematical binary form. Most often these binary representations are used to encode various sorts of information: written text, graphic representations, and increasingly, video images and audio sounds. Most information-processing technologies operate at these levels of electronic data and encoded information. As previously noted, it is only through the interpretation, analysis, and judgment of human interaction that such data and information is transformed into knowledge (which may itself be rerepresented as encoded information). In this sense, knowledge is a product of the process of interaction of humans with information-processing technologies.

Turning to communications technologies that send and receive information from one place to another, these include local area network (LAN) connections between computers and printers in an office, the server and transmission networks of the Internet, and satellite broadcast facilities like those of the Cable News Network (CNN).[2] It follows that an important aspect of communications technologies is the nature of the interactions they sustain. Since the process of communication consists of both the transmission and receipt of information, various sorts of communications technologies are better or worse suited to each of these tasks, and they also vary in terms of the number of individuals involved in the flow of communications.[3] At the most simple level, a communication technology might be suited only to transmission and reception between two individuals, or "single-to-single" communication, as with spoken language. (This is also the most common way in which telephone technology is used.) On the other hand, a more complex communication technology might be used for "single-to-many" communication in which transmission might originate from a single source, but be received by a variety of individuals, as with radio and television broadcasting. An example of "many-to-single" communication might be a toll-free telephone number or Web site form by which customers can transmit information to a business firm. Recently, we have witnessed the advent of complex "many-to-many" technologies such as the Internet in which there are not only large numbers of information transmissions and receptions but also great (and changing) diversity in the sources of transmission and reception.

Besides conceiving of information processing and communications technologies as technological products or artifacts, such technologies can also be viewed as processes or practices. The processes of information technologies extend beyond the use of technological artifacts and are representative of the practices of postindustrial, high technology in contemporary society. The practices of technology include all those processes through which technological artifacts become manifest.[4] These include the initial extraction from the environment and conversion of raw materials and energy; the invention, innovation, and diffusion of technological capabilities and knowledge; the production and manufacturing of artifacts; the distribution of technologies throughout society, including the provision of necessary infrastructure; the administrative and managerial integration of these technological activities; and ultimately the usage of the technological artifacts. A number of these broader practices of information technology have implications for world politics in terms of their tendency to centralize or decentralize information-processing technologies and the degree to which they foster or hinder one or more of the different types of communications transmission and reception.

The extraction and conversion of raw materials and energy has little impact upon the practices of information technologies that require relatively limited or readily available raw material inputs and that use relatively small amounts of energy. On the one hand, invention and product innovation tend to increase costs as new products initially appear. For information technologies, this increase in costs gives an advantage to large-scale, centralized producers, thereby favoring "single-to-many" communication technologies and centralizing and isolating the use of information-processing technologies in the development of knowledge. On the other hand, process innovation and technology diffusion tends to reduce costs, leading to small-scale and decentralized production that favors "many-to-many" communication technologies and diverse and interconnected uses of information processing in the development of knowledge.

Most information technology manufacturing and distribution systems are relatively simple and therefore have a limited impact upon the broader practices of information technology. Infrastructure, though, is enormously important in the processes of information technology. The provision of telecommunications transmission networks can be undertaken by both private or commercial entities as well as by public or governmental entities (or quasi-governmental private entities regulated by the government). The provision of private or commercial infrastructure fosters "single-to-many" communications technologies and centralizes and isolates information-processing technologies as multiple providers compete for users in the marketplace in order to recoup capitalization costs. Public or government infrastructure fosters "many-to-many" communications technologies and diverse and interactive information processing technologies as multiple users are able to take advantage of shared, common facilities.[5]

Administrative and bureaucratic integration affects the practice of information technologies in two principal ways. One important aspect of any technology is the development and propagation of standards that allow technologies produced by a variety of users to interoperate. Standards can be public (mandated by a government authority) or private (developed by one or more commercial entities) and in either case the advantages that result in terms of interoperability enhance "many-to-many" communications technologies and decentralized and interactive information-processing technologies. The need for standards represents just one of many sorts of "market failures" that may shape the practices of information technologies. To the extent that other sorts of market failures occur—for example, in terms of reduced commercial research and development efforts arising from the inability to recover costs—"many-to-many" communications technologies and decentralized and interactive information processing technologies will be restricted.

A main aspect of the practice of information technology is the dispersion and usage of technologies throughout the society. The market is the most widely used mechanism for the dispersion of information technologies. Therefore the spread of information technologies, both information-processing and communications technologies, will follow economic lines (not only in terms of traditional consumer-buying patterns, but also in terms of other economic activities like corporate donations to schools). In general, this means that information technologies will track with economic resources throughout a society (including global society). Where economic disparities exist, corresponding disparities in information technologies will exist. Nonmarket dispersion mechanisms can be used to disseminate information technologies (as has largely been the case with telephone service), but these sorts of public (governmental) efforts are likely to be much less common at the global level.

Tendencies toward centralization or decentralization of information-processing technologies will play an important role in globalizing and localizing tendencies in world politics. Similarly, different tendencies in communications transmission and reception will have different impacts upon the formation of

collectivities of individuals. We now turn to an examination of these tendencies—a result of the microelectronic revolution—upon world politics in
the context of postinternational theory.

Turbulence and Information Technologies in World Politics

With the distinction between information-*processing* technologies and *communications* technologies and the broader *practices* of information technology in mind, we can now turn to the task of assessing the impact of the
microelectronic revolution upon the course of world affairs. As noted, our
approach is to probe the impact as it is manifest in the transformation of the
three basic parameters of the turbulence model of world politics. Postinternational theory posits the onset of turbulence as occurring when all three of
the parameters enter a condition of high complexity (extensive interactions
among numerous, and interdependent actors) and high dynamism (extensive
variability in the way the actors conduct their affairs). It also presumes that
a worldwide condition of turbulence emerged in the 1950s and has continued to prevail and expand ever since, in part because turbulent conditions
feed on themselves and in part because the transformations at work have yet
to run their course. The three parameters central to the theory consist of a
microlevel skill parameter, a macrolevel structural parameter, and a macro-
micro-level relational parameter. As will be seen, information technologies
play an important role in the continuing transformation of each of the three
parameters.

The Microparameter

The transformation of the microparameter involves the increasing skills with
which people everywhere understand, both analytically and emotionally,
where they fit in world affairs. In every culture healthy adults today are
hypothesized to be better able to both focus their emotions and use their analytic skills to construct scenarios that link them to distant events than was the
case for, say, their grandparents.[6] Included among these expanded skills is a
greater capacity for appreciating the potential of collective action and, thus,
for knowing when to engage in it. The sources of these expanded emotional
and analytic skills are many. They include the world's trend toward more and
more education for more and more people; the increased rates of tourist and
business travel abroad; the need to adapt to ever more complex urban environments; and the growing exposure to computers, global television, and the
many other mechanisms of the microelectronic revolution.

It might be asked, How do information technologies contribute to the
emotional skills of individuals, to their ability to know more precisely what

they judge to be desirable or undesirable? One can readily grasp that the flow of information facilitated by various technologies enhances analytic skills, but why should emotional capacities be enlarged? The answer is implicit in our broad conception of information just noted, namely, that the information provided by the technologies consists of much more than the empirical materials that underlie analytic conclusions; its words and pictures are also laden with both the explicit and implicit values on which judgments are based, developed, and rendered.

Turbulence theory acknowledges that wide differences still obtain in the access people have to information technologies and thus in the analytic and emotional skills they have developed. Clearly, people in the developed world have much more access than those in the developing world.[7] But at the same time the skill revolution is hypothesized to be worldwide even though the differences continue to prevail. That is, people everywhere are expanding their skills, but it is likely that they are doing so at different rates. Furthermore, the theory does not presume that the skill revolution is leading to attitudinal convergence on a global scale. Rather, people are seen to be increasingly skillful in terms of their own cultures, with the result that the Islamic fundamentalist is more analytically and emotionally skillful than his or her grandparents, just as the same can be said for the Asian peasant, and the New York literate. Indeed, the granddaughter of Malay peasants today works at a Hewlett-Packard or Sony electronics assembly plant even as she rejects U.S. or Japanese conceptions of democracy in her political life.

The ways in which the information technologies contribute to the skill revolution are many and varied. Three are perhaps especially noteworthy. One is the "single-to-many" technology embedded in global television, another is the information-processing capabilities reflected in the computer, and the third is the "many-to-many" technology represented by the Internet and by its World Wide Web.[8] While the ensuing paragraphs explore these technologies separately, they are of course interactive and cumulative; more accurately, many people in the world have access to at least one of these technologies and more than a few are able to enjoy the advantages of all three. As will be seen, moreover, together these technologies have contributed to a freeing up of imaginations—the capacity to envision what heretofore had been beyond conjecture.

Turning to the "single-to-many" technologies as represented by global television, it can be noted that the skills of people everywhere have been enlarged by the availability of programming from and about other parts of the world. The data on the spread of television sets and the satellite dishes used to receive programming tell a consistent story of expansion, with every country in the world having progressively more sets since 1965 (Rosenau 1990, 338–352). Even the least-developed countries that have few homes with electricity are seeking to expand the capacity of their people to view the TV screen by opening community centers with television sets in rural areas (Daley 1996, A4). To be sure, "single-to-many" technologies do not allow for interaction among their users and they also make it possible for media owners to manipulate the values and perspectives of their viewers. Notwithstanding these possibilities, however, the spread of television on a global scale brings much more of the world into the homes of people than was ever the case in prior eras, and it does so with compelling images of distant places that are bound to open up new perspectives for viewers even if they may also be simplistic and skewed. As noted in the following section, moreover, the content of the images may be less important in terms of the skill revolution than are the ways in which they free up imaginations to roam across previously unrecognized vistas of possible experience.

As for information-processing technologies represented by the computer, they have contributed to the skill revolution by giving people an opportunity to use and process data much more extensively than was the case in earlier eras and, also, by facilitating more analytic modes of thought. Individuals are now able, even required, to develop new skills with which to cope with the availability of more refined data and with much greater amounts of them, but equally important, there is good evidence that both in the workplace and at home the computer provides challenges that engage the intellect of people, sometimes by posing puzzles they know to be solvable if they can get their programs to operate effectively (Zuboff 1988, 75–76) and sometimes by demonstrating ways of wording and handling ideas to which they would not otherwise be exposed (Papert 1993). It is even reasonable to anticipate that successive generations of ever more computer-literate people will, like new generations of computers, lead to individuals who are ever more playful with ideas and ever more competent in manipulating data. The future of the skill revolution is very bright indeed.

The construction of elaborate scenarios by individuals is directly affected by information-processing technologies that enhance their ability to generate and manipulate information. Communications technologies are used to enhance the ability of individuals to communicate with distant, diverse, and disparate others. Already there has been widespread diffusion of "single-to-many" communications technologies (traditional broadcast and print media). And more recently, effective and efficient communication has become available to elite users of emerging "many-to-many" technologies such as the Internet.

Since they involve "many-to-many" communications, it is hardly surprising that the Internet and its World Wide Web have undergone phenomenal growth in recent years, growth so phenomenal and "so fast and in so many places that no one really knows how big it is or how many people use it" (Deibert 1997, 133). One effort at measurement, for example, concluded that "the number of host computers, or network 'nodes,' around the world has grown from 1,000 in 1984 to 10,000 in 1987 to 100,000 in 1989, to 1,000,000 in 1992, to 4,851,000 in 1994, to 9,500,000 in January 1996, to 12,881,000 in July 1996" (Deibert 1997, 132). And these figures barely hint at the growth that lies ahead as the capacity, portability, and number of telephones (through which people are linked on the Internet) explodes and fosters a "wired world" that results in the "death of distance" (*Economist* 1995, 5–6). To be sure, until now the Internet and the World Wide Web has been an information technology predominantly used in the United States and in the developed world, with developing countries lagging far behind in their access to the facilities of the wired world. But while the developing world has a long way to go before it is substantially wired for "many-to-many" communications, the declining cost of telephones, the proliferation of satellite systems in a space-based geostationary orbit 23,000 miles above the earth's equator, and the burgeoning of fiber optic wires that can handle thousands of calls simultaneously all point to an increasingly rapid rate of growth of "many-to-many" channels throughout all regions of the world.[9] Again the figures tell the story succinctly:

> One million new hosts were added in the first six months of 1994 alone, many of which came from outside the United States. In that same first six months of 1994, Germany experienced a 51 percent increase in hosts; France 117 percent; Spain 96 percent; New Zealand 157 percent; Hungary 169 percent; Mexico 45 percent; Chile 170 percent; and Malaysia 204 percent. Although the figures are rapidly made obsolete by exponential growth, there may be as many as 90 million Internet users spread unevenly around the world. (Deibert 1997, 132)[10]

Viewed from the perspective of the turbulence model, data such as these only begin to depict the ways in which the Internet and the World Wide Web are contributing to the skill revolution.

What is less obvious, but even more important, are the consequences of the "many-to-many" technologies for how people perceive and relate to the world. These technologies not only provide, in effect, access to the world's accumulated knowledge, but they also enable people to be in frequent and continuous contact with colleagues, acquaintances, clients, competitors, like-minded professionals, and unknown others, interactions that are highly likely to expand their horizons and to enrich their grasp of how matters of concern are structured and function. The skills of people, in other words, seem bound to be honed the more they use the Internet. More than that, not only do "adults in the United States spend more time collectively browsing the Internet every week than they do watching videocassettes" (Specter 1996, 1), but the same is true for children, suggesting that future generations may be increasingly sensitive to the proximity of distant places and people. In the words of one observer, "I believe the on-line medium will be the dominant medium in children's lives in the 21st century, surpassing television. . . ."[11]

Hardly less important than the ways in which "many-to-many" technologies enhance the analytic and emotional skills of individuals is their potential for collective action. Since the Internet allows for the same message to be sent simultaneously to many receivers by many transmitters, it has become a prime instrument for the formation of groups that seek to coalesce and press their common concerns. As such, it is an indifferent instrument, usable to form hate groups as well as to enable persons with positive goals to come together. A report of the Anti-Defamation League, for example, observed that "hate organizations . . . have seized on the relatively low cost of using the Internet and its accessibility to a large audience worldwide to create a new vehicle for marketing their materials, exchanging information and attracting sympathizers" (Kovalski 1996, A4). On the other hand, when TWA Flight 800 exploded over the Atlantic and killed twenty-one people from Montoursville, Pennsylvania, messages began immediately arriving over the Internet from sympathizers all over the world, with the result that "the thousands of computer messages sent to condolences@pennet.net . . . helped the town begin to heal" (Meredith 1996, B4). In the words of the cofounder of PenNet, "We're going to have more E-mail than we have people."[12] We will return to the impact of "many-to-many" technologies as mobilizers of support in our discussion of the macro-micro parameter.[13]

Besides these examples of information technology dispersion and usage, the broader practice of information technology is an increasingly collective endeavor and provides experience in collective action. Individuals involved in information technology invention, in innovation and diffusion, in production and manufacturing, in distribution and the provision of infrastructure, and in the administrative and bureaucratic integration of these activities are also enhancing their general capabilities for collective action.[14]

Some critiques are less hopeful about the affect of information technologies on the intellectual skills of individuals. One observer, for example, sees a host of negative consequences. Most notably, powerful corporate interests, the government (especially the military), and the technical and scientific community, taken together, and

> aided by the persuasive skills of the advertisers, have fixed upon the computer as an education instrument; the machine brings that formidable constellation of social interests to the classrooms and

the campus. The more room and status it is given there by educators, the greater the influence those interests will have.

Yet these are the interests that are making the most questionable use of the computer. At their hands, this promising technology—itself a manifestation of prodigious human imagination and inventiveness—is being degraded into a means of surveillance and control, of financial and managerial centralization, or manipulating public opinion, of making war. The presence of personal computers in millions of homes, especially when they are used as little more than trivial amusements, does not in any way offset the power the machine brings to those who would use it for these purposes.

Introducing students to the computer at an early age, creating the impression that their little exercises in programming and game playing are somehow giving them control over a powerful technology, can be a treacherous deception. It is not teaching them to think in some scientifically sound way; it is persuading them to acquiesce. It is accustoming them to the presence of computers in every walk of life, and thus making them dependent upon the machine's supposed necessity and superiority. Under these circumstances, the best approach to computer literacy might be to stress the limitations and abuses of the machine, showing the students how little they need it to develop their autonomous powers of thought. (Roszak 1994, 241–242; see also Steele and Stein, in this volume)

On the other hand, as previously implied, the cumulative impact of the several types of information technologies on individuals is not confined only to analytic and emotional skills. It has been plausibly argued that the electronic media, along with extensive varieties of migration, have spurred the imaginations of people:

The first step in this argument is that electronic media decisively change the wider field of mass media and other traditional media. This is not a monocausal fetishization of the electronic. Such media transform the field of mass mediation because they offer new resources and new disciplines for the construction of imagined selves and imagined worlds. . . .

[Accordingly,] it is wrong to assume that the electronic media are the opium of the masses. . . . There is growing evidence that the consumption of the mass media throughout the world often provokes resistance, irony, selectivity, and, in general, agency. Terrorists modeling themselves on Rambo-like figures (who have themselves generated a host of non-Western counterparts); housewives reading romances and soap operas as part of their efforts to construct their own lives; Muslim family gatherings listening to speeches by Islamic leaders on cassette tapes; domestic servants in South India taking packaged tours to Kashmir; these are all examples of the active way in which media are appropriated by people throughout the world. T-shirts, billboards, and graffiti as well as rap music, street dancing, and slum housing all show that the images of the media are quickly moved into local repertoires of irony, anger, humor, and resistance. (Appadurai 1996, 3, 7)

In sum, due in good part to information-processing and communications technologies, the transformation of the microparameter has extended the ability of people to generate and manipulate information, to focus their emotions, and to explore their imaginations.[15] These same qualities have also contributed to the transformation of the macroparameter, to which we now turn.

The Macroparameter

The turbulence model postulates that global structures have undergone bifurcation with the advent of high complexity and dynamism. Where the long-standing arrangements of world politics were founded on an anarchic system of states, each of which was sovereign and answerable to no higher authority, the transformation of the macroparameter has occurred through the evolution of a multicentric world of diverse nongovernmental collectivities that are essentially autonomous and not necessarily subject to controls exercised by actors in the state-centric world. Sometimes the collectivities of the two worlds compete, sometimes they conflict, but at all times they are interactive. States are still central actors, in other words, but their capabilities have been diminished by the forces of globalization and, as a result, now they must be much more responsive than ever before to the demands and patterns that emanate from networks and coalitions of nongovernmental organizations (NGOs), multinational corporations (MNCS), ethnic minorities, professional societies, social movements, and many other collectivities that populate the multicentric world. Put differently, recent years have witnessed an associational explosion (Salamon 1994), a mushrooming of organizations at every level of community—neighborhood, local, provincial, national, regional, and global—that is both a source and a consequence of the high complexity that underlies the turbulence of our time.

Information-processing and communication technologies can enhance both the capabilities for cooperation and for conflict, and thereby interaction within both the state-centric and multicentric worlds as well as between them. Furthermore, as the practitioners of information technology engage in *competition* among each other rather than in conflict, they may find themselves, as collective globalizing forces, in conflict with localizing forces.

Among the many ways in which information and communication technologies have contributed to the bifurcation of global structures, perhaps the most notable is their role as a creator of channels for interaction among collectivities in the multicentric world and between the multi and state-centric worlds. As just implied, the coalitions and networks among diverse groups that lie at the heart of the multicentric world could not have been formed, much less sustained, without the availability and wide diffusion of "many-to-many" technologies. Indeed, so extensive is the use of information technologies in the multicentric world that many of its practitioners are themselves emerging as major players in that world. That is, having enhanced the capabilities of diverse multicentric actors by providing a multiplicity of channels through which the demands of individuals and groups can get onto the global agenda, the practitioners are relied upon to maintain and extend the technologies they developed.

The Macro-Micro Parameter

Concerned with the links between people at the microlevel and collectivities at the macrolevel, the focus of this parameter is the authority structures of both governmental and nongovernmental organization. People are conceived as having long been ready to comply with the directives of the authorities of the collectivities to which they belonged. With the onset of turbulent conditions on a worldwide scale, however, authority structures have been undergoing transformation from being in place to being in crisis. People are increasingly ready to defy, ignore, or otherwise challenge their authorities if the conduct of the latter is not regarded as minimally acceptable. In other words, legitimacy is decreasingly founded on tradition and increasingly attached to performance. The frequency with which the public squares of the world's cities have in recent years been filled with citizens protesting policies, demanding change, and in some cases toppling governments is a good measure of the extent to which the macro-micro parameter is undergoing transformation (Rosenau 1997, chapter 15).

The skill revolution is a prime source of this transformation. Not only are people more able than ever to discern where they and their interests fit in the unfolding of distant events, but these skills also include a growing capacity for recognizing how they might contribute to collective actions in the public arena. Clearly information and communication technologies are central to this expanding talent. They provide, as it were, the bases for knowing when and how to act in concert with others. The Internet and television news coverage supply the information and incentives through which individuals can come together and challenge their authorities. "Single-to-many" technologies provide the news and scenes of collective action being effective, or at least having consequences, and "many-to-many" technologies facilitate the networking necessary to mobilize like-minded citizens and to assign them specific tasks. One need only know about the role played by television and fax machines in the 1989 Tiananmen Square protests (*Europe* 1990, 40–41)[16] or the diverse ways in which the Internet sustained the Zapatista uprising in Mexico[17] and the peace movement in war-torn former Yugoslavia (Gessen 1995) to appreciate the large extent to which information and communication technologies are relevant to the transformation of the macro-micro parameter. Indeed, despite the hardening of factions in Bosnia, Croatia, and elsewhere in the former Yugoslavia, "people actually have ongoing conferences across these borders!" a dynamic described as "the most ridiculous, idiotic thing . . . a country at war with no money now has the highest percentage of e-mail users in the peace movement: every post-Yugoslav group active in environment, peace, et cetera, is on [the Internet]" (Gessen 1995, 160, 161).

Communication technologies enhance the ability of individuals to organize collectively in order to challenge traditional authorities. They also facilitate the formation of common values and interests, and hence, of performance criteria for authorities. Information-processing technologies enhance the ability to evaluate the performance of these new authorities. Finally, collectivities involved in the broader practice of information technology serve as a model for these new, performance-based authorities.

It follows that not only do information technologies enhance the skills of people individually and collectively, but they also affect the vulnerability of authorities to upheaval. Communication technologies make it difficult for authorities to control the flow of information. The greater diffusion of "single-to-many" technologies reduces monopolies held by central authorities while emerging "many-to-many" technologies add complexity to all communications. Information-processing technologies dilute the monopoly of authorities on information. This enhances the capabilities of decentralized groups while the increased complexity of information makes the refining of knowledge from data more difficult. The broader practice of information technology by commercial organizations—an increasingly well-established form of collective action—serves as one possible model for organizations seeking to deal with upheaval.

Quite apart from challenges to authority, moreover, the microelectronic revolution has been a major source of networks and networking having become a form of organization sustained by macro-micro interactions. It can even be said that the trend toward horizontal modes of organization have spread so rapidly that they are beginning to replace top-down, hierarchical modes in many realms of endeavor, a pattern that could hardly have accelerated without the advent of "many-to-many" technologies that enable substantial numbers of people to come together, concert their efforts, and move toward goals without ever being in face-to-face contact. Networks span national borders, issue boundaries, ideological divides, and professional communities, and they do so today much more effectively than in the past because of the availability of the networking capacities of the microelectronic revolution (Lipnack and Stamps 1994). The number of groups sharing common values and interests that have formed in cyberspace is beyond calculation, but surely it is enormous.

Stated differently, the networking phenomenon stimulated by the microelectronic revolution has undermined the attachment of people to territory. By making it possible for like-minded groups to form in cyberspace and for ethnic minorities and diaspora to sustain and extend their ties, the information and communication technologies have enabled communities to evolve and strengthen their ties.[18] Indeed, it has been noted that the microelectronic revolution has enabled groups to strengthen their ties by confining communications to their own limited audiences—what we might call "some-to-some" technologies. As one analyst puts it, "The key to these new uses of telecommunications technology lies in recognizing that mass media are steadily being replaced by targeted or 'addressable' media with specialized and more homogeneous audiences" (Elkins 1997, 139).

Change or Continuity?

The question remains whether the dispersion and usage of information-processing and communication technologies as well as the broader practices of information technology (and indeed high technology in general) will continue to stir the transformation of the three parameters posited by the turbulence model, or whether the dynamics of change have run their course to the point where patterns of continuity will evolve. Our take on the problem is clear-cut: there are no apparent reasons to believe that the circumstances of high complexity and dynamism will settle down. The skills and imagination of people, having been facilitated by both "many-to-many" and "single-to-many" technologies, can be expected to continue to expand as the microelectronic revolution yields ever more refined and powerful technologies, thereby raising ever higher the performance criteria demanded of leaders in both the public and private sectors.[19] Likewise the continuing refinement of information and communication technology seem likely to sharpen the bifurcation of global structures and to intensify the proliferation of organizations and networks.

More specifically, the impact of information technologies as sources of change or continuity need to be considered in the areas of international security and the world political economy, which have been the traditional interests of sovereignty-bound actors, as well as in the areas of human rights and the natural environment, which are increasingly of interest to emerging actors in the multicentric world.[20] Similarly, the impact of information technologies upon the incidence of conflict and cooperation should be considered not only in terms of conflict or cooperation between actors within the state-centric and multicentric worlds but also in terms of the likelihood of conflict between and cooperation among globalizing and localizing forces in both worlds.

International security has long been a traditional concern of sovereignty-bound actors. Information technologies will contribute to continuity in this area through the enhancement of the war-fighting, surveillance, and intelligence capabilities of states. Undoubtedly, these enhanced capabilities on the part of states will be used both for conflictual and cooperative ends. Nevertheless, advances in surveillance and intelligence capabilities may add to the enforceability of arms control agreements, thereby making such agreements more likely. In particular, advances in surveillance and intelligence capabilities will add to the ability of third parties, including actors in the multicentric world, to monitor military activities.

Perhaps the greatest likelihood of change in international security affairs stemming from the emergence of information technologies is the enhanced capabilities of sovereignty-free actors in the multicentric world.[21] The emergence of multicentric actors has added a new dimension to traditional forms of interstate conflict and cooperation: conflict between and cooperation among globalizing and localizing forces in the state-centric and multicentric worlds. While information technologies may allow multicentric actors to play a larger role in monitoring the military activities of states, ethnic conflict and other sorts of fragmentation within states are also influenced by the enhanced capabilities of these emergent actors.

Like international security, political economy has long been a traditional concern of states. Here again, as with international security, information technologies foster continuity by enhancing the capabilities of states to pursue their traditional interests in the world political economy. And as with international security, information technologies pose the greatest potential for change in the world political economy through the enhanced capabilities of multicentric actors.

The emergence of sovereignty-free actors changes the nature of political economy in the processes of globalization and localization as suggested by postinternational theory (Rosenau 1997). Indeed, it is in the world political economy that the impact of globalization is most apparent. The emergence of actors in the multicentric world has changed the nature of the world political economy from competition between economic actors (sometimes leading to conflict between states) to conflict between globalizing economic forces and local forces resisting such globalization. These localizing forces appear principally in three areas: economic and safety protection for labor forces, environmental protection, and protection for national currencies. In general, information technologies, because of their bias toward sophisticated (wealthy, educated) users, favor globalizing forces.

Another area in which the influence of information technologies can be expected to lead to change in world politics is human rights, including women's rights. Human rights has generated an emergent set of performance criteria. On the one hand, information technologies enhance the capabilities of human rights-oriented actors in the multicentric world, allowing them to press their case. On the other hand, information technologies enhance the capabilities of states (and certain NGOs as well) that deny human rights. Nevertheless, as with economic affairs, affluent, educated users are at the forefront of human rights advocacy and hence the information technology edge seems to rest with human rights advocates.

Similar to the situation of human rights, protection of the natural environment has given rise to an emergent set of performance criteria. And, similarly, information technologies enhance the capabilities of environmental protection-oriented actors in the multicentric world, allowing them to press their case. And again, as with those who commit human rights violations, information technologies enhance the capabilities of states and some multicentric actors to commit environmental damage. But unlike the situation with human rights, globalizing forces are at work on both sides of the environmental issue. In this case, globalizing norms of environmental protection are at odds with similarly globalizing forces intent on economic activity that is often damaging to the natural environment. Furthermore, the globalizing economic forces that are damaging to the natural environment are part of the larger practice of all sorts of other technologies, whether it be the extraction of oil deposits from the Arctic Ocean or Caspian Sea or the disposal of nuclear waste in the deserts of the American Southwest. Thus, despite the globalizing norm of environmental protection, the actual protection of the natural environment is, paradoxically, a localizing activity. Once again, information technologies are involved in the growing conflict between globalizing and localizing forces.

Information technologies seem to contribute to continuity in the areas of international security and in the world political economy by enhancing the capabilities of states while at the same time they seem to be an element for change in these traditional areas by enhancing the capabilities of actors in the multicentric world, particularly those involved in the world political economy. In fact, information technologies are central to the emergence of the multicentric world and to the forces of globalization, and, therefore, to the rise of multicentric actors that focus on new performance criteria such as human rights and protection of the natural environment. While information technologies enhance the capabilities of multicentric actors to cooperate with each other and with states, they also contribute to the conflict between globalizing and localizing forces. Information technologies may enhance the capabilities of both globalizing and localizing forces, but because of their bias toward sophisticated users, will tend to favor globalizing forces that are most able to take advantage of greater resources gained trough participation in the global political economy.

Put more challengingly, the future may be as unlike the present as the present is unlike the not-distant past. The processes of globalization and localization, and the tensions between them, will surely persist and, in so doing, sustain the turbulent processes that are transforming the human condition. Given the enhanced capacity of individuals to engage in collective action, it can even be speculated that new forms of political organization may lie ahead as the

> electronic mass mediation and transnational mobilization have broken the monopoly of autonomous nation-states over the project of modernization. The transformation of everyday subjectivities thorough electronic mediation and the work of the imagination is . . . deeply connected to politics, through the new ways in which individual attachments, interests, and aspirations increasingly crosscut those of the nation-state. (Appadurai 1996, 10)

However, to allow for the possibility that information and communication technologies may be linked to an

> emergent postnational order [that] proves not to be a system based on relations between homogeneous units (as with the current system of nation-states) but a system based on relations between heterogeneous units (some social movements, some interest groups, some professional bodies, some nongovernmental organizations, some armed constabularies, some judicial bodies). (Appadurai 1996, 23)

is not to slip subtly back into the presumptions of technological determinism. We repeat that the choices that may produce such outcomes will be made by people and by their institutions for making collective decisions. And surely the making of these choices will be embedded deep in both conflict and cooperation which, in turn, will be both amplified and modified by the information technologies that have become part and parcel of the global landscape.

Notes

1. For a thorough exploration of the diverse dimensions of the micro-electronic revolution see van Tulder and Junne (1988).

2. Television remains perhaps the most ubiquitous communication technology.

3. The following discussion emphasizes the relative complexity of the *use* of different technologies rather than the technological complexity of the technologies themselves.

4. The manner in which technologies become manifest in society is more complicated by technological change, a topic that is beyond the scope of this analysis.

5. While private entities increasingly provide "many-to-many" communications infrastructure their efforts continue to rely upon public/government provision of right-of-way access and other essential elements of the infrastructure.

6. For one inquiry that systematically and successfully tested the skill revolution across three cultures, three issue areas, and two widely separate time periods for a sample of elites, see Rosenau and Fagen (1997). A lengthy presentation of anecdotal data relevant to the hypothesis can be found in Rosenau (1990, chapter 13) and Rosenau (1997, chapter 14) offers a theoretical framework for assessing the attitudinal dimensions of the skill revolution.

7. Indonesia, the fourth most populous nation in the world, has 1 television set per 6.9 persons, 1 radio per 7.6 persons, and 1 telephone per 39 persons. Congo (formerly Zaire) has 1 radio per 13 persons and 1 telephone per 2,400 persons. By comparison, the United States has 1 television set per 1.3 persons, 2.1 radios for each persons, and 1 telephone per 1.6 persons (Famighetti 1999, 787–873). CNN television broadcasts are received on satellite TV in 1.4 million Chinese households and there are 7.3 million cellular phone subscribers in China. By comparison, the United States, with a population of roughly one fifth of China's approximately 1.2 billion, has 49 million cellular phone subscribers (Malik 1997).

8. It is not clear whether the World Wide Web is a dimension of the Internet, or vice versa. As one analyst puts it, "Although technically distinct, the World-Wide Web has grown with such rapidity and adaptability that it has practically subsumed the Internet entirely" (Deibert 1997, 133).

9. The diffusion of information technologies throughout the developing world can be expected to track closely with the pace of economic development

particularly given the predominance of the market mechanism as the principle means of diffusion of information technologies. According to Malik, "The yearly per capita income in China is less than $700. It should be no surprise, therefore, that most Chinese—except for corporations and the small but burgeoning middle class—can't afford costly new communications technology" (Malik 1997, 19).

10. For a specific example of what growth rates such as these can mean for a country, see the case of China as outlined in *Eastern Express* (1995, 9). These percentages may be misleading because for many countries, especially those in the developing world, they're tied to low overall numbers of host servers. For example, an increase from 20 to 29 hosts—a reasonable situation for a developing country with only a handful of major universities—would show the same 45 percent increase demonstrated by Mexico. According to the Ministry of Posts and Communications, the primary Chinese regulatory agency for the Internet, by the end of 1996 only 30 percent of the approximately 20,000 Internet accounts (on servers) went to local individuals. The remainder were bought by corporations (Malik 1997).

11. Kathryn C. Montgomery, quoted in Mifflin (1996, A16).

12. Scott A. Frye, quoted in Meredith (1996, B4). PenNet was an early Internet Service Provider (ISP) which is no longer doing business. Its domain name, www.pennet.net is now owned by the Korean ISP Chollian (www.chollian.net/eng/).

13. Another important example of such collective action would be the efforts to oppose the Organization for Economic Cooperation and Development's (OECD) Multilateral Agreement on Investment (MAI). See, for example, the Public Citizen Web site at www.citizen.org/pctrade/MAI/maihome .html and the MAI-NOT Project's Web site at mai.flora.org/mai-not/.

14. Admittedly, perhaps the most ubiquitous growth in the use of Internet/Web technologies in recent years has been in the areas of marketing and advertising.

15. Viewed in this way, perhaps it is more than coincidence that a recent AT&T advertisement listed the number to order a new wireless phone as 1–800–IMAGINE.

16. For a description of the role played by television and fax machine technology at Tiananmen see Rosenau and Durfee (1995, 151–157).

17. The role played by the Internet in the mobilization of support that brought the Mexican government military counterattack to a halt and helped force negotiations, for example, is described in Harry Cleaver, "The Chiapas Uprising and the Future of Class Struggle in the New World Order," February 1994, which is available on the World Wide Web site maintained by Cleaver of the University of Texas at Austin at: www.eco.utexas.edu/faculty/Cleaver/ zapsincyber.html.

18. Of course these conditions apply only to those groups that have access to information technologies. Thus, these networks and the delinkage to territory will track with economic development and with the corresponding diffusion of information technologies.

19. It remains to be seen whether these expanding skills and imagination and demands for higher performance will lead to a crisis of governance and possible repressive reactions.

20. See Rosenau (1990, 36), for the definition of "sovereignty-bound actors."

21. See Rosenau (1990, 36), for the definition of "sovereignty-free actors."

References

Appadurai, Arjun. 1996. *Modernity at Large: Cultural Dimensions of Globalization*. Minneapolis: University of Minnesota Press.

Daley, Suzanne. 1996. "Malawi Deprived? Well, TV's on the Way." *New York Times* (May 30).

Deibert, Ronald. 1997. *Parchment, Printing, and Hypermedia: Communication in World Order Transformation*. New York: Columbia University Press.

Eastern Express (Hong Kong). 1995. "Internet Thrives in Nation Starved of Information," 6 April.

Economist. 1995. "Telecommunications" (September 20, Survey).

Elkins, David J. 1997. "Globalization, Telecommunication, and Virtual Ethnic Communities." *International Political Science Review* 18, no. 2: 139–152.

Europe: Magazine of the European Community. 1990 (April).

Famighetti, Robert, ed. 1999. *The World Almanac and Book of Facts 2000*. Mahwah, NJ: Primedia Reference.

Gessen, Masha. 1995. "Balkans Online." *Wired* (November):158–162, 220–228.

Kovalski, Serge E. 1996. "Hate Groups' Internet Use Raises Alarm." *Washington Post* (November 3).

Lipnack, Jessica and Jeffrey Stamps. 1994. *The Age of the Network: Organizing Principles for the 21st Century*. New York: Wiley.

Malik, Arslan. 1997. "The Internet and CNN Won't (Soon) Free China." *Christian Science Monitor*, 15 August.

Meredith, Robin. 1996. "Global Village Comforts a Tiny Town." *New York Times*, 29 July.

Mifflin, Lawrie. 1996. "Advertisers Chase a New Target: 'Cybertots.'" *New York Times*, 29 March.

Papert, Seymour. 1993. *The Children's Machine: Rethinking School in the Age of the Computer.* New York: Basic.

Rosenau, James N. 1990. *Turbulence in World Politics: A Theory of Change and Continuity.* Princeton: Princeton University Press.

Rosenau, James N. 1997. *Along the Domestic-Foreign Frontier: Exploring Governance in a Turbulent World.* Cambridge: Cambridge University Press.

Rosenau. James N. and Mary Durfee. 1995. *Thinking Theory Throughly: Coherent Approaches to an Incoherent World.* Boulder, CO: Westview Press.

Rosenau, James N. and W. Michael Fagen. 1997. "Increasingly Skillful Citizens: A New Dynamism in World Politics?" *International Studies Quarterly* 41 (December):655–686.

Roszak, Theodore. 1994. *The Cult of Information: A Neo-Luddite Treatise on High-tech, Artificial Intelligence, and the True Art of Thinking,* 2d ed. Berkeley: University of California Press.

Salamon, Lester M. 1994. "The Global Associational Revolution: The Rise of the Third Sector on the World Scene." *Foreign Affairs* 73 (July/August):109–122.

Specter, Michael. 1996. "World, Wide, Web: 3 English Words." *New York Times,* 14 April, Sec. 4.

van Tulder, Rob and Junne, Gerd. 1988. European Multinationals in Core Technologies, Chichester, England: Wiley.

Waldrop, W. Mitchell. "The Trillion-Dollar Vision of Dee Hocks." *Fast Company* (October-November): 75–86.

Zuboff, Shoshana. 1988. *In the Age of the Smart Machine: The Future of Work and Power.* Basic.

CHAPTER FOUR

Globalization, Information, and Change

FRANK WEBSTER

Globalization and *information* have probably been the most widely used terms in social science over the last decade. Though it has been developing for centuries, the process of global integration and interpenetration has escalated dramatically in recent years. The collapse of the Soviet system and the accommodations within China have ensured that capitalism has been the major expression of this globalization. We may speak now, for the first time in human history, of the entire planet being organized around a single set of economic principles (profitability, private ownership, competition, and market criteria), which are increasingly capable of being operationalized in real time on a global scale. This process has major consequences for what we do and how we live, influencing economics, politics, and culture in profound and pervasive ways, touching everything from international affairs to everyday life and consciousness. It has led to heightened competition, hybrid cultures, increased uncertainty in many spheres of existence, and a dramatic acceleration of change itself, such that the last decade of the twentieth century is arguably undergoing the most wide-reaching and speedy transformations in human history.

Information has always been integrally linked to globalization. In the first place, globalization has necessitated the construction and maintenance of an information infrastructure that allows people and institutions to operate in a global milieu. This means that telecommunications and computing facilities are axiomatic to a globalized world, though we should be careful not to reduce this to a matter of information and communications technologies (I CTs). Globalization does require ICTs—satellites, videos, television, and computers—if it is to function effectively, but it also requires other technologies and techniques such as the improved means of travel and the establishment of common means of communication to facilitate the ready movement and interaction of people when required. Airlines are as expressive of a globalized world as are ICTs, as is the astonishing recent expansion worldwide of the English language.

Nonetheless, information flows have expanded enormously, both in volume and velocity, over recent years, propelled by the diverse forces of globalization. A good deal of comment has been made especially on the astonishing growth of financial information; daily trade in foreign currency exchanges, for instance, grew from $10 billion in 1973 to a breathtaking $1.3 trillion in 1995 (*Economist,* 1995). The general pattern is also evident elsewhere—in the growth of television output, in the expansion of telecommunications traffic, and in the spread of computer communications links around the world. The conception of a worldwide "network society" captures well the requirement of an integrated planet for sophisticated and intricate information webs to draw together institutions and actors.

Every so often commentators emerge who insist that all this is a consequence of the "information technology revolution." From the obvious starting point that information and communications technologies are necessary for the globalization process, the likes of Toffler (1990) and Negroponte (1995) readily ascribe change to "being digital." This genre of technological determinism is familiar and stale: technologies come along, impact us all, and transform life as we know it. This is an explanation of change being brought about by a *deux ex machina* that emerges from out of the blue yet has the most devastating social effects. In the current era of the "information superhighway" it is even claimed that this will even bring about a "second industrial revolution."

Such writing carries with it an authoritative air. Technology appears to be so substantial, so practical, and so real, that it can be hard to resist the view that this indeed is the primum mobile of change. After all, we readily conceive of history in these terms: *the world the steam engine made, the atomic age,* and *the automobile era.*" As we witness innovation upon innovation in the technological sphere—E-mail, the Internet, cable television services, and portable personal computers (PCs)—that facilitate and affect how we analyze situations and stay in touch with one other, then it seems obvious that it is indeed technology that causes change. Not surprisingly such a way of seeing has a particular appeal for practical men and women in business and politics who have a stake in persuading people to adapt to change.

However, such an approach is both intellectually facile and misleading (Webster 1999). It is facile because a moment's reflection leads one to realize that there can be no unicausal explanation for the dynamics of change, that economic and military factors play at least an important role in stimulating or blocking innovation. Furthermore, when it comes to consideration of globalization, one may pretty quickly appreciate that, while ICTs are crucial to its growth, recent technologies are by no means the singular factor. The telephone, and before that the telegram, have arguably played a more critical role in the genesis of an integrated world than the computer. Why then the current emphasis on the transformative capacity of ICTs? The emphasis on new technologies is also misleading because it tends simultaneously to isolate technology from social contexts and to ascribe technology as the major factor influencing society. But to regard technology as at once socially autonomous and yet of decisive social consequence is demonstrably wrong. Study after study of the history of technological innovations has shown that they are not socially autonomous, technologies being intricately intermeshed with economic, political, and cultural relationships. Bluntly, technological developments are always socially mediated, as studies by social constructivists (Woolgar 1988) and historians (Winner 1977) especially have demonstrated in recent years, so much so that it is now truistic in social science to ridicule naive technological determinism (Dutton, 1996).

The Prioritization of Information

This is by no means to deny that there is an intimate relationship between globalization and the spread of ICTs. It is clear that while not sufficient to account for globalization, the development of advanced ICTs is necessary to enable it to happen. However, it is noticeable in recent years that social scientists have themselves stepped away from prioritizing ICTs as the agent of change. While the desire to cut through all the potential variables to isolate the most determinant factor tempts social scientists toward searching out the bottom-line technologies, it has become increasingly clear that such a search is in vain. For a start, it is becoming more and more evident that it is not so much the hard technologies that matter, but more the flows of information, the contents of transmissions between networks, which matter most. One cannot get far in understanding the world today by identifying the computer communications links between nations' stock markets, but one can advance a long way by an examination of the amounts, patterns, and frequencies of trading along these routes. Similarly, the presence of satellites in geostationary orbit is necessary to globalization today; of much more real-world consequence, however, is the information those satellites receive and transmit, whether in terms of surveillance of regions or of distribution of particular types of programming.

More and more the talk nowadays is of information—rather than of information and communications technologies—as the key source of change. As we move toward the second millennium, the focus is now on the spread of "information capitalism," on the emergence of a "global information economy," and on the expectation that the future is one of "information societies." The main thrust of those who argue that it is information that is set to play an especially important role in the future lays stress on the expansion of a particular occupational category that has been variously referred to as the "symbolic analyst," the "cognitariat," and "informational labor." This group is prominent in a range of recent influential writing, from Reich's *Work of Nations* (1992), Thurow's *Future of Capitalism* (1996), Drucker's *Post-Capitalist Society* (1993), to Castells's important, indeed seminal, trilogy *The Information Age* (1996, 1997, 1998; Webster 1997). The suggestion implied by these authors is that developments are afoot that will result in the heightened importance of information/knowledge workers,[1] a promotion of such magnitude that established power relationships are overthrown. These accounts go so far as to suggest that informational labor will become the locus of wealth creation in the "information age," displacing established classes, and in consequence profoundly transforming the character of society. It is this arrestingly novel point of view, one that suggests that we are undergoing deep social change, which I will subject to critical scrutiny in this chapter.

While there are significant differences between each of these thinkers, it is hard not to be struck by the degree of unanimity as regards the central role of information and informational labor especially. I think that it is possible to identify a number of common themes in the reasoning offered for this development. They are as follows:

1. *Globalization* has led to a decline in the significance and sovereignty of the nation-state, has heightened competition between business players, and has accelerated the pace of change across and between world markets. At the same time it has placed a special emphasis on *networks* between organizations and actors within, between and across countries.

   Perhaps the starkest statement of this position comes from former secretary of labor Robert Reich. His argument is that, while once what was good for American corporations was good for America since their production was concentrated inside America (and hence provided jobs for Americans), globalization has transformed the situation. Today it is no longer possible to refer with any accuracy to distinct national economies. Such is the fluidity of capital and production that nowadays "the very idea of an American economy is becoming meaningless, as re the notions of an American corporation, American capital, American products, and American technology" (Reich 1992, 8).

Now the economy operates irrespective of national frontiers, held together by what Reich describes as a "global web" of relationships between, within, and even across corporate organizations that are owned by myriad and dispersed shareholders.

2. Impelled by globalization, corporations are *vertically disintegrating*, undergoing a unlayering of bureaucratic levels, which empowers the central players in these global networks. This process has been evidenced in a host of downsizing cases that have stripped middle management layers from the "reengineered" corporation. The long-held dogma of sociology, as well as of businesses, that bureaucratic organization was a requisite of efficiency since rules and procedures, combined with a distinct hierarchy of command, were essential for smooth operation, has been undermined. The globalized economy is too fast-paced to allow for such cumbersome arrangements, and too competitive to allow the luxury of layers of bureaucracy. The upshot is that these are cut away simultaneous with the enhancement of authority to those who remain and who are able to be successful in this new world.

   Castells describes this as the development of the "horizontal corporation," a "flat" organization that is best equipped to meet the challenges of globalization by effecting the "transformation of corporations into networks" (Castells 1996, 115) where alliances are constantly made and remade by people who are at home in the deal-making, fast-paced, and interactive realm that straddles the globe. These are key players who are infused with "the spirit of informationalism" (Castells 1996, 195), a "calling" that evokes Protestantism's contribution to the rise of capitalism and combines this with acknowledgment of the need to be constantly alert to new opportunities, something that requires the sort of "creative destruction" once identified by Schumpeter.

3. There has been a shift away from mass toward *high-value production and services*. This stimulates differentiation, innovation, and the contribution of knowledge to economic matters generally, and to work more specifically, since specialized markets are constantly being sought, novel products being permanently developed, and their symbolic import and/or technical sophistication always increased.

   The Fordist era of mass production is giving way in a globalized, but increasing specialized, market to flexible customization, something that is sensitive to market needs and sensibilities. Products are increasingly knowledge and information intensive. The design on the T-shirt (and the marketing that goes with it) are more valuable, for instance, than the actual materials used in manufacturing it (Lash and Urry 1994). In addition, operation in a global market places a premium on those capable of defining niche markets across the globe, of spotting opportunities wherever they might occur, of cutting costs by way of well-honed accounting or management skills. All of this prioritizes the contribution to products and services of those most capable of adding value. A mere capacity to fabricate is no longer sufficient; the crucial factor is the ability to increase the worth of the good and/or the success of the organization. More generally, this shift toward high value increases the contribution of what Thurow (1996) calls "brainpower industries," such as biotechnology, media production, and computer software, since these are the only sure bets in a global economy where cheap labor is abundant, but incapable alone of offering sophisticated new products that yet may come at prices lower than asked today since once designed and developed the costs of production are minimal.

4. Combined, these factors result in the *prioritization of certain types of occupations*—those that manage and operate across global networks, those that are capable of offering design intensity, those that can provide high added value to products and services through scientific excellence, imaginative skill, financial acumen, or even effective advertising.

   To Reich these are the 20 percent or more of all occupations that he terms *symbolic analysts*, who hold together and advance the "enterprise networks." They are the people who are "continuously engaged in managing ideas" (Reich 1992, 85) and who are in possession of the intellectual capital crucial for success in the twenty-first century. Symbolic analysts "solve, identify, and broker problems by manipulating symbols" (Reich 1992, 178) and are represented in occupations that place stress on abstraction, system thinking, experimentation, and collaboration. They are problem-solvers, problem-identifiers, and strategic brokers located in jobs such as banking, law, engineering, computing, accounting, media, management, and academe.

5. What all these jobs hold in common is that they are *informational*. Of course they hold expertise in particular areas, but precisely because they operate in a world of constant and fre-

netic change, their greatest quality is their high-level *flexibility*, hence a capacity to adapt their generalized abilities to ever-new circumstances. Information labor is always capable of retraining itself, alert to the latest thinking in its areas, holding a keen eye for shifts in fluid markets, watchful of changes in public feelings, constantly able to improve the product.

Castells estimates this informational labor at 30 percent of occupations in nations that are members of the Organization for Economic Cooperation and Development (OECD), and lays great stress on the flexibility of this sort of worker. It is what he calls "self-programmable," by which he means one who is equipped to constantly learn and relearn (in current educational parlance, "lifelong learners"), hence one who is able to sit comfortably within a constantly changing world. Castells (1998) contrasts this informational labor with inflexible—and thereby endangered—generic labor that is heavily represented in the declining skilled manual sector and in many routine clerical operations.

Other writers have stressed that the informational dimensions of most work have increased in significance. For instance, Block (1990) and Hirshhorn (1984), have testified that work operations increasingly provide "cybernetic feedback" to employees who are in turn required to understand complex systems and to rectify faults and to reorient production appropriately. Block wrote of "postindustrial possibilities" and Hirshhorn of "post-industrial technology," but both laid stress—along with the much-quoted Zuboff (1988)—on an upgrading of employees who must, as a matter of course, develop their informational skills to be able to retrain and readapt to a constantly changing situation. Such formulations are in close accord with the popular thesis of post-Fordist "flexible specialization" advocated by Piore and Sabel (1984; Webster 1995).

6. Thus equipped, symbolic analysts tend not to occupy permanent positions in a solid corporate bureaucracy, but more move around *from project to project* on short-term and consultant bases, drawing on their extensive networks and renewed knowledge to ensure effectiveness. Informational labor is characterized by that which moves from one research project to the next, from one marketing contract to another, from one media assignment to another. It features a portfolio career that is self-designed rather than a bureaucratized one proved by the corporation (Handy 1995).

To some this might appear to be a world without security and one that is characterized by increasing social fragmentation (Hutton 1995), but there are more positive versions of such developments. Fukuyama (1997), for example, considers the fact that the flat organization empowers its employees, so they may find satisfaction in their autonomy and, while there may be a diminishing commitment to the organization, the fact that these highly skilled freelancers combine with like-minded people on specific projects might actually stimulate social capital because there are ethical and professional bonds of loyalty between such actors. The image is conjured of the research professor closer to colleagues in California than to her own university in Cambridge, of the software engineer who ranks more highly associates in cyberspace than whomsoever is paying her salary at any given moment.

7. These occupations are estimated to account for between one in five and one in three of all positions today. And however differentiated they are, they share the characteristic of qualification by *high-level educational attainment*. For this reason, universities are integral to the global economy,[2] as is their ability to handle something like 30 percent of the age group. The development of the postmodern university, where established knowledge is overturned and new disciplines and subareas are being developed at breakneck speed, and where the stress is on "performativity" rather than on "truth," is indicative of this (Scott 1995; Smith and Webster 1997). Nonetheless, the greatest quality bestowed on graduates by the university is not specific abilities, but rather a clutch of "transferable skills," those capacities such as the ability to abstract and analyze, to solve problems, to communicate effectively, to be a team-player, yet also a self-starter, to be adaptable while entrepreneurial, about which universities in Great Britain and elsewhere have much concerned themselves in recent years.

Information as the Central Resource

It is worth emphasizing immediately that none of today's stress on the crucial role of information and informational labor has anything, at least in principle, in common with the recently and recurrently popular argument that the information age was being brought about by technological developments. To be sure, it is likely that informational labor will be adept at use of ICTs, but the emphasis on its contribution recurrently draws attention to the fact that, in the words of Castells (1998, chapter 6), it "embodies knowledge and information," a quality attained, as a rule, through high-level education. Remember, the recent emphasis is on the capacities of symbolic analysts to problem solve, to develop strategies, to think abstractly, and so on. Thus we are offered an explanation of change that hinges, not on technological innovation, but on the capacities of the education system to supply a particular type of labor force—namely, highly educated labor equipped with key transferable skills. In this regard it is striking that enthusiasm for the information age has shifted its ground, away from the argument that it is an outcome of information and communication technologies, toward the more general claim that the new age is announced through the changed characteristics of the occupational structure.

Education as Panacea

It is also worth reflecting on the policy implications of these analyzes. In this regard, Reich's analysis is especially pertinent, since he moved from academe to Clinton's Cabinet with a clear policy in mind. Given that the American economy was being undermined by globalization, he saw no progress in strategies that might serve to identify, still less promote, distinctly American economic interests. All that an American government may do, reasons Reich, is exercise leverage over that which it can influence. The educational system is crucial here because this is pretty much geographically fixed, unlike manufacture, finance, and the rest of business activity. A U.S. government keen to do its best by the American people must strive to ensure that the higher education system is capable of producing an attractive type and quantity of symbolic analysts so that they might find a disproportionate share of the 20 percent of these premier positions that are going worldwide. Because America is blessed by a high rate of participation in higher education, and because its universities are among the best in the world, Reich is rather sanguine about the possibilities of capturing a lion's share of the best jobs. Because "no other society prepares its most fortunate young people as well for lifetimes of creative problem-solving,—identifying, and brokering" (Reich 1992, 228), then it is feasible to imagine that the United States might end up with a concentration of symbolic analysts jobs. President Clinton appeared to agree, urging, in his 1997 State of the Union address, a national crusade to make a thirteenth and fourteenth year in education as universal as the first twelve, or college education routine.

There is a downside—and here Reich articulates what is fast coming a post-Reagan consensus—if America should continue to be polarized, then the symbolic analysts presently located there might just take off to live in more congenial climes. Since they are by nature cosmopolitan, symbolic analysts have few qualms about transferring abroad, hence should American cities continue to be plagued by high levels of crime, then the United States, in spite of its wonderful universities, might just lose its top earners by out-migration. The solution, of course, is the implementation of appropriate policies of welfare reform from a government that strives to include even the disadvantaged, not least because this may induce the symbolic analysts to remain, thereby providing the United States with a high proportion of high-earning professionals at ease with themselves and their neighbors (Webster 1999).

Castells might not follow precisely the same policy proposal as that of Reich, but he does foresee, in the long term, a global division of occupations as follows:

> What I call the newest international division of labor is constructed around four different positions in the informational/global economy: the producers of high value, based on informational labor; the producers of high volume, based on lower-cost labor; the producers of raw materials, based on natural endowments; and the redundant producers, reduced to devalued labor. (Castells 1996, 147)

Castells is at pains to emphasize that these divisions are not neatly reducible to territories. There will be pockets of the even the best-endowed nations where "redundant producers" are found (e.g., inside the ghettos of American cities), just as there will be sections of continents with huge numbers of people marginal to informational capitalism (Castells instances sub-Saharan Africa here as a place with little or no appeal to the world economy), yet where there are found segments of informational labor (e.g., clustered groups of highly educated professionals in the Cape area of South Africa are one such example). Nevertheless, while Castells is correct to place emphasis on the transnational dimensions of the global economy, he is aware of the fact that, in terms of occupations, there are "geographical concentrations in some areas of the planet, so that the global economy is not geographically undifferentiated" (Castells 1996, 147).

He is also sensitive to the capacity of governments to make a difference to their citizens in the "relentlessly variable geometry" (Castells 1996, 147) of the informational economy, and a good deal of his trilogy details both negative and positive consequences of political actions as we enter the information age, from the destructive, "predatory" regimes of much of Africa, to the successful "development" states of Pacific Asia:

> Because the position in the international division does not depend, fundamentally, on the characteristics of the country but on the characteristics of its labor (including embodied knowledge) and of its insertion into the global economy, changes may occur, and indeed do,

in a short time span. Actions by governments and by entrepreneurial sectors of society are critical in this matter. (Castells 1996, 147)

Writing this, Castells appears very close to Reich. Even closer to Reich is the present prime minister of Great Britain, Tony Blair, whose landslide victory in the May 1997 elections ensures that New Labor will lead Great Britain into the millennium. Where Reich may be seen as a reaction to Reaganism that has come now to express a contemporary orthodoxy, so might Blairism be regarded as the counterpoint to the Thatcherism that dominated the 1980s, and thereby to be indicative of a new consensus in Britain. The Blair debt to the U.S. Democrats, and notably to Reich, is quite explicit, and manifest in many particulars. The influence is so profound that the entire Blair strategy has been labeled *Reichian* by leading Conservative intellectual and former minister David Willetts (1997). In the context of this chapter it boils down to a prioritization of policy toward education, with the ambition of making Britain the "knowledge capital of Europe" (Labor Party 1995), hence able to enjoy a concentration of informational jobs (Webster 1996). Indeed, this emphasis became one of the very few positive features of Blair's election campaign, so much so that his alliterative insistence—that his top policy was "education, education, education"—came to be among the most memorable and most quoted phrases of the election. So enthusiastic is Blair about all this that he even discerns in Britain a "creative revolution" that is being led by the "best talents in fashion, architecture, product design, graphics, animation and film," a revolution so profound that Britain now has more people working in the film and television industries than in the car industry. Many more positions are promised in associated areas that call for "know-how, creativity, innovation, risk-taking, and most of all, originality" (Blair 1997). Informational labor is evidently the way forward, and government can play its role by improving the educational system.

It is worthwhile elaborating on this commonality of ambition and strategy between Britain and the United States. Recently, for example, two key codifiers of New Labor's electoral program described Reich as being "more responsible than anyone for stressing the primacy of investment in skills in the modern world" because of the "profound importance" of his diagnosis of today's economic realities (Mandelson and Little 1996, 89). The Commission on Social Justice, established by an organization intimately connected to New Labor (the Institute for Public Policy Research), reported this in 1993. Here was the same acknowledgment that "globalization is constraining the power of individual nation-states" (Commission on Social Justice 1993, 64), so much so that world trading in finance and currencies has "effectively created an international market in government policies" (65) that places a strait-jacket on indigenous politics. The commission did discern some leeway for economic policy at the pan-European level, but the thrust of its advocacy, at one with its American colleagues, leaned toward education as panacea. As Mandelson and Little candidly put it, "Governments can best promote economic success by ensuring that their people are equipped with the skills necessary for the modern world" (Mandelson and Little 1996, 89). Here it may not be quite so ambitious to aspire to create a nation of symbolic analysts, but New Labor's vision has the same concern for education as the central mechanism for improving national well-being. With New Labor the emphasis is on "cumulative learning" (Mandelson and Little 1996, 73), which encourages flexibility and retraining since these are key qualities required of a fast-changing global economy.

Blair voiced New Labor's position at his party's conference in Brighton in 1995:

> Education is the best economic policy there is for a modern economy. And it is in the marriage of education and technology that the future lies. . . . The knowledge race has begun. We will never compete on the basis of a low wage, sweat shop economy. . . . We have just one asset. Our people. Their intelligence. Their potential . . . It is as simple as that. . . . This is hard economics. The more you learn the more you earn. That is your way to do well out of life. Jobs. Growth. The combination of technology and know-how will transform the lives of all of us. Look at industry and business. An oil rig in the Gulf of Mexico has metal fatigue; it can be diagnosed from an office in Aberdeen. European businesses finalizing a deal with the Japanese. With simultaneous translation down the phone line, and the calls could even be free. Leisure too. Virtual reality tourism that allows you anywhere in the world. . . . Knowledge is power. Information and opportunity.

This strategy of relying on education, especially at the university level, but also to include a principle of lifelong learning, in order to seize the most desirable occupations for one's native population is not restricted to the United States and Britain. Indeed, it is a primary policy of just about every government of the advanced societies. The G7 member nations (United States, Canada, England, France, Germany, Italy, and Japan) committed themselves to developing a "worldwide information society" at their Naples summit in 1994, and high on their list of priorities is successful transition to the more skilled occupations that will become available. Moreover, it is well-known that the European Commission has for several years been devising policy toward the *global information society*. Bangemann of Germany produced an influential report entitled "Europe and the Global Information Society" in 1994. This tends toward emphasizing the need for technological change and the threat of outside competition, but since its production the European Union was worked assiduously to promote a market-based solution to the challenges the information revolution poses for its member states. Running through the strategy is a conviction that Europe will be able to capture the premier positions for its citizens, thereby to achieve a higher quality of life and greater choice of services and entertainment (Bangemann 1994).

It is hard to resist pointing out that this is a high-risk strategy for many nations. To be sure, there may seem to most to be no alternative since globalization appears to be irreversible and its pressures cannot be avoided. Nevertheless, there must be significant losers, even within the advanced societies. Furthermore, even the uppermost estimates put informational labor at 30 percent of the workforce. To remind oneself of the vast majority of the world's people that will be surplus to the running of the global economy does not refute the overall thesis, but it is sobering to acknowledge that the information age will be one that excludes a great many people, from entire populations in areas such as sub-Saharan Africa, to a large proportion of the undereducated and unskilled in the metropolitan societies.

New Times

Several of the writers to whom I have made mention may be distinguished from the more enthusiastic of futurist commentators on the information age (Webster and Robbins 1998). While the latter have a habit of announcing the information society as a decisive break with everything that went before, anticipating dramatic change in whatever we may do, Reich, Thurow, and Castells, among others, are under no illusions that capitalism persists—indeed, in their arguments it is in some ways, and especially in its globalized elements, more virulent and vigorous than ever. Thurow and Reich announce their recognition of the import of market factors in their very titles—*The Future of Capitalism* (1996) and *The Work of Nations* (1992)—and Castells recurrently refers to "informational capitalism" being the coming trend in his major trilogy.

Nonetheless, there are several shared traits among these writers that make it clear that we are undergoing a major and irreversible epochal change in the particular form of capitalism, one that hoists informational matters to the very core of the new and expresses several distinctive features. These include, first, the acknowledgment that *capitalism has won* the long battle with communism, and that thereby there is no credible alternative to the market economy. Today "survival of the fittest" capitalism stands alone. "There is no alternative," attests Thurow (1996, 5). Castells adds that globalization has brought into being a "hardened form of capitalism in its goals, but (one which) is incomparably more flexible than any of its predecessors in its means" (Castells 1998, 338). Margaret Thatcher put it more bluntly, but essentially no differently, in her famous acronym TINA (There Is No Alternative). Of course there is room for variants of capitalism—East Asian, European, or American—but all operate within the constraints of market economics and this cannot be challenged.

Second, the changed occupational structures of informational capitalism, in promoting symbolic analysts to the fore, advances the cause of *meritocracy* enormously. Since informational labor gains its position, power, and reward not by ownership of capital but by virtue of possession and achievement of intellectual capital that has, as a rule, been accredited by the university system, then, to an important degree we see evidenced in informational labor the rise of the meritocracy—those who deserve their positions because of a combination of ability and effort. Of course this does not mean that writers are complacent, notably about equal opportunities to perform in the educational race, but it does mean that, in key respects, the ideal of the meritocrats—that those most able would occupy the premier positions—has been met.

This is a close cousin to the death of communism, since one of the most important leftist criticisms of capitalism, that ownership of property massively advantaged the children of the privileged and was thus unjust, has been subverted. To the extent that informational capitalism relies on those who perform best in the education system, then a crucial plank of advocates of change has been removed since, so long as education is open, then who may complain about its unequal outcomes? As such the system of inequality is fixed since it is legitimated in ways that earlier forms of capitalism could never manage to be.

Third, connected to this is the recurrent theme that the *stratification system of capitalism has fundamentally changed*. Above all, the former divisions between capital and labor, which formed the basis of antagonistic classes, and in large part supplied the personnel and rationale for opposing political ideologies, are transformed. In Castells's comprehensive examination of the information age, class relations have been displaced as significant agencies of change, replaced by social movements such as feminism and environmentalism, which are so much more in tune with the network society than the old-fashioned working class (Castells 1997). Moreover, while entrepreneurs are in evidence today, a distinctive capitalist class, in the sense of an identifiable group of powerful property owners, has gone, even though capitalism continues to operate by what he terms a "faceless, collective capitalist" (Castells 1996, 474) system that is most evident, and most constraining, in the global financial markets that trade ceaselessly.

On the one hand, this is because symbolic analysts have taken over the reins of corporate (and other) endeavors and have thereby risen in the ranks, so much so that capitalists per se appear to have disappeared, replaced by these symbolic analysts who run corporations by virtue of their knowledge. On the other hand, precisely because informational labor has come to occupy the key positions, those remaining in the stratification system are in peril. Both Reich and Castells, with somewhat different terminology, divide one element of these into much the same thing—routine producers (Reich) and generic labor (Castells) who are threatened by the demands for flexibility that the new capitalism insists upon and who are projected to die away in the long run through automation.

The fear is that they will fall into the group that frightens all these commentators, namely the underclass, which has so exercised social science in recent years (see Gans 1995). Though it is given different names by each author, all share apprehension for those who are uneducated and inflexible, and hence unequipped, to survive in informational capitalism. Castells sees these as those who are excluded from the capitalist economy (those in the ghetto have little to give to the new labor market, and those in the poorest parts of the world have in addition nothing to buy with); while Reich stresses the possibilities of their getting along, occasionally with modest success, by providing in-person services to the affluent (and busy) symbolic analysts; and Thurow is worried especially by the creation of a new lumpenproletariat. All three are particularly concerned that this group, and the increased polarization of inequality that it represents, constitutes a threat because, in being irrelevant to informational capitalism, it is drawn to crime and to other antisocial behavior.

What seems to be especially important to note here is not merely that earlier class divisions inherent in capitalism have been overturned, but that those on the lower rungs, once regarded as the sources of wealth by analysts of capitalism, are now regarded as just about irrelevant. Indeed, they are often dependent on the symbolic analysts who frequently provide those at the bottom with casual jobs (cleaners, waiters, gardeners, etc.). though this dependency is not mutual. Meanwhile, symbolic analysts continue to replace middle-ranking generic labor with computerized machinery, thereby demonstrating the lack of need for manual work in the information age. The only people required by informational capitalism are the symbolic analysts. Marx's labor theory of value seems to have been outdated by the knowledge theory of value.

In sum, capitalist practices may still be around, and in key respects these are even more consequential than before, but the structure of inequality has been radically and irreversibly transformed because informational labor is ascendant and legitimate since it gets where it is chiefly through university and professional accreditation, while others are increasingly marginal to the requirements of informational capitalism. Moreover, capitalism has won through and, while today's commentators lack the triumphalism of the Thatcher-Reagan era, the sense of there being no feasible alternative is equally strong.

Potential Objections

While one may accept a good deal of this recent description of the role of information today, and while I welcome it as a counter to the obsession with technology that has dominated discussion of the future for far too long, I am skeptical of a good deal of its arguments. To avoid confusion, let me say immediately that I am an enthusiast for the periodization of capitalist development, but feel that too much of the writing on twenty-first-century capitalism lays stress on allegedly novel features. In what follows, I will draw attention to several characteristics of capitalism that suggest that long-established traits are still much in evidence and merit consideration in any calculation of the true extent of a transition to informational capitalism (Webster 2000). This is not to deny the realities of change—supporters and opponents agree that capitalism is by its nature a dynamic enterprise—but rather to lay emphasis on the weight of distinguishing features that have continued through time. In particular, I want to remind readers of the persistence of important class cleavages in the distribution of power, reward, and opportunity. I am not going to argue that these have not mutated, but I will suggest that they have remained consistent enough for us to cast doubt on the proposition that the stratification system—its primary features and legitimations—of the information age is something significantly new.

First, accepting that there is an increased representation of symbolic analysts in the labor force, one may ask questions both of its novelty, its size, and its significance for contemporary capitalism. The historian Harold Perkin's book, *The Rise of Professional Society*, is a useful source here, since it maps in detail the rise to prominence of professional occupations, not—as with information age analysts—during the last decade or so, but over the last century and more. The history of England since at least 1880, argues Perkin, may be understood as the emergence of "professional society" that claims its ascendancy, in particular, by virtue of "human capital created by education" (Perkin 1989, 2). Professionals are symbolic analysts, yet they have been on the rise, according to Perkin, for over a hundred years. There are here no compelling reasons to highlight their emergence in recent years as in some way indicative of change profound enough to merit the title "information age."

In addition, one might query the novelty of knowledge-intensive industries. Biotechnology and software engineering excite many commentators today, but there are equally obvious examples of important knowledge businesses in the past. Petrochemicals, pharmaceuticals, aerospace, electrical engineering, and even banking are industries with roots in the early decades (and before) of the century, ones that have made a significant contribution to the gross national product (GNP) as well as to employment. Giddens correctly observes that it was during World War I that we saw "the integration of large-scale science and technology as the principal medium of industrial advancement" (Giddens 1985, 237). It ought to be remembered that developments such as solid state physics, nuclear energy, radar, the jet engine, plastics, and television have been important industrially (and, indeed, in everyday life), and each had an important knowledge input, yet all date from at least the interwar period. This is echoed in the steady and sustained expansion of "professional and technical" occupations since the late nineteenth century. In the United States, for instance, they expanded from 4 to 15 percent of the workforce between 1900 and 1970, a percentage increase that underestimates the enormous growth in absolute numbers (Dunlop and Galenson 1978, 25). Similarly, Routh (1980) has calculated that the managerial and professional occupations grew from 4 percent of the British workforce in 1911 to 11 percent by 1971; and the 1981 census put the proportion at 27 percent. Of course, one may want to quibble about precise definitions, but this continuous growth of informational labor over the century must lead one to doubt the novelty of the symbolic analyst, and the argument that places such weight on the expansion of the category.

Second, it is useful to be reminded here of another dimension of Perkin's account. He baldly states that higher education, of itself, definitely does not lead to a privileged position. It may now be necessary to gain official accreditation, but at least of equal weight is one's location in the market and, notably, a profession's capacity to gain leverage over that market. If a profession can monopolize the market, and thereby exercise what Max Weber termed *closure*, then it certainly will see an enhancement of its status and privileges. In Britain the preeminent examples of this exercise of professional power has been law and medicine, both of which enjoy high status and rewards. If a profession cannot do this, however, it will be poorly rewarded and, in all probability, poorly regarded. Extrapolating from this, it requires little imagination to ask questions of the alleged influence ascribed to symbolic analysts by many information age thinkers. They may be indispensable to the market, but whether or not they are key power holders is quite another matter. A look around at the turbo-capitalism of the late-twentieth century suggests that most symbolic analysts are subordinate to the marketplace, far removed from the picture of the powerful brokers envisaged by their admirers. In Britain we have experienced over the last twenty years a sustained assault on many professions (not the least university teachers [Halsey 1992], researchers, and teachers), and we have also witnessed a manifest decline in the returns on higher educational certification. A great deal of this testifies to the power, not of symbolic analysts, but to that of the market system which—whatever the intellectual capacities of the employee—appears to be the most decisive factor. Bluntly, the rise of symbolic analysts has done little if anything to limit the determining power of capital in the realm of work, or anywhere else for that matter.

It may well be the case that the globalization of capitalism has placed an increased premium on informational labor, to help with necessary tasks such as the coordination and general management of contemporary business affairs. There may also have been some promotion of informational work as cultural industries have grown in economic value. However, neither of these developments says very much about the transformative capacities of information and knowledge. Rather both underscore the central shaping role of the dynamic capitalist economy and it is surely this, and its familiar imperatives, rather than attendant labor requirements on which analysts may most fruitfully focus (Schiller 1996).

Third, though it is undeniable that globalized capitalism is an unsettling and uncertain phenomenon for all concerned, including capitalist corporations themselves, there is good evidence to suggest that the main stakeholders are constituted by a propertied class that enjoys concentrated ownership of corporate stock. The work of Scott (1982, 1986, 1991, 1996, 1997), undertaken over many years and developed from a neo-Weberian perspective, is a crucial source in this regard since, while it does not directly address the question of the significance of informational labor, scotches many of the key claims of the likes of Castells and Reich with the evidence it presents. For instance, Scott demonstrates that an important change in capitalism has been the shift from personal to impersonal forms of control. That is, outright individual ownership of firms has declined relative to dispersed-share ownership. Thus nowadays typical corporations are owned by various institutions such as banks and insurance companies, with individual shareholders usually accounting for small percentages of total shares. However, this has not necessarily meant any major loss of control by the capitalist classes, since networks of relationships, based on intertwined shareholdings, link them together and ensure their position is maintained through a "constellation of interests." Contra Castells, it still appears that there is a capitalist class at the helm of the capitalist system, which is a good deal less anonymous than he believes.

That there is concentrated at the head of capitalist enterprise an elite of decision makers is not, of course, so much of an issue provided they are there by virtue of their attainments as symbolic analysts. Objections to their privileges must be muted if the capitalist leaders can demonstrate that they have attained their positions in an open meritocratic contest. And it is certainly the case that corporate leaders today increasingly do possess credentials won through (and beyond) the university system, and to this degree they do manifest knowledge attainments that are requisites for high-level work performance. However, the key question revolves around whether or not their educational success is genuinely meritocratic.

On this matter it is as well to say outright that the evidence is inadequate to make really authoritative statements. For rather obvious reasons research on the constitution, lifestyles, and decision making of economic elites is sparse, and still rarer is work on their composition over time. Nonetheless, what evidence we do have suggests that, while there has been a "partial dissociation" of "mechanisms of capital reproduction" and "mechanisms of class reproduction" (Scott 1997, 310)—that is, capitalists still appear able to pass onto their heirs their property, but they cannot guarantee to transmit the associated top management positions (something that owes a great deal to the demand for educational achievement), this "dissociation" does not seem to have extended very far. Indeed, Scott argues that the propertied class also "forms a pool from which the top corporate managers are recruited" (Scott 1997, 20).

This propertied class is especially advantaged in the educational system, so much so that it tends to emerge with the high level symbolic analytic skills so admired by Reich. As Scott points out, this "propertied capitalist class . . . is able to ensure its continuity over time through its monopolization of the educational system as well as its monopolization of wealth" (Scott 1997, 20). In the British context, Adonis and Pollard (1997) have recently documented the extraordinary success of private schools (which account for but 7 percent of the age group between the ages of five and sixteen) in gaining entry to Oxford and Cambridge, the two premier universities in the country, where they account for about half of all students. And the likelihood of entry to these prestigious institutions increases markedly with attendance at the most elite of the private boarding schools such as Eton, Harrow, Winchester, and Westminster (current annual fees about $25,000 per pupil). Let it be noted that these young people gain entry to Oxbridge on the basis of excellent performances in the open examinations available to all eighteen-year-olds in Great Britain. For that very reason candidates of exceptional ability may gain entry whatever their family circumstances may be, and a few do so. It just happens that, while merit is the criterion for selection, the most privileged in terms of family background are those able to attend schools with high expectations, excellent resources, and strong academic traditions. Not surprisingly, pupils educated in such situations are also the most likely to achieve well in the open examinations and to enter the best universities in vastly disproportionate numbers. From the top universities emerge the symbolic analysts who go on to occupy strategic positions in commerce and industry in later life (Adonis and Pollard 1997). This situation is similar else-where in Europe (Bourdieu 1996).

One is compelled to conclude that at the hub of globalized capitalism are indeed symbolic analysts, but for the most part they are where they are, and able to continue there, by virtue of privileged origins, privileged educa-tion, and the inestimable advantage of inherited wealth. To be sure, it is the case that, as capitalism has globalized, then so have patterns of capitalist classes around the world become more variegated. I would not want to pro-pose that there is at the helm of the world economy a self-reproducing and totally exclusive, class that steers the movements of globalized capitalism (Gill 1990). Important national differences, intense market competition, the demand for demonstrable talent in those who must try to manage in condi-tions of routine uncertainty, plus the sheer complexity and turmoil in the world today, ensure that the there is no single coordinating force and that those temporarily at the top of the tree cannot guarantee the transmission of their positions to their own kind. Nevertheless, while all of this may be readily conceded, what we cannot do is ignore the fact that, even on the world stage, we may discern signs of the emergence of transnational interest groups that reflect the disproportionate influence of propertied groups that manifest a marked degree of self-reproduction (Useem 1984; Useem and Karabel 1986).

Conclusion

The dual processes of globalization and informationalism are striking fea-tures of the contemporary landscape. It does not require very much persua-sion to acknowledge either that the tangential development of globalization has accelerated and deepened, or that there has been an explosive growth of ICTs and information flows around the world.

In this chapter I have centered attention on the emergence of a body of writing that emphasizes the rise to prominence, out of globalization and infor-mationalization, of a new occupational category—that of informational labor. At the least I believe this emphasis should be welcomed by social scientists after far too much writing from techno-boosters who, stuck inside a frame-work of technological determinism, offer what is quite simply an inadequate sociology.

More recent analysts such as Castells and Reich acknowledge that the context of change remains capitalism, yet still they stress the novelty of the present age, and particularly the role of symbolic analysts. However, the claims for the new are overstated. Against the assertions of profound change in power structures and in the organization of inequality, it still seems that the hold of privileged property owners in the corporate sector has been maintained, not least by a timely turn to higher education to equip their members with the symbolic analyst attributes required to run their affairs.

Notes

1. I do not distinguish between information and knowledge here because none of the writers under discussion do.

2. Reich pithily notes, "a world-class university and an international airport combine the basic rudiments of global symbolic analysis—brains, and quick access to the rest of the world" (Reich 1992, 238–239).

References

Adonis, Andrew and Pollard, Stephen. 1997. *A Class Act: The Myth of Britain's Classless Society*. London: Hamish Hamilton.

Bangemann, Martin. 1994. *Europe and the Global Information Society*. Brussels: Commission of the European Communities (June).

Blair, Tony. 1995. *Speech to Annual Conference*. Brighton, 3 October.

Blair, Tony. 1997. "Britain Can Remake It." *Guardian*, 22 July.

Block, Fred. 1990. *Postindustrial Possibilities: A Critique of Economic Discourse*. Berkeley: University of California Press.

Bourdieu, Pierre. 1996. *The State Nobility: Elite Schools in the Field of Power*. Trans. Lauretta Clough. Cambridge: Polity.

Castells, Manuel. 1996. *The Information Age*. Vol. 1, *The Rise of the Network Society*. Oxford: Blackwell.

Castells, Manuel. 1997. *The Information Age*. Vol. 2, *The Power of Identity*. Oxford: Blackwell.

Castells, Manuel. 1998. *The Information Age*. Vol. 3, *End of Millennium*. Oxford: Blackwell.

Commission on Social Justice. 1993. *Social Justice in a Changing World*. London: Institute for Public Policy Research.

Drucker, Peter. 1993. *Post-Capitalist Society*. New York: HarperCollins.

Dunlop, J. T. and W. Galenson, eds. 1978. *Labor in the Twentieth Century*. New York: Academic.

Dutton, William, ed. 1996. *Information and Communication Technologies: Visions and Realities*. Oxford: Oxford University Press.

Economist. 1995. "World Economy Survey," 7 October.

Fukuyama, Francis. 1997. *The End of Order*. London: Social Market Foundation.

Gans, Herbert J. 1995. *The War Against the Poor*. New York: Basic.

Giddens, Anthony. 1985. *A Contemporary Critique of Historical Materialism*. Vol. 2, *The Nation State and Violence*. Basingstoke: Macmillan.

Gill, Stephen. 1990. *American Hegemony and the Trilateral Commission*. Cambridge: Cambridge University Press.

Halsey, A. H. 1992. *The Decline of Donnish Dominion: British Academic Professions in the Twentieth Century*. Oxford: Oxford University Press.

Handy, Charles. 1995. *The Age of Unreason*. London: Arrow.

Hirshhorn, Larry. 1984. *Beyond Mechanisation: Work and Technology in a Postindustrial Age*. Cambridge: Massachusetts Institute of Technology Press.

Hutton. Will. 1995. *The State We're In*. London: Vintage.

Labor Party. 1995. *Information Superhighway*. London: Labor Party.

Lash, Scott and John Urry. 1994. *Economies of Signs and Space*. London: Sage.

Mandelson, Peter and Roger Little. 1996. *The Blair Revolution: Can New Labour Deliver?* London: Faber.

Negroponte, Nicholas. 1995. *Being Digital*. London: Hodder and Stoughton.

Perkin, Harold. 1989. *The Rise of Professional Society: England since 1880*. London: Routledge.

Piore, Michael and Charles Sabel. 1984. *The Second Industrial Divide*. New York: Basic.

Reich, Robert B. 1992. *The Work of Nations: Preparing Ourselves for 21st Century Capitalism*. New York: Vintage.

Routh, Guy. 1980. *Occupation and Pay in Britain, 1906–1979*. Basingstoke: Macmillan.

Scott, John. 1982. *The Upper Classes*. Basingstoke: Macmillan.

Scott, John. 1986. *Capitalist Property and Financial Power*. Hassocks: Wheatsheaf.

Scott, John. 1991. *Who Rules Britain?* Cambridge: Polity.

Scott, John. 1996. *Stratification and Power: Structures of Class, Status and Command*. Cambridge: Polity.

Scott, John. 1997. *Corporate Business and Capitalist Classes*. Oxford: Oxford University Press.

Scott, Peter. 1995. *The Meanings of Mass Higher Education*. Buckingham: Open University Press.

Schiller, Herbert I. 1996. *Information Inequality: The Deepening Social Crisis in America*. New York: Routledge.

Smith, Anthony and Frank Webster, eds. 1997. *The Postmodern University? Contested Visions of Higher Education*. Milton Keynes: Open University Press.

Thurow, Lester. 1996. *The Future of Capitalism*. London: Nicholas Brealey.

Toffler, Alvin. 1990. *Powershift: Knowledge, Wealth and Violence at the Edge of the 21st Century*. New York: Bantam.

Useem, Michael. 1984. *The Inner Circle: Large Corporations and the Rise of Business Political Activity in the US and UK*. New York: Oxford University Press.

Useem, Michael and Jerome Karabel. 1986. "Pathways to Top Corporate Management." *American Sociological Review* 51 (April): 184–200.

Webster, Frank. 1997. Analyst of the Information Age. *City* 7 (May): 105–121.

Webster, Frank. 1997. Is This the Information Age? Towards a Critique of Manuel Castells. *City* 8 (December): 71–84.

Webster, Frank. 1995. *Theories of the Information Society*. London: Routledge.

Webster, Frank. 1996. The Information Age: What's the Big Idea? *Renewal* 4: 15–22.

Webster, Frank. 1999. Information and Communication Technologies: Luddism Revisited. *Technocities: Culture and Political Economy of the Digital Revolution*. Eds. John McGuigan and Jim McGuigan, 60–89. London: Sage.

Webster, Frank. 2000. "Information, Capitalism and Uncertainty." *Information, Communication and Society* 3 (1): 69–90.

Webster, Frank and Kevin Robins. 1998. "The Iron Cage of the Information Society." *Information, Communication and Society* 1(April): 23–45.

Willetts, David. 1997. "Reich and Wrong." *Guardian*, 13 November.

Winner, Langdon. 1977. *Autonomous Technology: Technics-out-of-Control as a Theme in Political Thought*. Cambridge: Massachusetts Institute of Technology Press.

Woolgar, Steve. 1988. *Science: The Very Idea*. Chichester, England: Ellis Horwood.

Zuboff, Soshana. 1988. *In the Age of the Smart Machine: The Future of Work and Power*. London: Heinemann.

PART THREE

Contemporary Issues

CHAPTER FIVE

Coincident Revolutions and the Dictator's Dilemma

Thoughts on Communication and Democratization

CHRISTOPHER R. KEDZIE, WITH JANNI ARAGON

Totalitarian societies face a dilemma: either they try to stifle
these [information and communication] technologies and
thereby fall further behind in the new industrial revolution,
or else they permit these technologies and see their totalitarian control inevitably eroded

—George Shultz
former U.S. secretary of state

Mass information and transport have made the world so
visible and more tangible to everyone. International communication is easier now than ever before. Nowadays, it is
virtually impossible for any society to be "closed."

—Mikhail Gorbachev

Aristotle laid out the importance of communication to politics. The political essence of man, he said, stemmed from his faculty of speech (Bickford
1996). Many since Aristotle have also noted how significant communication
and attendant technology are to politics (Downing 1989; Haraway 1990;
Luke 1997; Mcluhan 1962). Coincident revolutions in information technology and democratization further demonstrate the contemporary relevance of
Aristotle and the insight of many others. Concomitant with the proliferation
of democratic regimes and prodemocracy movements, information technologies have democratized the information industries and made it exceedingly

difficult for governments to monopolize the political information markets. What I refer to as the "dictator's dilemma" has raised the opportunity costs of censorship, forcing despots to revisit their structure of preferences, make new choices, and expose themselves to the unintended consequences. These are, indeed, radical new developments for any examination of international politics, in particular, for any examination of how global politics change as we approach a new millennium due to innovations in information technologies.

The reinforcing principles of communications and democracy are restructuring the realities of world anarchy through the mechanism of popular participation in domestic and cross-national affairs. Still in their infancy as far as global use is concerned, information technologies are making the vision of world peace and governance through democracy feasible. The distance-dissolving technological advancements in communications may ultimately envision a globalized political community. Recalling Aristotle, Athenians, not Athens, constituted the polis (Arendt 1958). If, indeed, participation or people, not place, determine politics, the increasing levels of cross-border discussions and deliberations may indeed lead to the sustained public contemplation of the "good life" on a more global scale, that is, a world polis.[1] Wolin provides a contemporary expression of this point: "democracy is not about where the political is located but about how it is experienced" (Wolin 1996, 38).

By force of the diffusion of information technologies, the polis is the world, and the manner of the experience is becoming increasingly imbued with liberalism. This liberal vision for the future hinges on the premise that increased communication spreads liberal principles and supports democratic change (Dahl 1996). As a test of this foundational premise, the research problem addressed in this chapter is as follows:

Is there an empirical relationship between international communications, democracy, and democratic change; if so, can it be explained causally?

As such this chapter seeks to determine if information technologies are connected in principle and in fact with the spread of democracy. Democratic theory provides the analytic frame for structuring this study. The theoretical context supplies the rationale linking communication to economic efficiency and political efficacy, which together give rise to the "dictator's dilemma." Multivariate regression techniques are used to explore various forms of associations between both democracy and development to information flows. A variety of models are tested as a means of weeding out confounding effects. The resultant positive correlation between information technologies and democratic changes proves to be robust. Informed by democratic theory, the empirical findings suggest some readily feasible policy options for democracies to pursue from a self-interested perspective.

Theoretical Context: Economics and International Politics

Communication is the most important force for organizing political and social behavior.[2] This observation inheres from the uncertainty and lack of information that contextualize decision making. In economics, the positive relationship between information, efficiency, and growth is axiomatic, as is the imperfect information-uncertainty corollary (Mitchell 1998). A liberal mass communication system rests on the idea of private enterprise,[3] since many explain that capitalism is the most free and expansive of any economic system.[4] Development has typically been posited as either a cause of democracy (Comor 1999; Lipset 1959; Moravcsik 1997), or as its effect (Olson 1993). In either case, democracy and communication are necessarily linked.[5] By increasing communication, the proportion of public to private information grows; the rational domain for investments expands, which causes the production possibilities frontiers to shift out over time. This was observed in the concurrence between market expansion with the spread of early information technologies, such as telephones and radios (Jipp 1963; Ronfeldt, 1993).

As the world economy surges into the information age, the interactive media are set to become the dominant mode of communication.[6] Already, information technologies are integral to the increasingly interconnected infrastructure of the world markets. Given strong information technology growth multiplier effects (Hills 1993), they will attract considerable investment capital, which in turn extends their global reach and the range of political outcomes they may affect. Embodying the link between communication and efficiency, information technologies promise to be a continuing force for moving the world toward the liberal model.[7]

Democracy itself has eluded a universal definition (Chan 1997), but is generally defined by its processes. That is, democracy is a political system with constitutional procedures for leadership change and also a mechanism for translating suffrage into decisional influence. Its constitutive principles include citizen involvement in political decisions, equality, civil liberties, representation, and majority-rule (Lipset 1960; Sargent 1972). Moreover, democracy is embodied in communicative practices (Reisinger et al. 1995; Riker 1982). Liberals expect communication to preserve the central freedoms of democratic society: the freedom to know, share, and find out (Rivers and Schramm 1969). Absent communication between citizens on the issues, laws will lack social traditions, that is, legitimacy, and thus ultimately either fail (Kariel 1964), or engender more coercion.[8]

Liberals optimistically presume the universal appeal of liberalism to politics and to other spheres of life. Given participatory norms themselves developed through debate, more diversity is better.[9] The communication of disparate views increases the issues and groups around which deliberation occurs, improving the civic virtues, citizenry, and the polis.[10] Thus, democratic theory extols this form of "human development in its richest diversity."[11]

Past communication technologies, such as the newspaper, the radio, and satellite television, have easily increased the potential for state control.[12] How do information technologies, like the Internet, compare? In general, means of communication that are dispersed and accessible are freedom enhancing (Pool 1983). Media that tap new opinions increase self-efficacy and confidence in political processes (Roberts 1995), precisely because the deliberative construction of political information becomes democratized (Page and Tannenbaum 1996; see also McLean 1989). Communication via the Internet and associated media breeds efficacy. Personal efficacy, in turn, ideally encourages continued participation centered around the internalized norm of tolerance and civic-mindedness.

Ideas speak louder than actions in democratic politics (Roseman, Mayo, and Colinge 1966). And when people learn that there is an alternative to their way of life, revolution becomes possible (Wriston 1993). "New words" are crucial for sowing the discontent that initiates regime change (Hoffer 1951). According to liberalism's opponents, liberalism is a contagion that has now no foreseeable ideological antidote. A polity's exposure to liberalism can be deadly for illiberal regimes. Exposure to persuasive communication resulting in opinion change constitutes political learning, the key elements of which are the "recommended opinion' and source credibility (Hovland et al. 1953).[13] As recommended opinion, the universal appeal of liberalism is evident in the fact that the emergent world culture has already markedly Western traits.[14]

Information technologies are particularly well suited to carry the message of democracy abroad. The Internet bypasses authority structures; by going directly to the masses, creating visions of an interactive global democracy (Snider 1994; Varley 1991). Indeed revolutionary processes of communications have begun to impact the last bastion of realism—the international use of power, diplomacy, and propaganda.[15] With respect to the lawlike claim that democracies are unlikely to fight other democracies (Russett 1993; see Ward and Gleditsch 1998 on an important elaboration), electronic communication links are indirectly promoting pacific modes of international cooperation (Russett and Starr 1996; see also Fearon 1995), so much so that relations between developed democracies currently approach their own pacific intranational traits (Lebow 1994). More generally, information technologies are shattering states' privacy (Padelford and Lincoln 1967) and rendering governmental methods open to the scrutiny more characteristically associated only with democracy (Grossman 1995). The increase in transparency works to mitigate the harshness of world anarchy by opening new avenues for the evaluation of credibility and intent.

"In the long run, we will live in one integrated world shrunk by data links" (Halacy 1964). With interactive media, like two-way television, democracy becomes the most practical form of government for all people (Fuller 1964). "Intellectronic" legislation, it has been argued, will ultimately extend the areas of international cooperation and, through the rapid handling of information, more logical concepts and better world relations will result (Halacy 1964). Through communication come different and higher levels of consciousness, at which point people can begin to set the agenda of world politics and the parameters of discourse themselves (Gray and Mentor 1995; Neufeld 1995). This higher level of consciousness is interwoven with the increased access to information, the dissemination of information to others, and the ensuing communication between people.

Information technologies promote democratization by diffusing liberal ideas throughout the globe. The phenomenon of democratization should lead to the expansion of the democratic peace once the new liberal regimes are consolidated and established (Ward and Gleditsch 1998). If the democratic peace continues, concerns for welfare will supplant warfare in world culture (Noel and Therieu 1995). Humanity may indeed be at the point of "evolutionary decision between Homo Sapiens and 'Homo Cyberneticus'" (Aubrey 1996; see Resnick 1997 and Toulouse 1997 for a counterargument).

The Dictator's Dilemma

This discussion has thus far assumed that information technologies will have full, positive sway across the globe. Modern communication was born in the age of authoritarianism, when the state controlled all tools of persuasion and coercion (Rivers and Schramm 1969). States still make the rules by which other lesser political organs on their territory operate (Waltz 1979). However, the costs of isolation are now much higher than in the past. The opportunity costs are not just borne in subjective dimensions like questionable legitimacy, if ever they were, but now directly implicate economic competitiveness, and thereby military power also. The data-dependent character of development in the information and communication age creates the dictator's dilemma (DD).

DD: economic efficiency and political efficacy are positively related to each other, and negatively related to authoritarian control.

Under liberal principles, the efficiency of economic agents fosters the efficacy of political actors. The technology of modern communication makes authoritarian control over information far more difficult than in the past. Electronic networks necessarily couple decentralization of political power with economic growth. National economic competitiveness requires free access to information networks and computer technology, which degrades dictatorial control over domestic economic, cultural, and political events (Builder and Banks 1993). Free information flows drive the efficiency and growth on which nations' power rests.[16] Richards (in this volume) explains how the computer screen affords an examination into the condition of other peoples' lives. These impressions can accentuate similarities or differences in terms of standard of living or political rights. Formally, states have the power to refuse to "get connected," or to do so on their own terms.[17] Thus, squelching new information technologies arguably degrades a nation's political or military position, not to mention its position on human rights (see Richards, in this volume).

Data Analysis

The preceding theoretical discussion suggests that there may indeed be a relationship between information technologies and democracy. This section seeks to enhance our understanding of this relationship by examining empirical evidence. More specifically, democracy ratings for selected countries are regressed against correlates for democracy drawn from historical data. As a whole, the regression models employed here investigate a range of potential causal arguments, some of which would counter my thesis that information technologies, in part, explain democratic development. Yet in all cases, the results indicate that "electronic network connectivity" is a significant predictor of "democracy."

Before reviewing these results, however, it is important to note that causality, while implicitly central to my argument, is impossible to demonstrate with only the present nonrandomized observation study. Thus the objective of this analysis is to strengthen the policy-oriented argument that information technologies can be both an asset to the process of democratizing, and useful for improving extant democracies.

Logic of the Test Sequence

The statistical tests were selected specifically to investigate dominant causal premises, especially those that rival the thesis that information technologies have an important role in the process of democratic development. Furthermore, the research design employs a variety of models and functional forms for the main exogenous variable, electronic network interconnectivity. Results, therefore, have the broadest validity and do not rely on any particular model or functional form, which would be undoubtedly subject to dispute.

First, cross-sectional univariate analyses are used to confirm a strong correlation between levels of democracy and of network interconnectivity, both in an absolute sense and relative to democracy's other traditional correlates. Second, because this strong correlation could be the result of excluded variables, additional correlates are included in a supplementary multivariate analysis. Third, considering that the dynamics of technological and political change may vary with geographic region, categorical analyses are evaluated as a means of controlling for potential regional influences.[18] Fourth, because there are significant reasons to believe that democracy influences interconnectivity, systems of simultaneous equations are used to compare the possibility that this is, in fact, the case.

Data

Democracy. Although the concept of democracy may be difficult to describe explicitly, it is nonetheless well understood intuitively:

> [D]emocracy is a distinctive and highly coherent syndrome of characteristics such that anyone measuring only a few of the salient characteristics will classify nations in much the same way as will another analyst who also measured only a few qualities but uses a different set of characteristics, so long as both have selected their indicators from the same larger pool of valid measures. Far from being like the elephant confronting the blind sages, democracy is more like a ball of wax. (Inkeles 1990, 5)

In accordance with common academic practice, the metric for democracy in the following statistical analyses is derived from Freedom House data—specifically, the 1993/1994 report.[19]

Freedom House conducts annual worldwide surveys on political rights and civil liberties. Scores are assessed relative to checklists of questions. The checklist for political rights includes nine questions such as; "Is the head of state and/or head of government or other chief authority elected through free and fair election?" The checklist for civil rights includes thirteen questions, such as; "Are there free and independent media, literature, and other cultural expressions?" Each checklist item per country is assigned from "0" to "4" raw points relative to the degree the question can be answered affirmatively. The maximum raw score for political rights is "36"; for civil liberties, it is "52." In each survey, the range of possible scores is divided into seven nearly equal categories. Freedom House annually reports a rating from "1" to "7" for every country, from the greatest freedom to the least, respectively. The single measure for "democracy" in this study is the average between these two measures. This scale is then inverted and normalized to "100." The result of these cosmetic conversions is a metric with 13 discrete values, the maximum democracy rating is "100" (instead of "1"), and the minimum is "0" (instead of "7").

Interconnectivity. The presence of information technologies in a given nation might appear easier to quantify than "democracy," but construction of this variable is actually no less problematic. Some difficulties are definitional, while others are practical. As suggested in this volume, for instance, accessibility to information technologies is problematic in some regions. Moreover, answering the question of what ought to be included as an information technology is not trivial. This study focuses specifically on electronic mail, or E-mail, because it is the technology that enables people to engage in discourse across borders in ways that have never before been possible. Richards (in this volume) further articulates how E-mail has undermined the gate-keeping role of traditional print media and opened up new opportunities for communication and political participation. Thus, E-mail presents a new mode of communication *and* is expeditious.

The term given to the E-mail metric is *interconnectivity*.[20] Four E-mail networks are globally dominant: Internet, BITNET (a network created by Ira Fuchs in 1981 to connect IBM computers worldwide), UUCP (a tool for transferring files, sending mail, and executing remote commands invented in 1978 at At&T Bell Labs), and FIDONET (Framework for Interdisciplinary Design Optimization). As record keeping has not been consistent, regular, or accurate, the best data are for the number of nodes, which will constitute the basic unit of measure for interconnectivity. The Matrix Information Directory Service (MIDS) tracks and maintains data on these networks aggregated by country. These data were compiled in October 1993, by which time there was wide self-selected variation in the levels of connectivity.

The numerical value of a country's interconnectivity derived from these aggregated is calculated in three different ways. All three formulations are per capita measures that give equivalent weight to each of the four networks. For comparison among telecommunications media, the interconnectivity metric is the logarithmic transformation of the algebraic sum of the network nodes. The discontinuity at zero of the log transformation of the interconnectivity variable is problematic because the node count in 1993 was identically zero in approximately a third of the countries. Therefore an additional binary variable is paired with the log transformation of the interconnectivity variable, to indicate the existence, or not, of electronic mail networks in each country.

The second transformation is the square root of the sum of the nodes on all four networks. This transformation preserves some of the magnitude effects without the discontinuity at the origin. Thus, the level of interconnectivity associated with each nation may be described with just one variable.

This transformation is useful to describe the change in connectivity over time in the longitudinal analysis.

The final interconnectivity transformation is more computationally intensive than the other two. The data are transformed to yield a linear metric rating of countries according to their relative extent of interconnectivity. By network, countries are ranked and scored with a number from "0" to "4." The "0" is assigned to all countries with no nodes in a particular network. The numbers "1" through "4" are assigned by quartile. The lowest quartile countries with one or more nodes in a particular network receive a score of 1. The highest quartile countries receive a score of "4." The sum of the four scores determines the level of interconnectivity on a scale from "0" to "16." The resulting scale is a useful metric to evaluate the correlation between electronic mail network interconnectivity and democracy.

Note that the equal weights assigned in each of the three functional forms just described, are justifiable because the ability to exchange E-mail is relatively generic capability. However, assumed equivalence does introduce some theoretical difficulties. Despite the universal similarity in supporting E-mail, the networks are not necessarily comparable in other respects. For instance, the Internet, with specialized services such as the World Wide Web and remote logon, has more functional capacity than the others. Therefore, in each functional form, perverse results are theoretically possible. For example, a country with relatively fewer nodes and thus a lower interconnectivity score could potentially have more communications capability than a country with relatively more nodes if a higher percentage of the former's nodes were Internet nodes.

In practice, however, such complications are unlikely to occur. There are several reasons why this might be the case. First, E-mail, not necessarily the other services, offers the specific capability that is hypothesized to have dynamic implications for democratization: multidirectional discourse across borders in a timely and inexpensive manner, unbounded by geographic and institutional constraints. Second, interconnectivity evolves. Less capable systems are similarly less expensive and easier to implement, so initially they are more prevalent. Improvements ultimately incorporate Internet capabilities. This scale thus approximates a natural progression in the enhancement of interconnectivity. Furthermore, to the extent that interconnectivity as a predictor for democracy is measured imprecisely, the effect is reduced statistical significance of the predictor. Thus the conclusions would still be sound from the resulting a fortiori analysis.

Economic Development and Education. Economic development, reported here as per capita Gross Domestic Product (GDP), is measured as purchasing power parity. Education is commonly paired with economic development as a predictor of democracy. Of course, an educated public is likely to be both more aware of political events and more capable of intervening to influence them. Education also, indirectly, enhances democracy by contributing to economic growth. The average number of years of schooling across the entire population is considered to be the best measure of education for analyses such as these (Rowen 1995).

Human Development and Health. Human development and health indicators—"infant mortality" rates and "life expectancies," respectively—are also often correlated with democracy. It is reasonable to argue, for instance, that as citizens become more assured of their own well-being, they have more incentive and wherewithal to demand civil rights and political liberties. The United Nations Development Program (1993) is the source for the economic, education, and health data analyzed here.

Ethnicity and Culture. Cultural and ethnic factors may also play a role in the process of democratization. Some have argued, for example, that "[h]omogeneous national entities may be more likely to evolve into peaceable democracies than states rent by harsh linguistic and cultural antagonisms" (Gottlieb 1994, p. 101). The measure of ethnic homogeneity employed in this study is the percentage of the population that constitutes the largest ethnic group in a nation. Data are drawn from the CIA. *World Fact Book* (1994); in the few northern European and African cases for which data were not available, the percentages of largest religious affiliation serve as substitutes for the missing data.

It is not difficult to believe that cultural aspects influence the characterization of the political regimes and the appreciation of personal liberties. To account for these effects, the data set includes binary variables that indicate the culture with which each country most closely identifies. More specifically, six regional categories are defined on the basis of geography, history, and religion: Africa, Asia, Eurasia, Latin America, Middle East, and Western Europe. Western Europe includes countries that are not on the continent but that have a dominant Western European heritage: United States, Canada, Australia, and New Zealand. Israel also is included in the Western European category. The Middle East category is predominantly Muslim, and includes the Islamic North African states and extends from Morocco to Pakistan. Africa is defined in fairly obvious geographic terms including South Africa, minus the northern states grouped into the Middle East. Asia includes the Confucian countries and the Pacific islands, plus India and Japan, minus North Korea. Latin America stretches from Mexico through Argentina including all the Caribbean except Cuba. Cuba and North Korea, plus Albania and the splinter states of Yugoslavia, in addition to the members of the former Warsaw Pact countries, are all grouped in the Eurasian category.

Note that because cultural influences may also shape the ways in which various people utilize communications technologies, some of the regression models that follow include interaction terms that are the products of the binary regional variables and the interconnectivity scores. The resulting regression coefficients on this term describe region specific correlations between democracy and networked communications technologies.

Population. Presumably, a country's size may influence the type and effectiveness of its government (Alesina and Spoloare 1995). Since very small countries may be anomalous, only data for countries whose populations exceed one million, and for which data are available, in 1993 are included. Country populations have a skewed distribution that spans more than three orders of magnitude, so the variable is included in its logarithmic transformation.

Univariate Analysis

As indicated in table 5.1, there is a surprisingly powerful correlation between "interconnectivity" and "democracy." The correlation coefficient on interconnectivity is not only large; it is substantially larger than that of any other traditional predictors of democracy in this first-order analysis. Indeed, the coefficient on per capita GDP, which has often been considered the most important of democracy's correlates, is more than 20 percent smaller. This relationship is displayed graphically in figure 5.1.

Multivariate Regression Analysis

In large, complex systems such as international politics, a simple bivariate relationship can rarely tell the whole story. Multiple linear regressions can, therefore, be a powerful tool for providing insight into complicated interactions. Here several models provide a variety of perspectives on the hypothesized relationship between interconnectivity and democracy, which may be integrated into a single, comprehensive account of the role that electronic network connectivity plays in the development of modern democratic states. As a whole, these results suggest that the correlation between interconnectivity and democracy cannot be easily ignored.

Model I in table 5.2 represents an inclusive model involving six predictors—interconnectivity, GDP, population, "education, life expectancy, and ethnicity—that explains 58.3 percent of the observed variance in observed democracy. It is immediately obvious that interconnectivity is the dominant correlate. The level of certainty that interconnectivity is a valid predictor for

Table 5.1.
Matrix Showing First-Order Correlations

	Democracy	Interconnectivity	Schooling	Gross Domestic Product	Life Expect	Ethnicity	Log (Pop)
Democracy	1.00						
Interconnectivity	0.73	1.00					
Schooling	0.67	0.82	1.00				
Per Capita CDP	0.57	0.84	0.79	1.00			
Life Expectancy	0.53	0.71	0.87	0.71	1.00		
Ethnicity	0.42	0.27	0.26	0.35	0.23	1.00	
Log (Population)	−0.09	0.07	0.10	0.05	0.07	0.11	1.00

Sources: Freedom House, "1994 Freedom Around the World" (Democracy); Matrix Information and Directory Services, Inc. (Interconnectivity); United Nations Development Program (Per Capita GDP, Life Expectancy, Schooling); CIA World Fact Book (Ethnicity); World Telecommunication Development Report (Population).

Figure 5.1. Democracy and Interconnectivity

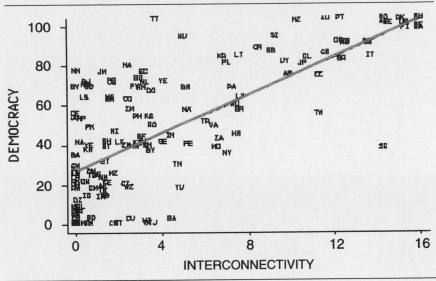

democracy is greater than 99.9 percent, higher than that for any other potential predictor. Furthermore, the coefficient on interconnectivity is large; a single point increase on the interconnectivity scale corresponds to an increase of four to five points in democracy rating.

As indicated in table 5.2, Model II retains as independent variables only GDP, population, and interconnectivity, and thus represents a more parsimonious characterization of the relationship between interconnectivity and democracy. Yet these three variables explain more than 50 percent of the variation in democracy for 141 countries. After excluding three predictors, the small drop in adjusted R-squared—0.007 to 0.536—arguably underlines the relative importance of interconnectivity. That is, interconnectivity alone may be more important for predicting level of democracy than these three independent variables combined.[21]

Models III and IV in table 5.2 are, given the addition of regional interaction terms, analogous to Models I and II, respectively. These models demonstrate that the correlation between interconnectivity and democracy is consistent across and within regions. For all of the regions, the regional coefficient is positive. For half of them, the regional coefficient is substantial and statistically significant. Overall, the relationship between interconnectivity and democracy is weakest in mature democracies and strongest in nascent democracies or those in the midst of political transformation. More

Table 5.2.
Regression Models

					Model			
	I	*II*	*III*	*IV*	*V*		*VI*	
LHS Variable	DEM	DEM	DEM	DEM	DEM	INT	INT	GDP
N	136	141	136	141	136			
Adj. R-square	0.583	0.536	0.643	0.588	0.583	0.832	0.833	0.597
Constant	61.7**	36.1**	35.59	85.40*	61.5**	21.14*	21.3	1407
	(3.21)	(8.58)	(1.41)	(2.13)	(3.19)	(21.68)	(21.56)	(1.34)
Democracy						0.0103	0.0126	-30.5
						(0.53)	(0.59)	(-0.71)
Interconnectivity	4.43***	5.57***			4.72**			1478***
	(5.81)	(7.99)			(3.06)			(7.69)
GDP	-0.0014*	-0.0008	-0.0006	0.0003	-0.0015		0.00009	
	(-2.09)	(-1.25)	(-0.64)	(0.37)	(-1.65)		(0.37)	
Log (Population)	-4.21**	-3.48**	-3.73**	-2.98*	-4.21**			
	(-3.07)	(-2.48)	(-2.71)	(-2.08)	(-3.07)			
Ave. School Yrs.	4.81**		4.81**		4.61**			
	(3.48)		(3.17)		(2.78)			
Life Expectancy	-0.076*`		-0.35		-0.75*			-288
	(-2.02)		(-0.74)		(-1.98)			(-1.15)
Ethnicity	0.13		0.18*		0.13			
	(1.59)		(2.17)		(1.58)			
Literacy						0.034**	0.033**	
						(3.23)	(3.08)	

Table 5.2. (continued)
Regression Models

| | Model | | | | | |
	I	II	III	IV	V	VI
Telephones					0.22*** (9.45)	0.19** (2.38)
Africa			0.11 (0.013)	-53.06 (-1.32)		
Asia			-dropped-	-44.98 (-1.11)		
Eurasia			-19.22* (-1.77)	-59.82 (-1.47)		
Latin America			15.1 (1.47)	-29.92 (-0.73)		
Middle East			-17.00* (-1.83)	-62.83 (-1.55)		
West Europe			30.98 (0.80)	-dropped-		
INT* Africa			7.02** (3.34)	7.15*** (3.41)		
INT* Asia			1.93 (1.25)	2.22 (1.40)		
INT* Eurasia			3.87** (2.97)	4.93*** (3.69)		
INT* Latin America			1.98 (1.36)	3.24* (2.15)		

Table 5.2. (continued)
Regression Models

			Model			
	I	II	III	IV	V	VI
INT* Middle East			3.87	2.63		
			(1.50)	(0.98)		
INT* West Europe			0.72	0.98		
			(0.25)	(0.33)		

t-statistics are in parentheses
*** = Significance at the 0.1 percent level
** = Significance at the 1 percent level
* = Significance at the 10 percent level

specifically the coefficient on the interaction term is highest for Africa; the t-statistics correspond to a one percent level of significance. The Eurasian results are quite similar. The Latin American coefficient is also substantial—at a 10 percent significance level in Model IV. Western Europe shows the most paltry correlation; that is, the interconnectivity levels do not vary much and the high democracy ratings move even less.

Multiple Endogeneity Analysis

Although it is tempting to infer causality from these strong correlations between interconnectivity and both the change and level of democracy, it would be wrong to do so because causality might easily flow in the opposite direction. Democracies rely on an informed public and uninhibited communication and may therefore seek interconnectivity. One way to explore this possibility analytically is through a system of simultaneous equations with multiple endogenous variables solvable by 2SLS estimation. The two-equation model employed here assumes that interconnectivity can influence democracy and vice versa, making it possible to compare the relative statistical significance and sizes of the coefficients on these variables in each of the two equations.[22]

As indicated by the results of Model V in table 5.2, interconnectivity remains a powerful predictor of democracy. The magnitude of the coefficient for interconnectivity on democracy is even greater than in the comparable OLS model and its significance level remains exceptionally high. Democracy, however, does not prove to have any significant effect on interconnectivity. Thus, the suggestion that democracy leads to interconnectivity is not supported while the hypothesis that there is no positive effect cannot be rejected. The coefficient on population is still negative and significant, while GDP is also still negative and nearly significant at the 10-percent level. The other outputs also closely parallels those of Model I.

The leading alternative explanation for the strong correlation between interconnectivity and democracy is that a third variable may influence both simultaneously. The obvious candidate is economic development, which is widely regarded as an important prerequisite for democracy. Here, the high correlation between interconnectivity and GDP—0.84—would support testing the hypothesis that economic development is *the* variable underlying the correlation between democracy and interconnectivity. More specifically, it is reasonable to include measures of communication, radios, telephones, and newspapers per thousand persons in an index for wealth (Lipset 1959). Equipment to communicate electronically is expensive, especially in the Third World. The same economic resources that can finance participation in the communications revolution thus should fuel demands for personal rights and freedoms.

Model VI in table 5.2 relies on a system of simultaneous equations in which the dependent variables GDP, democracy, and interconnectivity unravel these reciprocal effects. The model itself assumes that (1) economic development and interconnectivity predict democracy; (2) democracy and economic development predict interconnectivity; and (3) interconnectivity and democracy predict economic development. The results do not support the hypothesis that economic development is a confounding third variable. The regression coefficients for interconnectivity on democracy and GDP are both substantial and statistically significant, again above the 0.1 percent level. Democracy or GDP do not strongly influence interconnectivity. GDP is negatively correlated with democracy at a 10 percent significance level.

Interconnectivity, however, does correlate positively with democracy at high levels of significance in each model. Thus it is reasonable to suggest that country size and interconnectivity may share a common effect on democracy, much as smaller size and interconnectivity may be similarly conducive to democracy by facilitating coordinated civic action. Indeed, data links are shrinking the political space.

Conclusion

The purpose of the foregoing analysis was to examine the effects of a single source of political development to democracy—the revolution in personal communications. Despite the inherent limitations of statistical analyses, several analytic perspectives, every model, set of statistical tests, and functional form in this study is consistent with the hypothesis that interconnectivity is a powerful predictor of democracy, more than any of democracy's traditional correlates. In univariate analysis, the correlation coefficient for interconnectivity on democracy is larger than that of any other variable. As a variable in an ordinary least squares multiple linear regression, interconnectivity is exclusively the dominant predictor. As an interaction term in conjunction with regional categorical variables, the correlation of interconnectivity with democracy is everywhere positive, and has both the largest substantive value and greatest statistical significance in regions characterized by dynamic political transformations. Moreover, tests of alternative causal explanations invariably fail. As an endogenous variable in systems of simultaneous equations, interconnectivity always proves to be a significant predictor of democracy and economic development, but the reverse is never true.

Certainly these results reflect what we are coming to know about institutions of democracy and the process of democratizing. There are historic examples such as Gorbachev's Soviet Union in which it appears that information technologies played a role in supporting the emergence of democracy. Information technologies enable citizens of prospective democracies to learn more about how other societies operate. If they discover that others living elsewhere live more freely and appear to have a higher quality of life, they are motivated to seek more freedom and democracy for themselves. That is, there is indeed a connection between the revolution in information technology and democratic politics (see Baum and Richards, in this volume). Independent of whether one takes the position that freedom is inherently good or bad, this is precisely the reason why nondemocratic regimes, from the former Soviet Union to Singapore, have found it necessary to attempt to control communication and information.

Information technologies simultaneously empower citizens almost everywhere to broadcast charges that their own governments violate freedoms and human rights. The objective of such efforts is to bring unified world pressure and public opinion to bear against repressive regimes unable to hide their misdeeds as successfully as before. That demonstrators in Tiananmen Square chose to hold signs written in English had strategic implications.

As the "Dictator's Dilemma" formally suggests, governments that try to squelch the information technologies to protect their monopoly on power do so at the peril of economic growth within and outside of their borders. It is the message that Shultz shared with Gorbachev, and it is what leading analysts predict:

> For nations to be economically competitive, they must allow individual citizens access to information networks and computer technology. In doing so, they cede significant control over economic, cultural, and eventually political events in their countries. (Builder and Banks 1993, 160)

As it should be. Information technologies, which combine autonomy and influence in the same medium for the first time, thereby also couple decentralization of political power with economic growth. While some communications media tend to assist authoritarian regimes in maintaining control, the characteristics of electronic networks are exceptional in their theoretical and practical capacity to sustain the reciprocal communication on which democracy thrives.

Notes

1. One of the original intents for the ARPANET was to create the illusion that communicators were in the same room. See Baran (1964).

2. Deutsch (1953); McLuhan (1962). Note that by communications I mean a set of procedures by which minds are influenced.

3. Rivers and Schramm (1969). The price mechanism is itself a technological device to impart accurate information instantaneously.

4. Friedman (1962); Sargent (1972). With both development and democracy critically dependent on information, communication stands as a necessary variable for any formal study of democratic processes. Information and communications technologies (pamphlets, media, computers, conventions, and advertisements) factor heavily into the endurance equations for both political and economic markets. These technologies are directly relevant to democracy because of its emphasis on debates and deliberation. Market capitalism is also heavily reliant on communications issues, as evinced by mass advertising of differentiated goods, want-generation efforts versus need-satisficing on the part of firms, and so forth.

5. Optimal economic development requires allocative and productive efficiency, both of which are a function of information and, hence, communication. Information can be conceived as a stock at a given time or as a flow that is a process occurring over time. Information flows, of course, are synonymous with communication and free speech concerns.

6. Jost (1994). Technological productivity depends on the degrees of freedom in information flows. Rates of social change are changing the structure of world political and economic markets and cultures with unparalleled speed, leading even scientists to acknowledge their influence over an uncertain world.

7. Jost (1994); Smith (1999). To secure international competitiveness, some nations are attempting to manipulate information technologies as sources of comparative advantage (Sandholtz 1993).

8. Communication under democracy is the common good on which citizen-government relations hinge and ideas-in-common as the basis of political community are constructed (Bickford 1996; Beiner 1983; Nichols 1987). Under democratic forms of government, communication constitutes and organizes the deliberative polis and guards individual liberties (Tocqueville 1954). It is only through communication, that ideals like equality are constructed and institutionally materialized (Arendt 1958).

9. Legitimized norms of public participation, cooperation, and conflict (Dahl 1971) lead to the internalization of virtues like toleration and self-restraint (Rohrschneider 1996), and to the formation of collective preferences (Gibson 1992) that are to be transformed into law.

10. In modern democracies, opinion leaders do routinely influence mass belief systems through the selective interpretation and presentation of information (Gibson 1992). Nevertheless, common sense sets the terms of public discourse in civil society (Gramsci 1971). Ideas must first resonate with the masses (Risse-Kappen 1994) before they can be diffused. Given discursive space for criticism and learning, the best cure for biased communication structures is more communication from more sources.

11. Mill in Riemer (1962). That is, it perceives a need for at least a modicum of articulated disagreement to maintain public awareness and incentives for self-governance (Tocqueville 1954) required by human improvement.

12. In contrast with their capacity to even manage the Internet, governments may, with relatively little effort, control the newspapers read by its citizens, what they listen to, and what they watch on television.

13. Hovland et al. (1953). The credibility of liberalism surely stems in large part from the longevity and power of the U.S. government and other Western nations that employ variations on the liberal model. This would fulfill Thomas Jefferson's hopes that the United States would become a republican monument worthy of the world's emulation (Russel 1988).

14. Finnemore (1996). Scholars' recognition of liberalism's impact on events and discourses opens the door for various forms of communication to be used as political weaponry in the democratic cause. Gorbachev's foreign policy was dramatically affected by inputs from an international liberal community that had many academic, diplomatic, and cultural contacts with the Soviet intelligentsia (Risse-Kappan 1994; Rosenau 1984), which came to value free information flows, markets, and decentralization (Blum 1993). From spying every transparent aspect of the American social web, and U.S.-world relations, Soviet intellectuals accepted that the United States was not imperialist or war-prone and, most of all, that communism was not in Russia's best interest (Blaker 1993; Kennedy 1993; Stephanson 1998).

15. Electronic communications have already lessened diplomats' discretion and duties (Padelford and Lincoln 1967). Statecraft, thus, is more likely to reflect the truest and latest preferences of the home government, lessening the prospects of miscommunication.

16. Capitalist democracies have been found to experience faster economic growth (Leblang 1996), and technological innovation and economic position to predict military capability (Rasler and Thompson 1991). This helps explain why democratic initiators are most likely to win wars (Reiter and Stam 1998).

17. Most Asian countries seek to control information flows on the Internet for political reasons (Rodan 1998).

18. Elsewhere (Kedzie 1996), the author explores complementary longitudinal analyses to ensure that the cross-sectional results reviewed here are not circumstantial artifact, but rather an outcome consistent with systematic change.

19. The eight leading indicators of democracy from both Freedom House surveys are highly correlated; moreover, the correlation coefficient between the Freedom House data set and other ranged from .79 to .93 (Jaggars and Gurr 1995).

20. The term *interconnectivity* was popularized by Larry Landweber for his measures of the proliferation of global E-mail networks. For more general discussion about E-mail and politics see Leer (1999).

21. Note that the correlation matrix in table 5.1 reveals high correlations between many of the independent variables, particularly those of specific interest to this investigation: GDP, interconnectivity, and schooling. Colinearities between independent variables will tend to reduce the efficiency of predictors, but without bias. Reduced efficiency means that the reported statistical significance may be less than the actual because the standard errors will be excessively large. The absence of bias means that the estimated coefficients will be neither systematically higher nor lower than their "true" values. Correcting for the multicolinearity could result in an increase in the number of statistically significant predictors and further strengthen statistical inferences relative to those variables such as interconnectivity that are already significant. On the other hand, the effect of GDP might be unduly understated since some statistical significance is sacrificed to interconnectivity and to the other included variables with which GDP is colinear. The magnitude of the coefficient on GDP is, nevertheless, quite small and is presumably reported without bias in the inclusive Model I. Furthermore, comparing Models I and II, the coefficients do not vary much with the consecutive inclusion or exclusion of the other independent variables.

22. That is, both democracy and interconnectivity serve as dependent variables in the relevant model (Model V). To achieve a unique solution, at least one additional instrumental variable must be included in the interconnectivity equation; because electronic mail is text-based and travels over telephone lines, appropriate instruments are literacy or, alternatively, the number of telephone lines per capita. Relevant independent variables capture economic growth, human development, and ethnicity.

References

Alesina, A. and E. Spoloare. 1995. On the Number and Size of Nations. Working Paper no. 5050, National Bureau of Economic Research, Cambridge, MA.

Arendt, H. 1958. *The Human Condition.* Chicago: University of Chicago Press.

Arquilla, J. and D. Ronfeldt. 1997. *In Athena's Camp: Preparing for Conflict in the Information Age.* Santa Monica: RAND.

Aubrey, Singer. 1966. "Television: Window on Culture or Reflection in the Glass." *American Scholar* 35 (Spring): 303–309.

Baran, P. 1964. On Distributed Communications: XI. Working Paper no. RM–3767–PR. Santa Monica: RAND.

Bickford, Susan. 1996. "Beyond Friendship: Aristotle on Conflict, Deliberation, and Attention." *Journal of Politics* 58 (May): 398–421.

Blaker, C. 1993. *Hostage to Revolution: Gorbachev and Soviet Security Policy, 1985–91*. New York: Council on Foreign Relations.

Blum, D. 1993. "The Soviet Foreign Policy Belief System." *International Studies Quarterly* 37: 373–394.

Builder, C. and S. Banks. 1993. Artificial Societies: A Concept for Basic Research on the Societal Impact of Information Technology. Working Paper no. P-7740. Santa Monica: RAND.

Chan, S. 1997. "In Search of the Democratic Peace: Problems and Promise." *Mershon International Studies Review* 41: 59–91.

Central Intelligence Agency. 1994. *World Fact Book*. Washington, DC: Central Intelligence Agency.

Comor, E. 1999. "Governance and the Nation-State in a Knowledge-Based Political Economy." *Approaches to Global Governance Theory*. Eds. Martin Hewson and Timothy Sinclair, pp. 117–134. Albany: State University New York Press.

Dahl, R. 1971. *Polyarchy: Participation and Opposition*. New Haven: Yale University Press.

Dahl, R. 1996. "Democratic Theory and Democratic Experience." *Democracy and Difference: Contesting the Boundaries of the Political,* ed. Seyla Benhabib, pp. 336–339. Princeton: Princeton University Press.

Deutsch, K. 1953. *National and Social Communications*. Cambridge: Massachusetts Institute of Technology Press.

Downing, J. 1989. "Computers for Political Change: PeaceNet and Public Data Access." *Journal of Communication* (Summer): 154–161.

Fearon, James. 1995. "Rationalist Explanations for War." *International Organization* 49 (Summer): 391–410.

Finnemore, M. 1996. "Norms, Culture, and World Politics." *International Organization* 50 (Spring): 325–347.

Freedom House. 1993/94. Comparative Survey of Freedom.

Friedman, M. 1962. *Capitalism and Freedom*. Chicago: University of Chicago Press.

Fuller, R. B. 1964. *Education Automation*. Carbondale: Southern Illinois University Press.

Gibson, J. 1992. "Democratic Values and the Transformation of the Soviet Union." *Journal of Politics* 54 (May): 329–370.

Gottlieb, G. 1994. "Nations Without States." *Foreign Affairs* (May/June): 100–112.

Gramsci, A. 1971. *The Modern Prince*. New York: International Publishers.

Gray, C. and S. Mentor 1995. "The Cyborg Body Politic Version 1.2." *The Cyborg Handbook*. Ed. Chris G. Gray, pp. 453–467. New York: Routledge.

Grossman, L. 1995. *The Electronic Republic: Reshaping Democracy in the Information Age*. New York: Viking.

Halacy, D. S. 1964. *Computers: The Machines We Think With*. New York: Dell Publishing Co.

Haraway, D. 1990. "A Manifesto for Cyborgs: Science, Technology, and Socialist Feminism in the 1980s." *Feminism/Postmodernism*. Ed. Linda J. Nicholson, pp. 190–233. New York: Routledge.

Hills, J. 1993. "Telecommunications and Democracy: The International Experience." *Telecommunications Journal* 60 (January): 21–29.

Hoffer, E. 1951. *The True Believer*. New York: Harper.

Hovland, Carl, Irving L. Janis and Harold H. Kelly. 1953. *Communication and Persuasion*. New Haven, CT: Yale University Press.

Inkeles, Alex. 1990. "Introduction: On Measuring Democracy." *Studies in Comparative International Development* 25 (Spring): 3–6.

Jaggars, Keith and Ted Robert Gurr. 1995. "Tracking Democracy's Third Wave with Polity II Data." *Journal of Peace Research* 32: 469–482.

Jipp, A. 1963. "Wealth of Nations and Telephone Density." *Telecommunications Journal* (July): 199–201.

Jost, K. 1994. "Talk-Show Democracy." *Congressional Quarterly Researcher* 4 (April): 363–379.

Kariel, H. 1964. *In Search of Authority*. New York: Free Press of Glencoe.

Kedzie, C. 1996. Communication and Democracy: Coincident Revolutions and the Emergent Dictator's Dilemma. Typescript.

Kennedy, P. 1993. *Preparing for the 21st Century*. New York: HarperCollins.

Leblang, David. 1996. "Property Rights, Democracy and Economic Growth." *Political Research Quarterly* 49 (March): 5–26.

Lebow, R. 1994. "The Long Peace, the End of the Cold War, and the Failure of Realism." *International Organization* (Spring): 249–277.

Leer, A. 1999. *Masters of the Wired World: Cyberspace Speaks Out*. London: Pitman Publishing.

Lipset, S. 1959. "Some Social Requisites of Democracy: Economic Development and Political Legitimacy." *American Political Science Review* 53: 69–105.

Lipset, S. 1960. *Political Man: The Social Bases of Politics*. Garden City, NY: Doubleday.

Luke. Timothy W. 1997. "The Politics of Digital Inequality: Access, Capability and Distribution of Cyberspace." *New Political Science* 41–42 (Fall): 121–144.

Matrix Information and Directory Services. 1993. Data.

McLean, I. 1989. *Democracy and the New Technology*. Oxford: Polity.

McLuhan, M. 1962. *The Gutenberg Galaxy: The Making of Typographic Man*. Toronto: University of Toronto Press.

Mitchell, R. 1998. "Sources of Transparency: Information Systems in International Regimes." *International Studies Quarterly* 42: 109–30.

Moravcsik, Andrew. 1997. "Taking Liberal Preferences Seriously: A Liberal Theory of International Politics." *International Organization* 51 (Autumn): 513–533.

Neufeld. M. 1995. *The Restructuring of International Relations Theory.* Cambridge: Cambridge University Press.

Nichols, M. 1987. "Aristotle's Defense of Rhetoric." *Journal of Politics* 9: 657–677.

Noel, A. and J. Therieu. 1995. "From Domestic to International Justice." *International Organization* 49 (Summer): 523–553.

Olson, M. 1993. "Dictatorship, Democracy and Development." *American Political Science Review* 87 (September): 567–576.

Padelford, N. and G. Lincoln. 1967. *The Dynamics of International Relations,* 2d ed. New York: MacMillan.

Page, B. and J. Tannenbaum. 1996. "Populist Deliberation and Talk Radio." *Journal of Communication* 46 (Spring): 33–54.

Pool, Ithiel de Sola. 1983. *Technologies of Freedom.* Cambridge: Belknap Press.

Rasler, Karen and Will Thompson. 1991. "Technological Innovation, Capability Positional Shifts, and War." *Journal of Conflict Resolution* 35 (September): 412–442.

Reisinger, W., Arthur H. Miller and Vicki L. Hesli. 1995. "Public Behavior and Political Change in Post-Soviet States." *Journal of Politics* 57 (November): 941–970.

Reiter, Dan and Allan Stam III. 1998. "Democracy, War Initiation, and Victory." *American Political Science Review* 92: 377–390.

Resnick, D. 1997. "Politics on the Internet: The Normalization of Cyberspace." *New Political Science* 41–42 (Fall): 47–68.

Riemer, Neal. 1962. *The Revivial of Democratic Theory.* New York: Appleton-Century-Crofts.

Riker, W. 1982. *Liberalism Against Populism.* San Francisco: W. H. Freeman.

Risse-Kappen, T. 1994. "Ideas Do Not Float Freely." *International Organization* 48 (Spring): 185–214.

Rivers, W. and W. Schramm. 1969. *Responsibility in Mass Communication.* New York: Harper.

Roberts, S. 1995. "Open Arms for Online Democracy." *U.S. News and World Report,* 16 (January): 10.

Rohrschneider, R. 1996. "Institutional Learning versus Value Diffusion: The Evolution of Democratic Values among Parliamentarians in Eastern and Western Germany." *Journal of Politics* 58 (May): 422–446.

Ronfeldt, D. 1993. Institutions, Markets and Networks—A Framework about the Evolution of Societies. Working Paper no. DRU–590–RC/FF. Santa Monica: RAND.

Roseman, C. C. G. Mayo and F. B. Collinge. 1966. *Dimensions of Political Analysis*. Englewood Cliffs, NJ: Prentice-Hall.

Rosenau, J. 1984. "A Pre-theory Revisited: World Politics in an Era of Cascading Interdependence." *International Science Quarterly* 28: 245–305.

Rowen, Henry S. 1995. "The Tide Underneath the 'Third Wave.'" *Journal of Democracy* 6 (January): 52–64.

Russel, G. 1988. "The Ethics of American Statecraft." *Journal of Politics* 50: 503–517.

Russett, Bruce. 1993. *Controlling the Sword: The Democratic Governance of National Security*. Cambridge: Harvard University Press.

Russett, Bruce and Harvey Starr. 1996. *World Politics: Menu for Choice*. New York: W. H. Freeman and Company.

Sandholtz, Wayne. 1993. "Institutions and Collective Action: The New Telecommunications in Western Europe." *World Politics* 45 (January): 242–270.

Sargent, L. T. 1972. *Contemporary Political Ideologies*. Homewood: Dorsey Press.

Snider, J. 1994. "Democracy Online: Tomorrow's Electronic Electorate." *Futurist* 28 (September/October): 15–19.

Stephanson, Anders. 1998. "Rethinking Cold War History." *Review of International Studies* 24: 119–124.

Tocqueville, Alexis de. 1954. Democracy in America. Vol. 1. New York: Vintage Books.

Toulouse, C. 1997. "Introduction to the Politics of Cyberspace." *New Political Science* 41–42 (Fall): 1–16.

Varley, P. 1991. "Electronic Democracy." *Technology Review* 94 (November/December): 43–51.

Von Mises, L. 1935. "Economic Calculation in the Socialist Commonwealth." *Collectivist Economics Planning*. Ed. F. Hayek, pp. 87–130. London: Routledge and Kegan.

Waltz, K. 1979. *Theory of International Politics*. New York: Random.

Ward, M. and K. Gleditsch. 1998. "Democratizing for Peace." *American Political Science Review* 92 (March): 51–61.

Wolin, Sheldon S. 1996. "Fugitive Democracy." *Democracy and Difference: Contesting the Boundaries of the Political*. Ed. Seyla Benhabib, pp. 31–44. Princeton: Princeton University Press.

Wriston, B. 1993. "The Twilight of Sovereignty." *Fletcher Forum of World Affairs* 17 (Summer): 117–135.

CHAPTER SIX

The Communications Revolution and the Political Use of Force

MATTHEW A. BAUM

In summarizing one of history's most renowned theories of warfare, the legendary military strategist Karl von Clausewitz (1780–1831) asserted that war is an extension of politics by other means. To the extent that the decision to employ military force is, as Clausewitz claimed, a *political* act, then understanding the likely effects of the communications revolution on future trends in global conflict requires consideration of the effects of modern communications and information technologies on the *domestic* politics of military conflict. Combined with the near-simultaneous end of the post-World War II bipolar Cold War system, the communications revolution may indeed hold profound implications for the future of global conflict in general, as well as for the domestic politics of U.S. foreign policy, in particular.

An initial glimpse of the important relationship between these two historic developments came with the Persian Gulf War, which, thanks to modern satellite technology, was dubbed by Cable News Network (CNN's) Ted Turner a "ready-set-go" war, where hostilities were coordinated with calendar dates. (Bernstein 1991). Numerous analysts have documented the urgency placed by the Bush administration on achieving a quick, decisive victory over Iraq, lest images of bloody American soldiers and bodybags, broadcast live into America's living rooms, erode domestic support for the war. President George Bush himself noted, in January 1991, "I don't think that support would last if it were a long, drawn-out conflagration. I think support would erode, as it did in the Vietnam conflict."[1] Simply stated, massive, real-time media coverage of U.S. military actions abroad has become ubiquitous in the 1990s and will likely be factored into all future presidential decisions concerning the use of force.

A predominant hypothesis in the literature holds that the media does indeed influence public opinion, and that public opinion does, at least sometimes, influence foreign policy making in general (Hinckley 1992; Page and Shapiro 1992, 1983; Powlick 1995; Risse-Kappan 1991), and crisis decision making in particular (Fearon 1994; Gaubatz 1999, 1996; James and Oneal 1991; Levy 1989; Ostrom and Job 1986; Mueller 1973; Smith 1996; Zaller 1994; see also Gowa 1998). Yet no theory adequately explains the causal relationship between the media, public opinion, and policy outcomes, how such a relationship might evolve, or the implications of such an evolution for foreign policy. Elsewhere (Baum 2000a; Baum and Kernell 1999) I have argued that the media and the public have in fact evolved over the past fifty years. Modern communications technologies, such as cable and satellite television, have produced a revolution in mass media presentation of news and information, which, I have argued, is analogous to a revolution in direct marketing. The net result has been an increase in public attentiveness to foreign policy crises.

There exists no consensus concerning whether the breakdown of the bipolar U.S.-Soviet competition will lead to greater or reduced conflict in the international arena. Yet recent events in Bosnia, Iraq, and elsewhere attest to the continued potential for military conflict. Beyond the Persian Gulf War, the importance that recent presidents have placed on influencing public opinion concerning foreign crises, as well as the apparent impact of significant changes in public opinion on presidential decision-making, have been visible in such diverse U.S. military operations as those in Panama, Somalia, and Haiti. While scholars disagree on the nature and extent of the influence of public opinion on presidential decision making during these crises, both Presidents Bush and Clinton acted in a manner suggesting that the domestic political implications of their decisions were never too far from their minds. It is therefore critical that the implications of the communications revolution be systematically addressed alongside studies of conflict and cooperation in the post-Cold War era.

This chapter focuses on the policy implications of an increase in public attentiveness to foreign crises for presidential decision making. Drawing upon what has been termed the *audience cost* variant of democratic peace theory, most closely associated with Fearon (1994), I argue that high levels of public attentiveness to foreign crises represent a significant constraint on presidential crisis decision making.[2] Moreover, I argue that due to changes in how the mass media presents news and information, average levels of attentiveness to foreign crises have increased over time, thereby enhancing the constraining effect.

I begin with a brief review of my theory and supporting evidence concerning the effects of the communications revolution on the changing presentation of news and information by the mass media, and the resulting increase in public attentiveness to foreign crises (see Baum 2000a). Next, I develop and test hypotheses concerning the nature and extent of the influence of public opinion on presidential crisis decision making. In the course of my empirical testing, I compare the audience cost model with several other prominent theories purporting to explain the influence, or lack thereof, of domestic politics upon the conduct of foreign policy. The results are most consistent with my hypothesis, though I also find some limited evidence in support of several other arguments. I then consider the broader implications of enhanced public attentiveness for the future conduct of American foreign policy, and for the future of global conflict in general. Finally, I conclude the chapter with a summary of my findings.

A Revolution in Media Presentation of News and Information

In this section I briefly review my theory concerning the effects of a revolution in the mass media's presentation of news and information to the public (see Baum 2000a for a more systematic elaboration of the theory). I argue that the massive resources of the modern media have substantially increased the propensity of average individuals, and by extension the mass public, to pay attention to sufficient information regarding certain high-profile political issues—most notably foreign policy crises—to express an opinion if queried, say, by a polling organization.

My theory does not challenge the numerous studies (e.g., Delli Carpini and Keeter 1996, 1991) that have found no evidence of a general increase in factual information about politics in the post-World War II era. Nor do I address whether or not the public's understanding of political issues has increased, over time (e.g., Rosenau 1990, 1997). Rather, I focus upon the average propensity to accept and maintain an opinion, at least temporarily, with the availability of sufficient accessible information (Aldrich, Sullivan, and Borgida 1989; Iyengar 1990, 1992) about high-profile political issues. I argue that this propensity has increased, due, in part, to the effects a revolution in the mass media's presentation of news and information about politics.

For an individual to express an opinion about a given issue, it must be sufficiently compelling that he or she is willing to incur the cognitive costs associated with acquiring some minimal level of information about that issue. Because accepting—or paying attention to—new information is costly (we must ignore many other information stimuli to focus on any given piece of information), individuals must economize on the information they accept. As a result, individuals tend to accept only information that they believe is likely to result in beneficial new knowledge, and for which the expected benefit outweighs the expected costs of paying attention (Lupia and McCubbins

1998).[3] It is therefore not necessarily relevant that far more information is available in the "information age," as individuals can simply raise an ever-higher perceptual "screen" with which to effectively screen out the vast majority of information to which they are exposed. In fact, the previously noted absence of an increase in average levels of factual information about politics suggests that individuals have indeed expanded their perceptual screens in response to the explosion of available news and information brought about by the communications revolution.

The theory consists of both a supply- and a demand-side argument. I shall briefly review each. Beginning with the former, I consider the impact of what is best described, in economics and management, as a revolution in direct marketing. To extend this borrowed analogy, it is useful to consider the media marketplace—particularly television—as having evolved over the past fifty years from an oligopoly to a competitive market. The "oligopolistic" television industry of the 1950s, and into the 1960s, presented political information primarily through the largely undifferentiated network news programming of the three broadcast networks. By contrast, in the 1990s, the communications revolution has created a highly competitive television marketplace. Between 1969 and 1998, the number of American households subscribing to cable television expanded from about 6 percent to almost 70 percent. The average number of channels available to cable subscribers has also expanded dramatically, from less than 15, in 1983, to over 45 in 1997 (Lowry 1997; Webster and Lichty 1991). Thanks to fiber optics and digital satellite broadcasting, many consumers now receive in excess of one hundred channels. Combined, these developments represent an explosion of consumer choices.[4]

In order to remain competitive, television broadcasters have adapted their programming to appeal to smaller niche audiences with particularistic tastes and preferences. In an era of increasingly fragmented television audiences—due to rising competition, primarily from cable television, but also, more recently, from the Internet—television networks have been forced to abandon their traditional "lowest common denominator" mass appeal strategy in favor of increasingly differentiated programming, a strategy analogous to niche marketing (Webster and Lichty 1991).

Traditional "informational" programming (e.g., network evening newscasts) has been both supplemented and supplanted in many respects by "reality" programming (e.g., *Cops*); "infotainment" news broadcasts (e.g., *Hard Copy*); news magazines (e.g., *Dateline NBC*); TV talk shows (e.g., *Oprah*); roundtable debates (e.g., *Crossfire*); and "newslight" newspapers (e.g., *USA Today*)—designed to appeal to the more narrow interests of smaller niche markets. The overall volume of news and information-oriented programming has expanded dramatically as well. For instance, NBC has increased its production of news programming from three to twenty-seven hours per day just since 1996 (Kalb 1998). The result of this revolution is that relative to the 1950s and 1960s, a larger percentage of the public is attentive to some element of the mass media—primarily television—with the potential to provide news and information about political issues, in some format—be it the Lifetime Network, Music TV, C-SPAN, The Discovery Channel, Nickelodean, Arts & Entertainment, CNBC, MSNBC, or Cable News Network—than was the case in the 1950s and 1960s. Simply stated, like direct-mail marketers, television broadcasters—including profit-conscious news organizations—have, out of necessity, grown increasingly adept at providing something for everyone, that is, a channel that caters to virtually every type of programming taste and preference.

Under normal circumstances, given the logic of Lupia and McCubbins (1998), this development is unlikely to produce a public that is better informed about political issues than were earlier generations. In fact, the highly segmented modern television marketplace allows individuals to escape news and information more effectively than was the case in the 1950s. However, under certain exceptional circumstances—such as a military conflict—the highly segmented modern media may focus its massive resources upon a single policy issue (albeit varying aspects of that issue). When the diverse elements of the mass media unify their focus, I expect the public to be more attentive to a given issue in the current era than to comparable events in the 1950s and 1960s. This, I argue, is exactly what occurred in such foreign crises as the 1991 Persian Gulf War and the 1992–1993 Somalia intervention.

I now briefly turn to the demand-side of the equation. Here, I draw upon cognitive psychology, in order to derive the conditions under which individuals, and by extension the mass public, are likely to perceive the expected benefits of paying attention to news and information about a foreign policy crisis as outweighing the expected costs of doing so. My theory posits a decision-theoretical model of individual information consumption. The argument rests upon individuals' efforts to maximize their overall utility derived from consuming information, given the finite volume of information that they are able to consume, as well as the inherent trade-off between consuming a given piece of information and doing other things, within a given time period.

I argue that by repackaging news and information about politics into multiple entertainment-oriented formats (i.e., "infotainment") the mass media has successfully reduced the expected costs of paying attention to what has traditionally been, for many citizens, mundane and uninteresting, while at the same time—by transforming political information into highly compelling human-drama (i.e., entertainment)—increasing the expected benefits of paying attention. In effect, individuals are able to accept substantial information about a given issue at virtually no cost, as political information (e.g., concerning a foreign crisis) is "attached" to a piece of information that is consumed purely for entertainment purposes. Political information is thus initially consumed as an incidental by-product of seeking entertainment.

Drawing from Popkin's (1994) theory of "causal narratives," I further argue that by inducing more individuals to pay attention to news and information about politics, when presented in entertainment-oriented formats, the mass media also facilitates the ability of average individuals to more easily integrate additional information about a given foreign crisis into a preexisting mental image or framework.

A causal narrative is an informational shortcut whereby individuals create "scripts" or "scenarios" about issue areas, general beliefs, and values. The narrative is a basic story line concerning how the individual "feels" about a given issue area. Subsequent information that concerns that issue area is evaluated through what Popkin calls a "goodness-of-fit" test—that is, an assessment of how the new information relates to the individual's preexisting beliefs—or narrative—concerning that issue. Information that is consistent with a preexisting narrative is more easily incorporated (accepted), particularly if the pertinent narrative has been recently used, and is thus more readily accessible (Popkin 1994, 72–73; for related perspectives, see also Conover and Feldman 1981; Lodge, McGraw, and Stroh 1989; Lodge, Stroh and Wahlke 1990; and Tetlock 1984, 1985, 1986).

I argue that by reducing the expected costs of paying attention to some initial information about a given foreign policy crisis, the media, in effect, renders the individual's causal narrative(s) concerning related issues (e.g., war and patriotism) more accessible, thereby further reducing the cognitive costs of paying attention to subsequent information about the crisis. Moreover, as more information is accepted, an expanded causal narrative is able to more easily integrate additional information about a given issue without provoking substantial (costly) cognitive conflict.

I will now summarize one element of a more extensive study as a sample of the evidence supporting the theory (see Baum 2000a). To substantiate my theory, I investigated public attentiveness to the three major post-World War II U.S. military conflicts—Korea, Vietnam, and the Persian Gulf.[5] I compared "no opinion" and "don't know" responses to a series of identical, or nearly identical, survey questions across the several periods.[6] The questions employed for this analysis were as follows:

- "Do you think the United States made a mistake in going into the war in Korea, or not?"

- "In view of the developments since we entered the fighting in Vietnam, do you think the United States made a mistake sending troops to fight in Vietnam?"
- Do you think the United States made a mistake in [getting involved in the war in/sending troops to fight against] Iraq, or not?"

My hypothesis in this investigation was that responding "no opinion" or "don't know" to a survey question represents unfamiliarity with the issue addressed by that question, and can thus be taken as indicating a lack of awareness of the issue.[7]

There are clearly a number of factors that complicate any attempt to compare these quite-different conflicts, such as the possibility that the greater controversy surrounding the Vietnam conflict could inflate the percentage of Americans responding "don't know" due to ambivalence rather than ignorance. I thus included public opinion during the Korean War as a control. While the Korean War became somewhat controversial, opposition to that war never reached the magnitude of the Vietnam conflict. As a result, the "ambivalence versus ignorance" critique makes my hypothesis—that levels of opinionation (i.e., the percentage of respondents expressing an opinion) during Vietnam should be stronger than during Korea—a particularly difficult test for my theory.

The results of this investigation indicated that the mean level of "no opinion" responses during the Persian Gulf War (5.3%; N = 12 surveys in 1991) was approximately one-third of that from a near-identical survey question asked repeatedly during the Korean War (15.3%; N = 13 surveys between 1950 and 1953), and less than one-half of that recorded during the Vietnam War (12.0%; N = 23 surveys between 1965 and 1971). Additionally, the Vietnam War garnered approximately 22% fewer "no opinion" responses than the Korean War, suggesting that greater ambivalence or "cognitive conflict" cannot explain the result.

As additional evidence, I identified a number of major foreign policy-related issues that have remained highly salient to the U.S. public for an extended period of time, and that are related to the public's attention to, and interest in, foreign crises. One such issue is U.S. involvement in the United Nations. Several major U.S. survey organizations, including the General Social Survey (GSS) and the National Opinion Research Council (NORC) have repeatedly asked Americans whether or not the United States should remain a member of the United Nations. At Figure 6.1 I report the annual aggregate overtime trend, between 1951 and 1994, in levels of opinionation on this question. The data clearly indicates a substantial overtime decline— from about 9 percent in 1951 to just over 4 percent in 1994—in average levels of "don't know" responses to the United Nations membership question

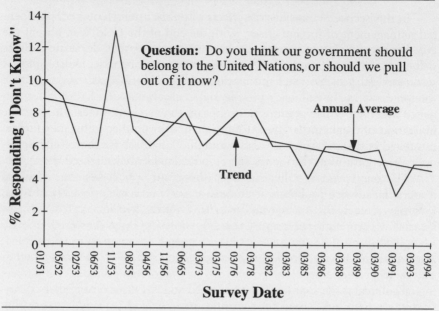

Figure 6.1.
Trend in "Don't Know" Responses for U.N.
Membership Question, 1951–1994 (N = 23 Polls)

Question: Do you think our government should belong to the United Nations, or should we pull out of it now?

Annual Average

Trend

% Responding "Don't Know"

Survey Date

Note: in addition to GSS surveys, graphic includes 8 NORC surveys & 1 SRS survey, covering the period 1951 to 1965.

(N = 23 polls). This suggests the public attentiveness to the question of U.S. involvement in the U.N., has increased substantially, over time.

The preceding discussion was intended to present a broad intuitive overview, along with some limited supporting evidence, of the "information-processing" theory underlying my argument. This discussion was merely intended to be suggestive and to provide a framework for understanding the overall argument. I now turn to my primary task for this chapter: considering the effects of the communications revolution on U.S. foreign crisis management, as well as some basic tests of my theory's implications.

Public Attentiveness and the Escalation of Foreign Crises

Ultimately, the notion that Clinton will be hobbled on the
world stage [by a wave of scandals] rests upon the idea
that his foreign policy needs public support. That's an

> understandable assumption, but one of limited value. In
> fact, what often counts is not so much lining up public
> support as defusing any active, determined opposition.
> —Jim Mann, "Clinton's Pain Hasn't Hurt Foreign Policy"

In this section, I consider the effects of public attentiveness on presidential management of foreign crises. With the end of the Cold War, absent the U.S.-Soviet competition, some scholars have argued that domestic politics will play an increasing role in U.S. foreign policy making (e.g., Holsti 1996). I assess several possible mechanisms through which public attentiveness to a foreign crisis might influence presidential decision-making. I then offer evidence that high public attentiveness appears to exert a stronger effect on the likelihood of escalating a given dispute than several other influential factors presented in the literature (see also Baum 2000a, 2000b for more fully developed presentations of the theory and empirical evidence presented here.)

The controversial "diversionary" theory of war holds that political leaders, faced with problems at home, are likely to act aggressively abroad, in order to create a "rally-round-the-flag" effect (Mueller 1973), thereby increasing their domestic popularity (e.g., Stoll 1984 and Russett 1990; see Levy 1989 for a thorough review and critique of diversionary war theories). Recent studies have continued the long-running debate concerning whether and by what means domestic politics affects the foreign policy decision making of political leaders, at least in democratic states. One recent large-N quantitative study found democracies significantly less likely to enter wars during election years, when leaders were presumably most accountable to their electorates (Gaubatz 1999). Another study employed a formal model to demonstrate that this phenomenon may be attributable to conciliatory behavior by potential adversaries during democratic election years, due to the fear that democratic leaders running for reelection are likely to fear the political consequences of backing down, if challenged (Smith 1996). Others have found high levels of public approval of the president's job performance to be positively related to the president's ability to carry out his policy agenda effectively, in general (Kernell 1997; Mondak 1993; Neustadt 1961; Page, Shapiro, and Dempsey 1987), as well as his willingness to use force in a crisis (e.g., Ostrom and Job 1986) in particular. Additional research has shown that presidential candidates are justifiably responsive to the public's foreign policy preferences (Aldrich, Sullivan and Borgida 1989). However, one recent quantitative study compared traditional neorealist international factors with domestic political factors and found that the domestic political variables, such as the electoral cycle, had no substantial effect on the decision to escalate militarized interstate disputes (Gowa 1998).

My argument concerning the effect of domestic public attentiveness on presidential crisis decision making, while it makes no attempt to prove or disprove each of these arguments definitively, does suggest a different mechanism by which presidential decision making in foreign crises might be influenced by domestic politics. My theory draws most heavily upon what has been termed the *audience cost* variant of democratic peace theory (Fearon 1994). Fearon argues, in a game theoretical analysis, that due to elections—through which democratic leaders are answerable to their publics via the ballot box and must therefore maintain public support to stay in power—democratic leaders are able to make more credible commitments than are leaders of nondemocracies (i.e., send more credible signals of resolve) in potential conflict situations. This is because democratic leaders, upon engaging in a potential crisis, must absorb immediate domestic audience costs that make it more difficult to back down from a commitment (lest she be voted out of office). Recognizing the costs borne by the democratic leader, the other actor in the negotiation will view a threat or escalatory step as a credible signal of resolve. The point is that public opinion creates domestic audience costs for leaders of democratic states, which, by constraining their range of action, makes their threats more credible. In the international bargaining literature, this is frequently referred to as "narrowing the win-set" (e.g., Putnam 1988). One study of the media's discovery of famine in Ethiopia in the mid-1980s offered the following summary of this argument:

> Public opinion may not direct government action, and its substance indeed may be dependent on the actions and words of political and media elites, but concerted public *attention* to an issue certainly narrows the range of options a government can take. (Bosso 1989, 172–73)

To the extent that this hypothesis is valid, it appears to follow that the greater the public's focus upon a given issue, the greater the domestic audience costs, and thus the stronger ought to be the constraint upon decision makers. Such constraints should be evident in presidential decision making during foreign crises. By escalating a foreign crisis to the use of force, the president is taking a political risk. If he uses force, and fails to achieve his objective, he will suffer politically at home. His political opponents will likely seek to exploit a foreign policy failure to help defeat the president and/or his party in the next election. Moreover, the more attention the public pays to the president's actions in a given crisis, the greater the likely domestic political cost to the president of failure. Given the increased potential political risk to the president of using force when the public is paying close attention to his actions, one would anticipate that as public attention increases, ceteris paribus, his willingness to use force, and thereby risk suffering substantial domestic political/electoral costs, ought to decline.

To understand why public scrutiny might be a more influential factor in creating domestic audience costs than, say, presidential approval ratings, it is useful to more closely examine the logic of Fearon's (1994) audience cost argument. Upon making a public demand of a foreign country, the president is likely to face substantial domestic audience costs, regardless of whether the general public is largely approving or disapproving of the policy. Public approval of a president's foreign policy is fickle. Should the crisis turn out badly, strong public support is likely to turn rapidly into strong disapproval of the president's performance. Similarly, as the dramatic increase in support for President Bush's war policy in the Persian Gulf War—once the public recognized the inevitable triumphant outcome—clearly demonstrated, there is no cure for ambivalence or disapproval like a decisive victory. As a result, the key to creating domestic audience costs appears to lie less in the ratio of support-to-opposition for the president's policy than in the percentage of the public paying attention to the crisis. Referring to this phenomenon, Zaller (1994) argues that politicians are primarily concerned with "prospective" public opinion—or anticipation of the likely future degree of public support for a policy—which, he argues, exerts a much greater influence on policy-makers than current public opinion. It is this anticipation of future public support or opposition that creates politically relevant domestic audience costs.

My argument presents an opportunity to differentiate between several of the competing arguments just cited. If the influence of domestic public attentiveness exceeds that of presidential approval, then this represents some evidence contrary to both the Ostrom and Job argument (hereafter referred to as the "political capital" theory), which suggests a positive relationship between presidential popularity and willingness to use force, and the diversionary theory of war, which implies a negative relationship between presidential popularity and the decision to use force abroad.

In order to conduct such a test, however, it is first necessary to identify an appropriate indicator of the domestic public salience of foreign crises. Fortunately, such an indicator is readily available. The Gallup organization has regularly asked Americans for their opinion concerning the president's job performance throughout most of the post-World War II era (eight to forty-two times per year).

In the context of studying foreign crises, I believe this question is a useful indicator of the salience of such crises. Because of the president's status as the nation's most high-profile national figure, an individual's opinion about the president tends to represent the sum total of his or her assessments about the state of the nation, and the world (Kernell 1978). The president is a lightning rod for everything citizens consider wrong or right about the country. As a result, one might imagine that to the extent that citizens have an increased propensity to evaluate the president's performance based upon foreign policy in the midst of a foreign policy crisis (see, e.g., Krosnick and Brannon 1993), one would expect levels of opinionation on this question to reflect attentiveness to such a crisis. Thus, rather than the traditional focus upon spikes in presidential approval during foreign crises, I instead examine levels of "no opinion" responses in Gallup's presidential approval question. By examining the effects of foreign crises on levels of opinionation in presidential approval polls, we may gain leverage into the question of how public opinion concerning foreign crises constrains presidential decision making. My data set begins with the Truman administration in 1946 and runs through the Bush Administration in 1992.

By analyzing presidential approval polls during U.S. military crises, it is possible to test my hypothesis against the other previously noted explanations for how domestic politics influences presidential crisis decision making, as well as against the Gaubatz (1999) electoral cycle argument. Specifically, I look at the presidential approval poll immediately preceding the onset of military action in a crisis. The logic is that a president takes a reading of the public's interest in a dispute prior to determining whether or not to initiate a military action, or to escalate the dispute. For this analysis I looked at U.S. militarized interstate disputes (MIDs) between 1946 and 1992. Data on U.S. militarized disputes between 1816 and 1992 is available as a part of Singer & Small's Correlates of War Project. By combining the MID data with presidential approval poll data, I am able to investigate whether levels of opinionation in presidential approval polls in the period immediately prior to the onset of militarized action were significantly related to the likelihood of escalating a given dispute.

Each U.S. MID is coded for the highest level of escalation reached during the course of the MID. The MID dataset divides MIDs into five categories. If the highest level of hostility reached in a conflict did not involve any military action, the MID is coded "1"; if the highest level was a threat of force, the MID is coded "2"; if force was deployed, the MID is coded "3"; if force was used, short of war as defined by the Correlates of War Project, the MID is coded "4";[8] and if the MID resulted in war, it is coded at level "5."[9]

Table 6.1 presents the results of four pooled time-series cross-section analyses. The first (Model 1) employs an ordered logit analysis on the full five-category MID escalation scale as the dependent variable, while the second collapses all U.S. MIDs into two categories: those in which force was employed (MID levels 4-5) and those in which force was not employed (MID levels 1-3). A logit analysis (Model 2) was conducted on the resulting dichotomous dependent variable. All MIDs involving the United States between 1946 and 1992, in which the highest level of hostility is available, are included in the ordered logit analysis. MIDs in which the hostility level was coded as "missing" are excluded from this analysis. However, all MIDs were included in the logit analysis.

There are two reasons for conducting the dichotomous logit analysis in addition to the more fully specified ordered logit. The most basic reason is simply that a dichotomous dependent variable allows inclusion of forty-five additional observations for which the hostility level was coded as "missing." Since it is highly improbably that this data would be unavailable for any U.S. disputes in the post–World War II era in which force was actually employed, it seems reasonable to include these cases as instances in which force was not used. The second reason is that some studies (e.g., Gaubatz 1999) have suggested that while leaders of democracies may be constrained in their actual use of force by domestic political pressures, they are less restrained in engaging in lower-level disputes, which are more likely to yield political benefits with minimal risk. The key independent variable is the percent of "no opinion" responses to Gallup's presidential approval poll immediately prior to the initiation of militarized action.

Included as controls are the MID's duration (DURATION) and the number of fatalities suffered in the MID (FATALITY LEVEL). A series of dummy variables are also included as controls. The first, "COLDWAR" (coded "1" from 1946 to 1988 and "0" from 1989 to 1992), is intended to partially control for the neorealist argument that conflict behavior is primarily determined by systemic factors, such as the U.S.-Soviet competition, which should have profoundly influenced all U.S. decision making concerning military activity abroad during the Cold War years (Waltz 1979).[10] The second dummy is included to account for the oft-cited "Vietnam syndrome" (a dummy variable, POST VIETNAM, coded "1" for the period 1974–1988 and "0" otherwise) which holds that U.S. policymakers in the post-Vietnam era have been fearful of taking military action due to the failure in Vietnam. The third dummy variable, "PRES. ELECTION YEAR" (coded "1" in presidential election years and "0" otherwise), is included to test the Gaubatz (1999) argument that democracies are less likely to fight wars in the period immediately prior to an election. For my purposes, I focus on all disputes, including those in which force was not used (Gaubatz conducted separate analyses upon all MIDs, as well as upon wars—i.e., level 5 MIDS—only). Gaubatz hypothesized, and found some supporting evidence, that while democracies my be unwilling to fight wars prior to an election, they may be quite willing to engage in lower-level disputes, intended to gain political advantage at minimum risk. The logic of Smith's (1996) argument—though he focuses overtly upon democratic war behavior—suggests that democracies ought to be less likely to engage in any displays or uses of force in an election period, simply because a potential adversary, knowing that a democratic leader cannot afford to back down prior to an election, would be unlikely to challenge a democracy in the first instance in an election year. My analysis should therefore allow a limited test of my hypothesis (which predicts that attentiveness will matter more than the electoral cycle) against those of both Gaubatz (who predicts an electoral effect primarily upon higher-level MIDs) and Smith (whose argument appears to predict an electoral cycle effect on all disputes).

Additional dummy variables included as controls are "ORIGINATOR" (coded "1" if the United States was involved on the first day of a MID and "0" otherwise), "REVISIONIST" (coded "1" if the United States sought to change the policy or territorial status quo in the MID, and "0" otherwise) and "NEW PRESIDENT," included to control for the first three months of a new presidency, during which the level of "no opinion" responses likely reflect the public's lack of familiarity with a new president, rather than attention to a crisis. The final independent variable is the percent approving of the president's performance in the Gallup poll immediately prior to the MID (% "APPROVE"). Both the political capital theory and the diversionary war theory would predict that presidential approval rates ought to exert a stronger influence on the decision to use force than my proxy for issue salience, albeit in opposing directions. While the political capital theory would anticipate a positive and significant coefficient on % "APPROVE," the diversionary war theory would predict a negative and significant coefficient.[11]

Table 6.1 indicates that under both specifications of the dependent variable—either the four-category scale representing increased escalatory steps or the dichotomous indicator of whether or not force was employed—the percent of "no opinion" responses to Gallup's presidential approval poll in the period immediately preceding a MID is positively and significantly related to the likelihood of escalating a given dispute ($p < .05$, for both the ordered logit and logit analyses). In fact, the coefficient on percent responding "no opinion" (17.672 and 16.470, respectively) are substantially larger than those on percent responding "approve" (1.662 and 4.380, respectively), which fails to achieve significance in the MID escalation model, suggesting that attentiveness to an issue is more important than the president's current approval rating in determining whether or not to escalate a crisis. However, the positive and significant coefficient on % "APPROVE" in the logit model appears to support the prediction of the political capital theory rather than that of the diversionary theory of war. Presidents are modestly more likely to use force when their approval ratings are high. These results were highly resilient to various specifications of either model, including exclusion of extreme values of "no opinion" levels, both low- and high-end, and exclusion of the three level-5 MIDS (Korea, Vietnam, and the Persian Gulf).

Similarly, the failure of PRES. ELECTION YEAR to achieve standard levels of statistical significance in either model suggests that once the other

Table 6.1. Likelihood of Escalating MIDs or Using Force, as "No Opinion" Rates Vary, 1946–1992

Independent Variables	MODEL 1 Ordered Logit on Likelihood of MID Escalation		MODEL 2 Logit Analysis[a] on Likelihood of Using Force		MODEL 3 Ordered Logit on Likelihood of MID Escalation		MODEL 4 Logit Analysis[a] on Likelihood of Using Force	
	Coef.	Std. Error	Coef.	Std. Error	Coef.	Std. Error	Coef.	Std. Error
% "NO OPINION"	17.672*	7.858	16.470*	8.348	—	—	—	—
CABLE REGIME	—	—	—	—	3.704	1.652	-2.510**	.793
% "APPROVE"	1.662	1.682	4.380*	1.802	-2.072**	.655	5.591**	1.950
PRES.ELECTION YEAR	.535	.539	.906^	.517	2.346	1.802	.780	.545
COLDWAR	-3.885**	1.392	-3.103**	1.014	.399	.551	-4.851***	1.109
DURATION	.001*	.001	.003**	.001	-4.825***	1.373	.003***	.001
FATALITY LEVEL	.592	.422	.421^	.241	.001*	.001	.516^	.300
REVISIONIST	.523	.440	1.460**	.470	.707	.583	1.790***	.495
NEW PRESIDENT	-2.319^	1.308	-2.846	1.988	.808^	.440	-2.056	1.436
ORIGINATOR	1.060*	.522	1.230	.829	-1.178	1.026	1.193	.914
POST VIETNAM	1.088*	.510	1.760**	.572	.797	.539	3.173***	.824
CONSTANT1	-1.872	1.336	-5.830***	1.753	2.169***	.677	-2.692^	1.623
CONSTANT2	2.251	1.271	—	—	-4.991	1.685	—	—
CONSTANT3	6.758	1.476	—	—	-.795	1.548	—	—
Pseudo R²	.19	(N = 121)	.28	(N = 166)	.21	(N = 121)	.32	(N = 166)

(^ p .10; * $p < .01$; *** $p < .001$)

[a] All models employ White's heteroscedasticity-consistent "robust" standard errors.

factors included in the model are taken into account, the United States is neither significantly more nor less likely to engage in a militarized dispute, or to use force, in an election year. The coefficient on PRES. ELECTION YEAR in the logit model, however, is positive and significant at .10, indicating that the United States may be somewhat *more* likely to use force in election years. This result appears inconsistent with both Gaubatz and Smith's predictions. (Recall that Gaubatz draws a clear distinction between low- and higher-level MIDs, with significant results, in the opposite direction, predicted only in the latter instance, a distinction seemingly not drawn in Smith's theory.) The coeffiicent on POST VIETNAM is significant in both models, suggesting that, contrary to the logic of the Vietnam syndrome, the United States was more, not less, prone to enter disputes, and to use military force, in the years following Vietnam. This, of course, may be attributable to the logic of anticipated reactions, as argued by Smith. According to that argument, potential adversaries may have anticipated that the United States would be less willing to resist challenges following its humiliation in Vietnam. Hence, the United States may have found itself facing more *opportunities* to escalate disputes, and to use force.

Finally, the coefficient on COLDWAR is negative and significant in each model. This suggests, contrary to Gowa's finding of a strong positive relationship between the Cold War period and U.S. participation in international disputes, that, after controlling for several additional domestic political factors, crisis escalation—including uses of force—was in fact deterred during the Cold War, perhaps by a fear that even low-level peripheral conflicts might escalate into a general superpower war.[12] Figures 2 and 3, respectively, present the results from the ordered logit and logit models at Table 6.1, transformed into probabilities that a MID reaches each level of escalation or that force is used.

Figure 6.2 indicates that with all control variables held constant at their mean values, as the percentage of "no opinion" responses increases, the probability of a MID escalating to the level of issuing threats (MID level 2), and no further, declines substantially. The probability of a MID escalating to the level of force deployments (MID level 3) drops off even more rapidly as "no opinion" rates increase (i.e., as attentiveness declines). The pattern, however, is strikingly different for the probability of using force (MID level 4), which increases monotonically as attentiveness declines (i.e., "no opinion" rates increase), from about 11% at the lowest "no opinion" rates, to about 73% when "no opinion" rates reach 26%. However, when the "no opinion" rate reaches its highest level (36%), a MID's probability of escalating to open warfare—which remains less than 1% at all other levels of attentiveness—increases substantially, to 34%, while the probability of escalating

Figure 6.2. Probability of Escalating U.S. MIDs as "No Opinion" Rates Vary, 1946–1992
(Ordered Logit Analysis; Pseudo R^2 = .19, N = 121)

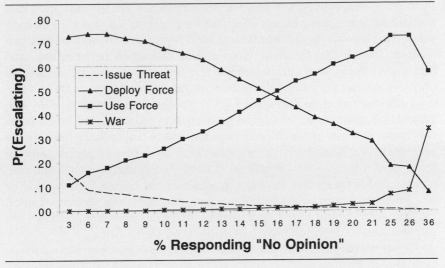

to the next highest level (the use of force) falls commensurately (to around 58%). The results from the logit model, transformed into probabilities parallel those from figure 6.3.

Figure 6.3 indicates that as "no opinion" rates increase from their lowest (3%) to their highest (36%) levels, the probability of using force in the MID increases from 7% to about 83% (though the increase is only to 65% at the next-highest "no opinion" rate of 26%). While this represents only one, limited, empirical analysis of the implications of the theory, these results do suggest that an increase in public attentiveness to a given crisis—that is, decreases in "no opinion" responses—is a substantial deterrent to using force; apparently more so than approval ratings or the electoral cycle.

This result appears to lend support to the audience cost argument, which holds that an attentive public effectively constrains the president's freedom of maneuver in a foreign crisis, by raising the possibility of incurring substantial domestic political costs should he back down. This, in turn, is likely to deter crisis escalation, given an attentive public, for at least two reasons. First, as Fearon (1994) argues, an attentive public allows the president to send credible signals of resolve, without having to escalate to the use of force. A potential adversary, seeing the president make a public commitment to respond forcefully to a given challenge (e.g., President Bush's 5

Figure 6.3. Probability of Using Force in U.S. MIDs as "No Opinion" Rates Vary, 1946–1992

(Logit Analysis; Pseudo R^2 = .28, N = 166)

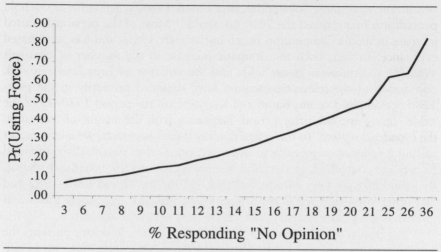

August, 1990 statement on the White House lawn regarding Iraq's August 1990 invasion of Kuwait that "This will not stand."[13]), will recognize that the president's threat is most likely not a bluff, given the political cost to the president of making a public promise and then reversing course. This, in turn, ought to make the president's threat highly credible, thereby deterring all but the most determined—or foolish—adversaries. A second factor, however, that most likely also comes into play is presidents' aversion to risking substantial political harm, should a conflict turn out badly for the United States. As the public's attentiveness to a crisis increases, the potential political damage to the president resulting from a bad outcome increases commensurately. This is likely to induce greater caution in presidents contemplating crisis escalation under conditions of intense public scrutiny. These two factors, in combination, appear capable of producing the empirical results just presented.[14] In addition to observing the hypothesized relationship between public scrutiny and crisis escalation, to the extent my theory is correct, we ought also to observe a significant relationship between changes in the mass media and the tendency of U.S. presidents to use force in foreign crises. Previously in this chapter and elsewhere (Baum 2000a; Baum and Kernell 1999), I have hypothesized that the rise of cable television, more than any other factor, has brought about a revolution in the mass media's presentation of news and information to the public, which has in turn led to an increase, over time, in average levels of public salience of foreign crises. To the extent this is accurate, we might expect to see a reduced propensity to use force in a crisis in the postcommunications revolution environment.

Baum and Kernell (1999) argue that the effects of the communications revolution were most substantial after about 1980, when cable household penetration first crossed the 20% threshold.[15] Most of the previously noted increase in media competition began in the early 1980s and has accelerated ever since. In fact, both the dramatic increase in the number of channels available to American households and the collapse of broadcast network dominance of the television medium have occurred primarily in the post-1980 period. As a result, Baum and Kernell term the period 1980–1998 the *cable regime* and the prior period, beginning with the advent of television, the *broadcast regime*. To the extent that my theory is correct, we might expect to find a reduced propensity to use force, once other potentially influential factors are controlled, in the cable regime relative to the broadcast regime. By including a dummy variable—coded "1" for the period 1980–1992 and "0" otherwise—in place of my attentiveness indicator in Models 1 and 2 at table 6.1, it is possible to conduct a crude test of this prediction.

The results again support my hypothesis. Table 6.2, below, presents the results from the ordered logit analysis (Model 3), translated into probabilities, with all control variables held constant at their mean values.

As Table 6.2 indicates, while the propensity to deploy force in a MID has increased (from 43% to 75%) in the post-1980 period, the probability of actually using force has declined substantially, from about 54% prior to 1980, to around 14% in post-1980 MIDs. These results suggest that while there has been no significant empirical secular decline in the U.S. propensity to either escalate MIDs or to use force, after controlling for a wide range of causal factors, one finds a substantial decline in the probability of escalating a MID, or using force, in the post-1980 period—the period in which the communications revolution, and with it a revolution in the mass media, became a prominent social force in American society. The logit analysis (Model 4), translated into the probability of using force, produced similar results.

Implications for the Future of Global Conflict

The preceding analysis, though focused upon the U.S. case, holds potentially significant implications for the future of global conflict for several reasons. First, and most obviously, because the United States is, for the time being, the sole superpower, and therefore tends to be involved in virtually all large-scale military conflicts around the globe, a change in America's crisis behavior will almost certainly affect the nature and frequency of military conflicts worldwide. To the extent that an attentive public does indeed deter presidents from escalating foreign crises—either because they are less likely to need to

Table 6.2. Probability of MID Escalation:
Broadcast Regime vs. Cable Regime

	Highest Level of Escalation Reached by MID			
	Threat	Deploy Force	Use Force	War
Broadcast Regime (1946–79)	.02	.43	.54	.02
Cable Regime (1980–92)	.10	.75	.14	.003

resort to force to appear credible, or because of the heightened potential political consequences should the conflict turn out badly for the president, or both, then this suggests that the frequency of lower-level military conflicts involving the United States—at least those involving the actual use of force—is likely to decline in the future. For, as I have argued, as the communications revolution continues to expand, and as more and more households gain access to the diverse resources of the modern mass media, the likelihood that the public will be attentive to a given military crisis increases. This trend is likely to accelerate in the future, thereby making public opinion an even greater constraint on presidential decision making during future foreign crises.

Second, and perhaps more importantly, the communications revolution —and the resulting revolution in the mass media presentation of news and information, though at its most advanced stage in the United States, is gradually spreading around the world. Over time, more and more of the world's citizens will gain access to the vast resources of the modern media. Along these lines, in a recent interview on PBS's *News Hour* with Jim Lehrer, Egypt's President Hosni Mubarak commented that with the advent of satellite television broadcasting, it was no longer possible for Egypt's president to conduct the Arab-Israeli peace process out of the view of average Egyptian citizens, who, thanks to CNN satellite broadcasts, are now able to learn of events on the ground in near-real time, at virtually the same instant as the government.

To the extent that my hypothesis—drawn in part from Fearon's audience cost argument concerning the effects of public scrutiny on the management of foreign policy—is correct, one would expect that, ceteris paribus, as more and more countries—particularly democracies—gain access to the modern mass media, the incidence of military conflicts ought to decline. Of course, all else is rarely equal, and there are numerous potential causes of conflict. Nevertheless, this argument is also consistent with those of recent "rationalist" theories of war (e.g., Fearon 1995 and Lake and Rothchild

1996), which argue that one primary cause of war is information failure—or the existence of private information by one or both sides in a conflict, combined with the incentive for one or both sides to misrepresent their private information. The media revolution, in effect, reduces the likelihood of information failure, by making available more information about all actors in a conflict—including the level of domestic audience costs absorbed by a leader who publicly threatens to use force.

While these arguments appear, on one level, to represent a hopeful finding for the future of global conflict, these developments may, upon closer scrutiny, represent a double-edged sword. Given the prominent U.S. role in virtually all post-Cold War multinational humanitarian relief, security, and peacekeeping operations (e.g., Bosnia, Iraq, Haiti, Somalia, and Rwanda), should U.S. presidents become increasingly hesitant to place U.S. troops in harm's way, out of fear of a domestic backlash, it is unclear whether such operations—which by most accounts are indispensable to international security—will be sustainable in the future. Signs of this emerging trend abound. For example, Congress recently passed legislation making it illegal for American forces to be placed under the command of a non-American in any UN operation. Moreover, as the communications revolution expands to more and more nations, there is no reason to believe that the restraining effect I have attributed to the mass media and public attentiveness will be unique to the United States. More and more nations, particularly given the increasing number of democracies, are likely to face similar constraints on their freedom of action, thereby compromising even further the ability of the international community to take decisive, cooperative action to contain emerging threats to international security.

Conclusion

Fearon (1994) argues that because leaders of democracies are accountable through elections to their domestic populations, they are better able to send credible signals of resolve to potential adversaries, without resorting to force, than are authoritarian leaders. Democratic leaders are thus less likely to need to resort to force to appear credible. I have argued that American presidents' ability to generate substantial domestic audience costs—thereby sending credible signals of resolve—without resorting to the use of force has been significantly enhanced by changes in the relationship between media coverage and public scrutiny of foreign crises. Additionally, because greater public attentiveness represents greater potential political damage in the event of a foreign policy failure, presidents are increasingly reluctant to risk the consequences of escalating foreign disputes. To test my predictions, I conducted ordered logit and logit analyses of all U.S. militarized interstate disputes between the Truman and Bush administrations (1946–1992). My results indicate that U.S. crisis behavior has followed trends largely consistent with my theory's predictions.

The present analysis does not allow a distinction between Fearon's logic, and my refinement of the audience cost argument; however, the empirical testing in this chapter has compared the audience cost model with several other prominent theories purporting to explain the influence, or lack thereof, of domestic politics on foreign crisis decision-making.[16] My results offered stronger support for the audience cost model, at least for the U.S. case, than for, respectively, political capital theory, the diversionary theory of war, the electoral cycle hypothesis, or the traditional neorealist argument. Nevertheless, this evidence must be considered preliminary, as far more extensive testing on a much wider range of cases would be necessary to convincingly demonstrate the superiority or inferiority of any of these several theories.

I have further argued that this finding may hold significant implications for the future of international conflict. For, as the media revolution follows democratic revolutions into more and more countries, the ability of leaders to conduct foreign military operations free from domestic public scrutiny shall likely be increasingly eroded. This will almost certainly alter the decision calculus of democratic leaders in determining whether or not to pursue military operations whether unilaterally or as part of a multinational force.

Contrary to the frequent pronouncements in the popular press that the U.S. public has largely tuned out from foreign affairs, I have argued—with the support of convincing evidence—that the contemporary U.S. public is in fact more attuned to foreign crises than at any time in the post-World War II era. The evidence reported in this chapter suggests that this heightened awareness—which is not necessarily accompanied by heightened understanding—is likely to increasingly constrain the freedom of action of future presidents facing crisis situations. Whether enhanced public scrutiny is normatively "good" or "bad" is a subject best left to philosophers and democratic theorists. Only time and additional research will tell whether this phenomenon is likely to result in a decline or increase in the prevalence of international conflict. What seems almost certain, however, is that the communications revolution brings an entirely new context to Clausewitz's legendary assertion; a context that shall likely demand substantial scholarly attention.

Notes

1. Excerpted from Mueller (1994, 121).

2. Fearon's "audience cost" argument is a variant of what Maoz and Russett (1993) term *structural* (i.e., institutional) explanations for Democratic peace theory.

3. A large literature in social psychology on individual media uses and gratification (e.g., Katz and Foulkes 1962; Katzman 1972; and Katz, Blumler, and Gurevitch 1973–1974) argues that individuals "use" the media to fulfill various social and psychological needs, including diversion, easing of social tension and conflict, establishing substitute personal relationships, reinforcing personal identity (e.g., value reinforcement), gaining comfort through familiarity, learning about social problems, and surveillance.

4. Even with the addition of two new broadcast networks in the 1990s (FOX and WB), there has been some consolidation among major broadcasters in recent years. Nevertheless, programming content has continued to expand and diversify.

5. Data regarding public opinion during the Persian Gulf conflict is drawn from Mueller (1994), who presents an impressive catalog of Gulf War survey data from numerous sources. Data from the Vietnam War era, also regarding public opinion, was collected through on-line Nexus retrieval of survey results (mostly conducted by Gallup or the Roper Center). Finally, additional data for the Vietnam era, as well as data from the Korean War era, is drawn from Mueller (1973).

6. While I am sensitive to the striking difference in survey responses that can be produced by seemingly minor variations in question wording, I believe the minor differences in questions employed in this analysis are unlikely to produce the striking substantive variation reported in the next section. In fact, any such bias seems likely to bias the results against my argument, thereby making the comparison a particularly difficult test for my theory. For instance, the Vietnam-era question includes a much longer preface, thereby likely priming (or focusing) respondents more substantially on the issue being queried than did the comparable Gulf War-era question. Ceteris paribus, it seems unlikely that a less-strongly primed question would induce stronger manifestations of public opinion. Nevertheless, because evidence drawn from multiple surveys and multiple survey organizations clearly does not meet the conditions of a controlled experiment, such evidence—absent additional supporting evidence—must be interpreted with caution. Substantial additional supporting evidence is, however, presented in Baum (2000a).

7. Zaller (1991) found a strong monotonic relationship between "no opinion" and/or "don't know" responses and political awareness (as proxied by several scales that he constructed) during the Vietnam War. Similarly, Page and Shapiro (1983) argue that issue salience can be most directly, though not perfectly, measured by the proportion of respondents answering "don't know" or "no opinion" to survey questions. A low-"no opinion/don't

know" proportion, they assert, is evidence of relatively high-issue salience. Conversely, a high proportion is evidence of relatively low salience. Additional evidence in support of the validity of this proxy for salience is available in Baum (2000a).

8. The Correlates of War data set defines an interstate war as involving a minimum of one thousand battle deaths.

9. Note that there are no "level 1" MIDs included in the data set. However, there are a substantial number of MIDs for which the highest level of force is coded as "missing." Since any such instances involving the United States in the post-World War II era can be reasonably presumed not to have involved the actual use of force, they are included in the dichotomous analysis (whether or not force was used), but excluded from the scaled analysis (which focuses specifically on the level of hostility reached in each MID).

10. Note that other studies have defined the onset of the Cold War slightly differently. For instance, Gowa (1998) treats 1949 as the initial year of the Cold War. I separately retested my model with the Cold War dummy variable recoded using each year between 1946 and 1950 as the first year of the Cold War. The substantive results reported in Models 1 through 4were nearly identical, regardless of the year (1946–1950) selected as the first year of the Cold War.

11. Though diversionary war arguments generally argue that overseas "diversionary" uses of force are usually conducted in response to poor economic conditions, or other domestic crises, such as political scandals (James 1988; Levy 1989; Mueller 1973; Russett 1990) the validity of my test merely rests upon the modest assumption, widely accepted in the extant literature, that poor economic performance and/or other types of domestic crises are likely to be reflected in the public's expression of approval or disapproval of the president's job performance (e.g., Kernell 1978).

12. While I have coded the years 1946–1989 as the Cold War period, Gowa (1998) defined the Cold War period as starting in 1949. As she indicates, any year between 1945 and 1950 could be considered reasonable. However, altering the start of the Cold War to 1949 had no substantive impact on my statistical results. Colinearity with the post-Vietnam variable could be producing inefficient results. Removing the latter variable, however, does not materially effect the coefficients on COLDWAR.

13. Quoted in Gaubatz (1999).

14. See Baum (2000a, 2000b) for additional statistical testing intended to test a series of hypotheses distinguishing between my argument and previous theories addressing domestic audience costs.

15. Cable Household Penetration increased from roughly 9% to 20% in the period 1969–1979. Between 1980 and 1990, the increase was approximately twice as large, from about 20% to 60%.

16. My refinement of the audience cost argument refers to the pacifying effect of the fear of domestic consequences of failure. This is the subject of related research (Baum 2000a, 2000b).

References

Aldrich, John H., John L. Sullivan, and Eugene Borgida. 1989. "Foreign Affairs and Issue Voting: Do Presidential Candidates 'Waltz Before a Blind Audience'?" *American Political Science Review* 83: 123–141.

Bartels, Larry M. 1991. "Constituency Opinion and Congressional Policy Making: The Reagan Defense Buildup." *American Political Science Review* 85 (June): 457–474.

Bartels, Larry M. 1993. "Messages Received: The Political Impact of Media Exposure." *American Political Science Review* 87: 267–285.

Baum, Matthew A. 2000a. "Tabloid Wars: The Mass Media, Public Opinion and the Use of Force Abroad." Ph.D. diss., University of California, San Diego (June).

Baum, Matthew A. 2000b. "Foreign Policy in the Public Eye: The Audience Cost Dilemma and the Use of Force Abroad." Unpublished Manuscript.

Baum, Matthew A. and Sam Kernell. 1999. "Has Cable Ended the Golden Age of Presidential Television?" *American Political Science Review* 93 (March): 99–114.

Berelson, Bernard R., Paul F. Lazarsfeld, and William N. McPhee. 1954. *Voting: A Study of Opinion Formation in a Presidential Campaign.* Chicago and London: University of Chicago Press.

Bernstein, Sharon. 1991. "Networks Gird for 'Ready-Set-Go' Gulf War." *Los Angeles Times*, 1 October.

Bosso, Christopher J. 1989. "Setting the Agenda: Mass Media and the Discovery of Famine in Ethiopia." *Manipulating Public Opinion: Essays on Public Opinion as a Dependent Variable.* Eds. Michael Margolis and Gary A. Mauser. Pacific Grove, CA: Brooks/Cole Publishing Company.

Campbell, Angus, Philip E. Converse, Warren E. Miller, and Donald E. Stokes. 1960. *The American Voter.* New York: Wiley.

Conover, Pamela and Stanley Feldman. 1981. "The Origins and Meaning of Liberal/Conservative Self-Identification." *American Journal of Political Science* 25 (November): 617–645.

Converse, Philip E. 1964. "The Nature of Belief Systems in Mass Publics." *Ideology and Discontent.* Ed. David E. Apter. New York: Free Press.

Delli Carpini, Michael, X, and Scott Keeter. 1991. "Stability and Change in the U.S. Public's Knowledge of Politics." *Public Opinion Quarterly* 55: 583–612.

Delli Carpini, Michael, X, and Scott Keeter. 1996. *What Americans Know about Politics and Why it Matters*. New Haven: Yale University Press.

Fearon, James. 1994. "Domestic Political Audiences and the Escalation ofInternational Conflict." *American Political Science Review* 83: 577–592.

Fearon, James. 1995. "Rationalist Explanations for War." *International Organization* 49: 379–414.

Gaubatz, Kurt Taylor. 1996. "Democratic States and Commitment in International Relations." *International Organization* 50: 109–139.

———. 1999. *Elections and War: The Electoral Incentive in the Democratic Politics of War and Peace*. Stanford: Stanford University Press.

Gowa, Joanne. 1998. "Politics at the Water's Edge: Parties, Voters, and the Use of Force Abroad." *International Organization* 52: 307–324.

Hinckley, Ronald H. 1992. *People, Polls and Policy-Makers: American Public Opinion and National Security*. New York: Lexington Books.

Hoffmeister, Sallie. 1996. *Public Opinion and American Foreign Policy*. Ann Arbor: University of Michigan Press.

———. 1997. "Networks Try to Find Niches." *Los Angeles Times*, 23 January 23.

Holsti, Ole R. 1996. "Public Opinion and Foreign Policy: Challenges to the Almond-Lippmann Consensus." Mershon Series: Research Programs and Debates. *International Studies Quarterly* 36: 439–466.

Hovland, C. I., A. A. Lumsdaine, and F. D. Sheffield. 1949. *Experiments on Mass Communications*. Vol. 3. New York: Wiley.

Iyengar, Shanto. 1987. "Television News and Citizens' Explanations of National Affairs." *American Political Science Review* 81: 815–831.

Iyengar, Shanto. 1990. "Shortcuts to Political Knowledge: The Role of Selective Attention and Accessibility." *Information and Democratic Processes*. Eds. John A. Ferejohn and James H. Kuklinski. Urbana and Chicago: University of Illinois Press.

Iyengar, Shanto. 1992. "The Accessibility Bias in Politics: Television News and Public Opinion." *The Mass Media*. Ed. Stanley Rothman. New York: Paragon House.

Iyengar, Shanto. 1993. "Agenda Setting and Beyond: Television News and the Strength of Political Issues." *Agenda Formation*. Ed. William H. Riker. Ann Arbor: University of Michigan Press.

Iyengar, Shanto and Donald R. Kinder. 1987. *News that Matters*. Chicago: University of Chicago Press.

Jagger, Keith and Ted Robert Gurr [producers]. 1996. *Polity III: Regime Type and Political Authority* [Computer File]. Second ICPSR Version. Interuniversity Consortium for Political and Social Research [distributor].

James, P. 1988. *Crisis and War*. Kingston, Ontario: McGill-Queen's University Press.

James, P. and J. R. Oneal. 1991. "The Influence of Domestic and International Politics on the President's Use of Force." *Journal of Conflict Resolution* 35: 307–332.

Jones, Daniel M., S. Bremer, and S. Singer [producers]. 1996. *Militarized Interstate Disputes, 1816–1992.* [Computer File]. Produced as part of David J. Singer and Melvin Small. 1993. *Correlates of War Project: International and Civil War Data, 1870–1992.* [Computer File], Ann Arbor, MI [producers]. Inter-university Consortium for Political and Social Research [distributor].

Kalb, Marvin. 1998. "Get Ready for the *Really* Bad News." *Los Angeles Times*, 10 July.

Katz, Elihu, Jay G. Blumler, and Michael Gurevitch. 1973–74. "Uses and Gratifications Research." *Public Opinion Quarterly* 37: 509–523.

Katz, Elihu and David Foulkes. 1962. "On the Use of the Mass Media as 'Escape': Clarification of a Concept." *Public Opinion Quarterly* 26: 377–388.

Katzman, Natan. 1972. "Television Soap Operas: What's Been Going on Anyway?" *Public Opinion Quarterly* 36 (Summer): 200–212.

Kernell, Samuel. 1978. "Explaining Presidential Popularity." *American Political Science Review* 72: 506–522.

Kernell, Samuel. 1997. *Going Public: New Strategies of Presidential Leadership*, 3rd ed. Washington, DC: Congressional Quarterly Press.

Krosnick, Jon A. and Laura A. Brannon. 1993. "The Impact of the Gulf War on the Ingredients of Presidential Evaluations: Multidimensional Effects of Political Involvement." *The American Political Science Review* 87 (December): 963–975.

Lazarsfeld, Paul F., Bernard R. Berelson and Hazel Gaudet. 1948. *The People's Choice.* New York: Columbia University Press.

Levy, J.S. 1989. "The Diversionary Theory of War: A Critique." *Handbook of War Studies.* Ed. M.I. Midlarsky. New York: Unwin-Hyman.

Lodge, Milton, Patrick Stroh, and John Wahlke. 1990. "Black-Box Models of Candidate Evaluation." *Political Behavior* 12: 5–18.

Lodge, Milton, Kathleen Mcgraw, and Patrick Stroh. 1989. "An Impression-Driven Model of Candidate Evaluation." *American Political Science Review* 83: 399–419.

Lowry, Brian. 1997. "Cable Stations Gather Strength." *Los Angeles Times*, 2 September.

Lowry, Brian. 1998. "With Clinton Under Fire, Viewers Vote for the News." *Los Angeles Times*, 30 January.

Lupia, Arthur and Matthew D. McCubbins. 1998. *The Democratic Dilemma: Can Citizens Learn What They Need to Know?* Cambridge: Cambridge University Press.

Mann, Jim. 1998. "Clinton's Pain Hasn't Hurt Foreign Policy." *Los Angeles Times*, 28 January.

Maoz, Zeev and Bruce Russett. 1993. "Normative and Structural Causes of Democratic Peace." *American Political Science Review* 87 (September): 624–638.

Miller, Joanne and Jon Krosnick. 1996. "News Media Impact on the Ingredients of Presidential Evaluations: A Program of Research on the Priming Hypothesis." *Presidential Persuasion and Attitudinal Change*. Eds. Mutz Diana C. and Paul M. Sniderman. Ann Arbor: University of Michigan Press.

Mondak, Jeffrey J. 1993. "Source Cues and Policy Approval: The Cognitive Dynamics of Public Support for the Reagan Agenda." *American Journal of Political Science* 37 (February): 186–212.

Mueller, John. 1973. *War, Presidents and Public Opinion*. New York: Wiley.

Mueller, John. 1994. *Policy and Opinion in the Gulf War*. Chicago and London: University of Chicago Press.

Neustadt. Richard E. 1990 (1961). *Presidential Power and the Modern Presidents: The Politics of Leadership from Roosevelt to Reagan*. Revised edition. New York: Free Press.

Ostrom, Charles W. Jr. and Brian L. Job. 1986. "The President and the Political Use of Force." *American Political Science Review* 80: 541–566.

Page, Benjamin I. and Robert Y. Shapiro. 1983. "Effects of Public Opinion on Policy." *American Political Science Review* 77: 175–190.

Page, Benjamin I. and Robert Y. Shapiro. 1992. *The Rational Public: Fifty Years of Trends in Americans' Policy Preferences*. Chicago: University of Chicago Press.

Page, Benjamin I., Robert Y. Shapiro, and G. Dempsey. 1987. "What Moves Public Opinion?" *American Political Science Review* 81 (March): 23–44.

Popkin, Samuel. 1994. *The Reasoning Voter*, 2d ed. Chicago: University of Chicago Press.

Powlick, Philip J. 1995. "The Sources of Public Opinion for American Foreign Policy Officials." *International Studies Quarterly* 39: 427–452.

Putnam, Robert D. 1988. "Diplomacy and Domestic Politics: The Logic of Two-Level Games." *International Organization* 42 (Summer): 427–460.

Risse-Kappen, Thomas. 1991. "Public Opinion, Domestic Structure and Foreign Policy in Liberal Democracies." *World Politics* 43 (July): 479–512.

Rosenau, James N. 1990. *Turbulence in World Politics: A Theory of Change and Continuity*. Princeton: Princeton University Press.

Rosenau, James N. 1997. *Along the Domestic-Foreign Frontier: Exploring Governance in a Turbulent World*. Cambridge: Cambridge University Press.

Russett, Bruce. 1990. "Economic Decline, Electoral Pressure and the Initiation of Interstate Conflict." *Prisoners of War?* Eds. E. S. Gochman and A. N. Sabrosky. New York: Lexington Books.

Smith, Alastair. 1996. "Diversionary Foreign Policy in Democratic Systems." *International Studies Quarterly* 40: 133–154.

Sniderman, Paul. 1993. "A New Look in Public Opinion Research." *Political Science: The State of the Discipline II*. Ed. Ada Finifter. Washington, DC: American Political Science Association.

Sniderman, Paul, Richard Brody, and Philip Tetlock. 1991. *Reasoning and Choice: Explorations in Political Psychology*. New York: Cambridge University Press.

Sniderman, James M. Glaser and Robert Griffin. 1990. "Information and Electoral Choice." *Information and Democratic Processes*. Eds. John A. Ferejohn and James H. Kuklinski. Urbana and Chicago: University of Illinois Press.

Stimson, James A. 1990. "A Macro Theory of Information Flow: Information and Electoral Choice." *Information and Democratic Processes*. Eds. John A. Kuklinski and James H. Kuklinski. Chicago: University of Illinois Press.

Stoll, R. J. 1984. "The Guns of November." *Journal of Conflict Resolution* 28: 231–246.

Tetlock, Philip E. 1984. "Cognitive Style and Political Belief Systems in the British House of Commons." *Journal of Personality and Social Psychology* 46(2): 365–375.

———. 1985. "Integrative Complexity of American and Soviet Foreign Policy Rhetoric: A Time-Series Analysis." *Journal of Personality and Social Psychology* 49(6): 1565–1585.

———. 1986. "A Value Pluralism Model of Ideological Reasoning." *Journal of Personality and Social Psychology* 50(4): 819–827.

Waltz, Kenneth. 1979. *Theory of International Politics*. New York: McGraw-Hill Publishing Company.

Webster, James G. and Lawrence W. Lichty. 1991. *Ratings Analysis: Theory and Practice*. Hillsdale, New Jersey: Lawrence Erlbaum Associates.

Woodward, Bob. 1991. *The Commanders*. New York: Simon & Schuster.

Zaller, John. 1991. "Information, Values, and Opinion." *American Political Science Review* 85: 1215–1237.

Zaller, John. 1992. *The Nature and Origins of Mass Opinion*. New York: Cambridge University Press.

Zaller, John, R. 1994. "Elite Leadership of Mass Opinion: New Evidence from the Gulf War." *Taken by Storm: The Media, Public Opinion and U.S. Foreign Policy in the Gulf War*. Eds. Lance W. Bennett and David L. Paletz. Chicago and London: University of Chicago Press.

Zaller, John and Stanley Feldman. 1992. "A Simple Theory of Survey Response." *American Journal of Political Science* 36: 579–616.

CHAPTER SEVEN

Making the National International

Information Technology and Government Respect for Human Rights

DAVID L. RICHARDS

Globalization, or the rapid and wide diffusion of capital, culture, and information, is perhaps the most significant and dynamic process shaping political events in the post-Cold War world. It is, therefore, appropriate to be concerned with its effects on important government policy outputs, such as respect for human rights. While many have investigated the effects of foreign capital on government respect for human rights, much less attention has been paid to the effect that the increasing ease and speed of information dissemination has, or could have, on government respect for these rights. This chapter examines the relationship between the globalization of information and the level of government respect for a subcategory of internationally recognized human rights known as "physical integrity rights."[1] Physical integrity rights include the freedoms against extrajudicial killing, disappearance, torture, and imprisonment for political or religious beliefs.

Current information globalization is driven by information technologies that are allowing the dissemination of information at volumes, in speeds, and with spatial coverage never before witnessed. While many forms of information technology exist (including paper and pen), in popular culture the term *information technology* has become almost synonymous with the Internet. It is important to remember, however, that the Internet is actually only one component of a larger entity known as the "Global Information Infrastructure" (GII). The *GII* is actually a slightly more precise term for what many commonly refer to as the "information superhighway." It is a network of different computer networks; a matrix of separate communications networks such as the Internet, Bitnet, Fidonet, and the UUCP. We can call access to the GII, "connectivity." In this chapter, a state's level of connectivity will refer to its level of access to the GII through information technologies. In using connectivity as a proxy for actual information globalization, it is assumed that the greater a state's level of connectivity, the greater the volume of, and speed with which, information will flow across that state's borders. That is, the greater the level of connectivity, the more globalized a state is with regard to information.

This chapter begins by exploring three different perspectives about the possibility of, and nature of, a relationship between the globalization of information and government respect for human rights. This preliminary exploration is followed by a simple empirical test that addresses these perspectives by examining the association between the globalization of information and government respect for human rights in seventy-three states for the years 1991–1996. The chapter concludes with a discussion of test results, which emphasizes the finding that connectivity may, only by fostering democratization, indirectly increase government respect for human rights.

The Positive Perspective on Connectivity and Human Rights

The positive perspective asserts that connectivity may be associated with improved government respect for human rights. How might connectivity improve government respect for human rights? Simply, connectivity can increase the amount of information coming into states and coming out of states. By letting information in, connectivity exposes information of external origin to a domestic audience. By getting information out, connectivity internationalizes previously domestic information.

Letting Information In

The size of the world is not only measured in miles or kilometers, but also in terms of how that physical distance prevents people from communicating with each other on a regular basis. From the positive perspective, connectivity is viewed as having shrunk the world, enhancing the ability of average persons to communicate with others across state boundaries. Communication is a "process in which people create shared meanings" (Lustig and Koester 1996, 29). Information must be exchanged in order for these shared meanings to be created. However, much of the world where the most gross levels of government-sanctioned violations of human rights take place is a world where many people are not aware of what life is like outside of their own society. Thus, should connectivity be able to increase a shared understanding of ideals or values related to human rights by letting information into formerly closed states, then changes in respect for human rights may be seen.

The idea of spurring domestic change from externally derived information is certainly not new. It is no secret that governments all over the world systematically attempt to influence citizens, and thus, events, elsewhere by "sharing meanings." During the Cold War, the United States used the Voice of America to promote dissatisfaction with Communist ideals and to promote democratic ideals by broadcasting radio programs to Communist and other nondemocratic societies. This explicit use of information designed to change the nature of citizen-government relations of other states, of course, immediately brings up the issue of state sovereignty. From the positive perspective, however, it is argued that within the confines of international law, it is appropriate to pursue internal change in other states when human rights are at stake. Donnelly (1989), among others, argues that a large body of international law establishes clear parameters on what is acceptable state behavior toward persons in a state's territory, and by doing so, establishes the treatment of those individuals as a legitimate topic of international politics.

Given that from this perspective connectivity increases the ability to let information into a society, and that it is justifiable to do so with the hope of changing citizen-government relations, what values or ideals would be most usefully promoted to increase the level of government respect for human rights? The most important finding from the scientific human rights literature is that democracy is more reliably associated with higher levels of government respect for human rights than any other regime type (Poe and Tate 1994; Poe, Tate, and Camp Keith 1999). That is, where we see increases in democracy, we would expect to see corresponding increases in government respect for human rights. In 1993, Boutros Boutros-Ghali, while United Nations secretary general, said,

> The process of democratization cannot be separated, in my view, from the protection of human rights. More precisely, democracy is the political framework in which human rights can be best safeguarded. . . . It is not possible to separate the United Nations' promotion of human rights from the establishment of democratic systems within the international community. (Moore 1998, 3)[2]

For many potential victims of human rights abuse, the assessment that "The uninformed human organism is not capable of surviving. If each of us had to acquire the information necessary for survival on our own, none of us would be alive" (Couch 1996, 15) may be accurate. Thus, if the dispensation of democratic ideals is associated with actual democratization, the diffusion of these ideals may help human rights. Indeed, Kedzie (1996, and in this volume) finds a reliable relationship between connectivity and democratization. This would not surprise some. Huntington (1993), posits five changes in the world that played important roles in the most recent wave of democratic transitions. One of these is what he called "snowballing" or "demonstration effects," where, enhanced by international communication, transitions to democracy in some states served as models for their neighbors. Kedzie states,

> Information revolution technologies enable citizens of prospective democracies to learn more about how other societies operate. If they discover that others living elsewhere live better thanks to democratic governance, they are likely to seek democratization. (Kedzie 1996, 10)

The promotion of democracy, however, is not the only manner in which, by letting information in, connectivity could affect government respect for human rights. That is, certain ideals may have a more direct effect. The idealist term *Global Village*, when used in relation to connectivity posits that information globalization will make the world's diverse peoples into codependent neighbors in the same global community. Moore points out that

> In a global village, to deny people human rights or democratic freedoms is not to deny them an abstraction they have never experienced but the established customs of the village. It hardly matters that only a minority of the world's people enjoy such freedoms or the prosperity that goes with them. Once people are convinced that these things are possible in their village, an enormous burden of proof falls on those who would deny them. (Moore 1998, 7)

That is, the penetration of information into previously isolated areas is a major step forward in those people being able to judge their existence by means of comparison to other parts of the world. One computer connected to the GII is worth more in these terms than many, many, books, as it provides a window to daily (or even more precise) updates of information about the world. A book is only as current as its publishing date. And, what would be worth more in the currency of hope than finding out that movements for reforms protecting human rights have been successful for other people in other countries?

Constantly updated information used for the comparison of one's life with the lives of those living in any section of the world is available for the first time without constant travel or face-to-face encounter with those who do. In 1965, Malcolm Hews (rather callously) reported, "To the average Saudi . . . the world outside his vast sun-baked sand pit is probably as insubstantial and dubious as a traveller's tale. 'And are there deserts in London? one old sheikh asked me.'" (Cherry 1978, 166). Such a statement would be unlikely today, due mostly to connectivity and to its abilities to take information on a regular basis to places where ordinary persons could not go, and to take it there at amazingly high speeds.

Even more important here than how fast information is conveyed, multimedia resources such as the Internet provide a range of information that no other single source can provide. In looking at "information as a thing" Michael Buckland finds five types: (1) data: records that can be stored on a computer; (2) text and documents: papers, letters, and books—that may be on paper, microfilm, or in electronic form; (3) spoken language in any medium; (4) objects: dinosaur bones, rock collections, and skeletons; and (5) records of events: photos, news reports and memoirs (Wresch 1996, 7).

Couch (1996) says that information technologies increase the amount of information we preserve, the amount of information in circulation, or both. As well, he notes that historically, different information technologies favor some types of information and disfavor others. Looking at Buckland's typology, it seems that with the exception of objects like dinosaur bones, the Internet can convey all of these types of information—no other communications medium can currently approach the Internet in the comprehensiveness of the information it can convey. In addition, finding this information gets easier as the Internet continues to grow at an astounding rate. Statistics from the Internet Software Consortium (2000, www.isc.org/ds/hosts.html) indicate that the number of hosts has grown from less than five million in 1991 to over one hundred million in 2001.[3] Keep in mind that these figures are estimates of the minimum size of the Internet, as there are always some hosts that are not picked up and new ones are always being added.

A further benefit of electronic information is that it can slip in between cracks where printed matter cannot. This principle is not new, however. Stonier notes that "the Shah of Iran kept tight control over the press, radio and television. He overlooked cheap portable tape recorders which carried the Ayatollah's messages from mosque to mosque" and thus, endangered himself because "when it is no longer possible to control information flows . . . it becomes almost impossible to control public opinion" (Stonier 1983, 145).

Governments may restrict access to information from outside by restricting connectivity, but once connectivity to the "outside" is established, it is harder for governments to censor E-mail or World Wide Web access than it is to censor books:

the gale of uncontrolled information available online is causing the (Saudi Arabian) ministry of information to fret. The ministry's all-male employees now do nothing but sit in rooms and tear out news articles critical of the leadership and ink out pictures of nudity in fashion magazines. But they don't know how to control the internet. (Ambah 1995, 1)

Metzl (1996, 720–721) describes how when Amnesty International was having a difficult time distributing paper copies of its 1994–1995 annual human rights reports in Indonesia because of government interference, electronic copies were able to be slipped through to domestic human rights nongovernmental organizations (NGOs), resulting in even wider distribution than expected because the reports were on floppy disk, and easily reproducible.

Satellite-based communications compound the problems for potential censors trying to tap into phone-line based communication resources. Hegener (1999, URL: http://www.isoc.org/oti/articles/0399/hegener.html) notes that very small aperture terminals (VSATs) can bring "full, almost impossible-to-monitor Internet access." He gives as an example the case of the Kurds in northern Iraq, where VSATs are being used to access the Internet.

Getting Information Out

As well as bringing information into a society, connectivity can get information out. In a sense, connectivity can help "make the invisible visible" (Wresch 1996, 17). That is, those experiencing or having firsthand knowledge of human rights abuses can make a problem previously unknown to the rest of the world into an acknowledged situation by attracting relief from external actors. Human rights NGOs such as Amnesty International and Human Rights Watch, as well as others in the world human rights community, can benefit from connectivity's ability to help monitor human rights situations in particular places via the information that is being sent out of that country by observers or witnesses. Indeed, connectivity also helps speed the dissemination of information from origin to recipient. Metzl gives the following example illustrating both the ability of connectivity to get information out and to disseminate this information in a uniquely expedient manner:

when six Cambodians were arrested for disseminating pamphlets critical of the Phnom Penn government, a trusted expatriate human rights worker sent an alert via E-mail. One informal copy was passed to the relevant desk officer in the [U.S.] State Department, and another went to the worker's home office, which called the State Department expressing concern. Two others were sent to Amnesty International and Human Rights Watch, both of which made public statements on the issue. From the concern of one individual, a seeming international campaign had instantaneously developed. (Metzl 1996, 713)

If connectivity can shorten the time frame of information diffusion, then the time frame of international reaction to a domestic event can also be shortened. The positive perspective holds that this would serve to benefit victims and potential victims of human rights abuse by government.

In Mexico is based a women's-issues E-mail activist network named ModemMujer. Smith describes how, in defending a woman imprisoned for killing her rapist (during the attack), ModemMujer sent out an E-mail to "hundreds of women and women's organizations in Mexico, Latin America, and North America" (Smith 1997, URL: http://www.isoc.org/oti/articles/1197/smith.html). Both persons and letters of protest flooded in from Mexico, Cuba, Argentina, Colombia, Bolivia, Canada, and the United States. The woman was freed. Smith correctly notes that the Internet itself did not free this woman. However, by facilitating networking and rapid information exchange among advocacy groups, connectivity played a great role in freeing the woman.

Bollen (1992) points out that one of the problems with information about human rights abuse itself, is that before it ends up anywhere of use, it goes through filters such as the domestic and world media that slow dissemination and dilute content. Abuses not egregious enough to captivate a wide audience may never be broadly reported. However, Metzl (1996) points out that the information technology supporting connectivity helps bypass such traditional information filters. For example, there was no filter in-between, or delays in, the information the Tupac Amaru put on their World Wide Web page while holding the Japanese embassy hostage in Peru, while I was viewing that same information from my web browser in my office.

The Negative Perspective on Connectivity and Human Rights

The negative perspective asserts that connectivity may be associated with diminished government respect for human rights. This relationship may exist for at least three reasons. First, if connectivity can function as a tool of the oppressed, it can just as well serve the oppressor. This principle is not new. Radio was used in an inflammatory manner in Nazi Germany. Gourevitch (1999) describes how Rwandan radio was used as a tool to stimulate, maintain, and intensify a desire among Hutus to kill Tutsis in 1994. The diffusion ability of connectivity could just as well enable threatening domestic actors to communicate among themselves, as it would enable transnational human rights groups to communicate among themselves.

Second, the positive perspective set out that connectivity could bring to the oppressed awareness of the concept of human rights, information about life in democratic or other societies, news of successful human rights campaigns, and possibly the hope of external help. From that perspective, connectivity would lead citizens living under abusive regimes to become increasingly dissatisfied with their treatment and emboldened by the hope of help and by tales of others' successes. Consequently, these people might be more likely to actively voice discontent to government and to actively—and possibly violently—press for reform, perhaps appealing to powerful external actors. If true, this may be dangerous, as Poe and Tate (1994); Poe, Tate, and Camp Keith (1999); and Richards (1999a, 1999b), among others, have found strong empirical support for the idea that the higher the level of domestic threat faced by governments, the lower the level of respect for human rights manifested by those governments.

This assumes that connectivity, or its corollaries, can incite internal conflict and that internal conflict, in turn, leads to repression (government violations of human rights). The possibility of connectivity, or its corollaries, causing internal unrest is reasonable. Brown posits four types of factors underlying internal conflict: structural, political, economic/cultural, and cultural/perceptual. He notes that democratization, posited here as a corollary of connectivity by the positive perspective, "can be destabilizing in the short run even if it promises stability in the long run" (Brown 1996, 17). As well, the perception of economic inequality, another corollary here, can "generate feelings of resentment and levels of frustration prone to the generation of violence" (Brown 1996, 19). This is similar to a type of relative deprivation that Gurr (1970) called "aspirational deprivation." Regarding connectivity, citizens would become upset because they feel they have no means of satisfying the new desires or increased expectations they have acquired through connectivity's ability to bring in information about the outside world. Furthermore, Muller (1972) adds that, combined with relative deprivation, if groups in society believe that the use of violence by other groups has been successful in their causes, violence is even more likely. Certainly, the positive perspective assumes that connectivity can carry information about successful social movements to nascent movements in other places.

It is also reasonable to suppose that rebellion may cause repression. For Tilly (1978), the decision of a government to repress existing domestic unrest generally depends on three factors: the power of the group threatening the government, the scale of action that group is engaging in, and the capability of the government involved. For example, a weak government will repress even small-scale actions of weak groups, because it feels threatened. On the other hand, a more powerful government can tolerate a higher level of domestic threat while still feeling that its authority is secure. This is especially important in the post-Cold War, where many governments that violate human rights are not fully secure in their position of power, and thus might repress even new, weak groups that form due to corollaries of connectivity. In a study of Chile over twenty years, Davis and Ward (1990) found that indeed, rebellion increased the propensity of government to engage in repression. This provided some backing for Gurr's supposition that "the greater the threat posed by the challengers, the greater the likelihood that the regime will respond with violence" (Gurr 1986, 51).

Finally, connectivity may be directly related to human rights abuse by governments. Human Rights Watch (1999 www.hrw.org/worldreport99/special/internet.html) has noted several such instances:

1. In July 1998, China arrested and charged a software engineer with subversion for supplying e-mail addresses to a U.S.-based prodemocracy magazine and Web site.
2. In August 1998, Malaysian police arrested three people for posting what authorities called "false reports" about riots in the capital. Although the Malaysian government said it had no intention of practicing Internet censorship, these people were tracked down with the help of the Malaysian Institute of Microelectric Systems, the sole Internet access provider in that country.
3. A Bahraini engineer Jalal Sharif was arrested in March 1997 reportedly on the grounds that he was transmitting information to the London-based Bahrain freedom movement via the Internet. He remained in detention awaiting charge and trial at the time of the Human Rights Watch publication.
4. In June 1998, a Turkish court sentenced a teenager to ten months suspended jail time for criticizing the rough police treatment of blind people while he was participating in an on-line daily forum.

The Null Perpective on Connectivity and Human Rights

The null perspective posits that connectivity may have no effect whatsoever on government respect for human rights. Both the positive and negative perspectives have at their core the assumption that the associated good/bad effects of connectivity happen because connectivity is able to deliver information into, or get it out of, a given state, or society. The null perspective would counter that governments may make it very difficult, or even impossible, for any exchange of information to take place. Many governments proactively try to censor information from connectivity, or even deny connectivity altogether. For example, Human Rights Watch (1996) notes that

1. China requires users and Internet service providers to register with authorities.

2. Singapore, which has chosen to regulate the Internet as if it were a broadcast medium, requires political and religious content providers to register with the state.
3. Vietnam and Saudi Arabia only permit a single, government-controlled gateway for Internet service.
4. India charges exorbitant fees for international phone access through the state-owned phone company.
5. Germany has cut off access to particular host computers or Internet sites.
6. New Zealand has classified computer disks as publications and has seized and restricted them accordingly.

In Great Britain a law is being considered that would give the British government "broad powers to intercept and decode e-mail messages and other communications between companies, organizations and individuals. The measure . . . would make Britain the only Western democracy where the government could require anyone using the Internet to turn over the keys to decoding e-mails messages and other data" (Lyall 2000). Indeed, the latest trend in government restriction or denial of electronic information is the use of filtering software. Filtering software was first developed to allow parents to prevent their children from accessing unsuitable material. Governments have refined this software to make possible the wholesale censorship of electronic information.

Great Britain is certainly not alone in its efforts. According to Human Rights Watch,

1. In June 1997, the South Korean government blocked access to the GeoCities online community because of a site that espoused North Korean beliefs.
2. In March 1998, the Russian Duma proposed a plan to monitor every piece of data sent over the Internet within Russia's boundaries.
3. In Bahrain, Iran, Saudi Arabia, the United Arab Emiretes, and Yemen, all Internet service providers block Web sites on the basis of cultural and/or political content due to government order or pressure.
4. Tunisia, Iran, and Bahrain are explicit in their filtering of Web sites containing criticism of government human rights practices. (Human Rights Watch 1999, www.hrw.org/worldreport99/special/internet.html)

The technologies these governments employ can be used "to track which computer terminals are accessing which web sites and for how long. In Saudi

Arabia . . . users who request a site that is blocked get a message on their screen warning that all access attempts are logged" (Human Rights Watch 2000, www.hrw.org/advocacy/internet/mena/filters.htm).

Hegener (1999, URL: http://www.isoc.org/oti/articles/0399/hegener .html) points out that many governments have even gotten wise to the trick of using satellite-based connectivity to bypass filtering. The anonymity of VSAT satellite technology depends, to some extent, on wide-beam satellite broadcasting. However, more than worrying about Internet-based dissidents, small states were worried that wide-beam broadcasting was allowing too much pirating and loss of revenue. So, in an agreement under the auspices of the International Telecommunications Union, 183 countries agreed to move toward narrow-beam broadcasting to increase revenue for small countries who had no other antipirating mechanisms available. What many of these countries found out as a bonus, Hegener reports, is that narrow-beam broadcasting allows the "spotting" of illegal users within a two hundred square-kilometer area. Further, he points out, if the broadcasting satellite is a low-orbiting satellite, on-board Doppler devices can enable authorities to locate any user within the range of a single kilometer.

The null perspective does not necessitate a government pro-actively interfering with electronic communications. Those who stand to benefit the most from increased government respect for human rights are those who are most at risk of having their human rights violated. Richards (1999a) has noted that those most at risk in society are the poorest in that society. Thus, the null perspective asks, Do those who are at the greatest risk of having their human rights violated have access to the connectivity that is supposed to help reduce or end such abuse?

Information is a commodity. Some have more; some have less. Wresch calls the have-nots "information exiles" and notes that in our gushing over computer-based information technology, we have forgotten a few things. He points out that in the middle of the information age, "half the Americans living on Indian reservations have no telephones. What information will they be downloading? . . . [W]e may also forget to notice that millions of people around the globe never saw *Schindler's List*—their governments would not let them" (Wresch 1996, 12). Human Rights Watch points out that

> Access requires a telephone. Forty-nine countries have fewer than one telephone per 100 people, 35 of which are in Africa. India, for example, has 8 million telephone lines for 900 million people. At a global level at least 80 percent of the world's population still lacks the most basic telecommunications. (Human Rights Watch 1996, (www.epic.org/free_speech/intl/hrw_report_5_96.html)

The Internet Society reports that

1. Africa has the least developed telecommunications infrastructure with only 2% of the world's telephones and 12% of the population.
2. Asia has 13% of the telephone lines of the world, and 57% of its population.
3. Latin America has 6% of the telephone lines in the world and 8% of the population. (2000, URL: http://www.isoc.org/isoc/publications/oti/ tocs/africa.shtml)

From those figures we see that 69% of the world's population has only 15% of its phone lines. This does not bode well for connectivity.

In addition, while we know that virtually every state in the world has some degree of connectivity, we do not know anything about the distribution of the access to connectivity in any given state. Obviously, distribution of access is important if connectivity is to help ameliorate human rights abuses by governments. In addition, language barriers may have something to do with the inability of international information to have an impact on human rights. In many societies, groups may speak in vaguely common dialects but not the national language used for business—nonetheless the predominant languages on the Internet. Data from Global Reach (2000, www.glreach.com/globstats/index.php3) show that 51% of the online population communicates in English, 8.1% in Japanese, 5.9% in German, 5.8% in Spanish, 5.4% in Chinese, and 3.9% in French. What we see is that in the on-line community, the languages (especially English and Japanese) of several developed nations are greatly overrepresented in relation to the actual percentage of the world population that speaks them.

Furthermore, the null perspective would posit that connectivity will have no effect on government respect for human rights in those places with high illiteracy rates and small percentages of the population with a formal education. In addition, connectivity will have no effect in those places lacking a certain population density where communication about ideas from electronic information can take place between the informed and uninformed, and the literate and illiterate, or the educated and uneducated.

A Simple Empirical Test

What follows is a simple empirical test designed to see if there exists any statistically reliable association between a country's level of connectivity and its level of government respect for human rights. Included in the sample for analysis are 73 states randomly drawn from the population of states with a population of 500,000 or more. The time-frame at which this relationship is looked at is 1991-1996. The following model will be used to test for any association between connectivity and government respect for human rights.

> Government Respect for Physical Integrity =
> (+/-) Level of Connectivity - Refugees
> Internal Conflict - External Conflict –
> Population + Economic Development +
> Level of Democracy - (Connectivity *
> Internal Conflict) + (Connectivity *
> Democracy)

All signs are as hypothesized or as previous research would lead us to expect. A (-) sign indicates an expectation of decreased government respect for human rights, whereas a (+) indicates an expectation of increased government respect for human rights. Level of connectivity is preceded by a (+/-), as both positive and negative possibilities have been presented.

This model will be analyzed using the maximum likelihood technique of ordered logit analysis with robust standard errors. Ordered logit analysis is very useful for estimating models of government respect for human rights using ordered dependent variables, as it takes into account the unique error structure that accompanies this type of indicator (Richards 1999a; Richards, Gelleny, and Sacko 2001). Robust standard errors are employed to account for the potential deflation of standard errors due to pooling effects (Beck and Katz, 1995).

Measuring Government Respect for Physical Integrity Rights

Physical integrity rights are a subset of internationally recognized human rights. They include the freedom against extrajudicial killing, disappearance, torture, and imprisonment for political or religious beliefs. The duty of governments to respect physical integrity rights is laid out in the Universal Declaration of Human Rights (1948), the International Covenant on Civil and Political Liberties (1966), and many regional pacts. I use Cingranelli and Richards's (1999a) measure of government respect for physical integrity rights as my measure of the same. Their indicator is a nine-point additive scale derived from a Mokken scale analysis of four ordinal indicators of government respect for physical integrity—the rights against torture, extrajudicial killing, disappearance, and political imprisonment.[4] This index ranges from "0" (no respect for any of the four physical integrity rights) to "8" (full respect for all four physical integrity rights). It is important to remember that this scale measures respect for human rights. That is, high scale scores indicate favorable amounts of respect for these rights and not high levels of violations of these rights. Thus, were connectivity to be associated with an increase in human rights, for example, we would see a positive relationship (reflected in a positive ordered logit coefficient).

These human rights scores indicating the level of government respect for physical integrity rights are based on information about government respect for these rights found in both Amnesty International's *Annual Report* and the U.S. State Department's annual *Country Reports on Human Rights Practices*.

Measuring Connectivity

Connectivity is a country's level of access to the GII. Access is defined as the ability to connect to a component of the GII by means of a computer, and to receive and send information electronically. Like Kedzie (1996, and in this volume), the base element of the measure of connectivity used in this study is a country's level of connectivity to each of the four largest distributed networks in the GII. The minimum criterion of inclusion is that these networks must allow the exchange of E-mail. The raw information used to create this study's measure of connectivity was collected by Lawrence H. Landweber of the Internet Society.[5] Landweber provides ordinal information on the number of sites that are connected to a network. For instance, to measure the level of connectivity to the FIDONET network, each country is assigned an *f*, *F*, or nothing at all. No assignment indicates no connection to this particular network. An *f* indicates minimal connection, or the existence of from one to five domestic FIDONET sites. An *F* indicates widespread connection, or more than five domestic FIDONET sites. The same is done for the UUCP and BITNET networks. The Internet is coded dichotomously as operational, or not operational.[6]

To create a scale of connectivity, each of the four networks was assigned an ordinal score from "0" to "2," with a "0" indicating no connectivity, a "1" indicating moderate connectivity (one to fve domestic sites), and a "2" indicating a high level of connectivity (more than five domestic sites). This categorization scheme comes from Landweber and the Internet Society. Both the Internet and BITNET were weighted twice as heavily as UUCP and FIDONET. This is due to the asynchronous (noninteractive) nature of UUCP and FIDONET. They support E-mail or news list service, but not gopher, telnet, ftp, or World Wide Web services. Mokken scaling analysis, a probabilistic scaling technique for polychotomous items, was used to construct a scale of connectivity ranging from "0" to "12," and empirically confirmed the strong unidimensionality of this index. In this index of connectivity, a score of "0" indicates no connectivity whatsoever, while a score of "12" indicates a high level of connectivity to all four components of the GII.

Figure 7.1 shows the number of countries falling into each connectivity score in each year from 1991 to 1996. It is notable that in this brief time period, the number of countries having no connectivity has decreased by a full two-thirds. The number of countries having total access has remained stable at about fifteen, or about 20 percent, of the countries in this sample. The number of countries falling in categories between have and have-not, indicating some viable level of connectivity, has markedly risen, especially since 1995.

Control Variables

To control for the effects of factors other than connectivity, I have included several independent variables that have been shown by previous research to have an impact on government respect for human rights. These include level of democracy (Henderson 1991, 1993; Poe and Tate 1994; Hofferbert and Cingranelli 1996; Poe, Tate, and Camp-Keith 1999; Cingranelli and Richards, 1999b); level of economic development (Henderson 1991; Mitchell and McCormick 1988, Poe and Tate 1994; Poe, Tate, and Camp-Keith, 1999; Richards 1999a, 1999b); level of domestic conflict (Poe and Tate 1994; Poe, Tate, and Camp-Keith 1999; Richards 1999a,b); level of interstate hostility (Poe and Tate 1994; Poe, Tate, and Camp-Keith, 1999; Richards, 1999a, 1999b); and population size (Henderson 1993; Poe and Tate 1994; Poe, Tate, and Camp-Keith 1999; Richards 1999a, 1999b).

Drawing on this previous research, the Polity III index (Jaggers and Gurr 1996) is used as the indicator of level of democracy; logged GNP per capita in thousands of dollars is used as the indicator of level of economic development; and the log of total population is used to measure population size. The measure of domestic conflict is a logged, weighted index of the number of contentious domestic political events occurring in a given country-year (Richards 1999a, 1999b; Cingranelli and Richards 1999a, 1999b; Richards, Gelleny, and Sacko 2001). It is constructed using variables from Banks's Cross-Polity Time-Series Data (1971).[7] The external conflict indicator is a dichotomous variable indicating whether or not a country was militarily involved in an external militarized action in a given country-year. Some examples of this would be all-out war, sending peacekeeping troops into hostilities, or perhaps border skirmishes with a contiguous sovereign country. The variable is adapted from the "Hostility Level" variable contained in version 2.10 of the Militarized Interstate Dispute (MID) data collection compiled by the Correlates of War (COW) Project.[8]

Refugees

This study includes one indicator controlling for alternative explanations that has not been included in previous empirical studies of government respect for human rights. Although they fall within the protection of various international

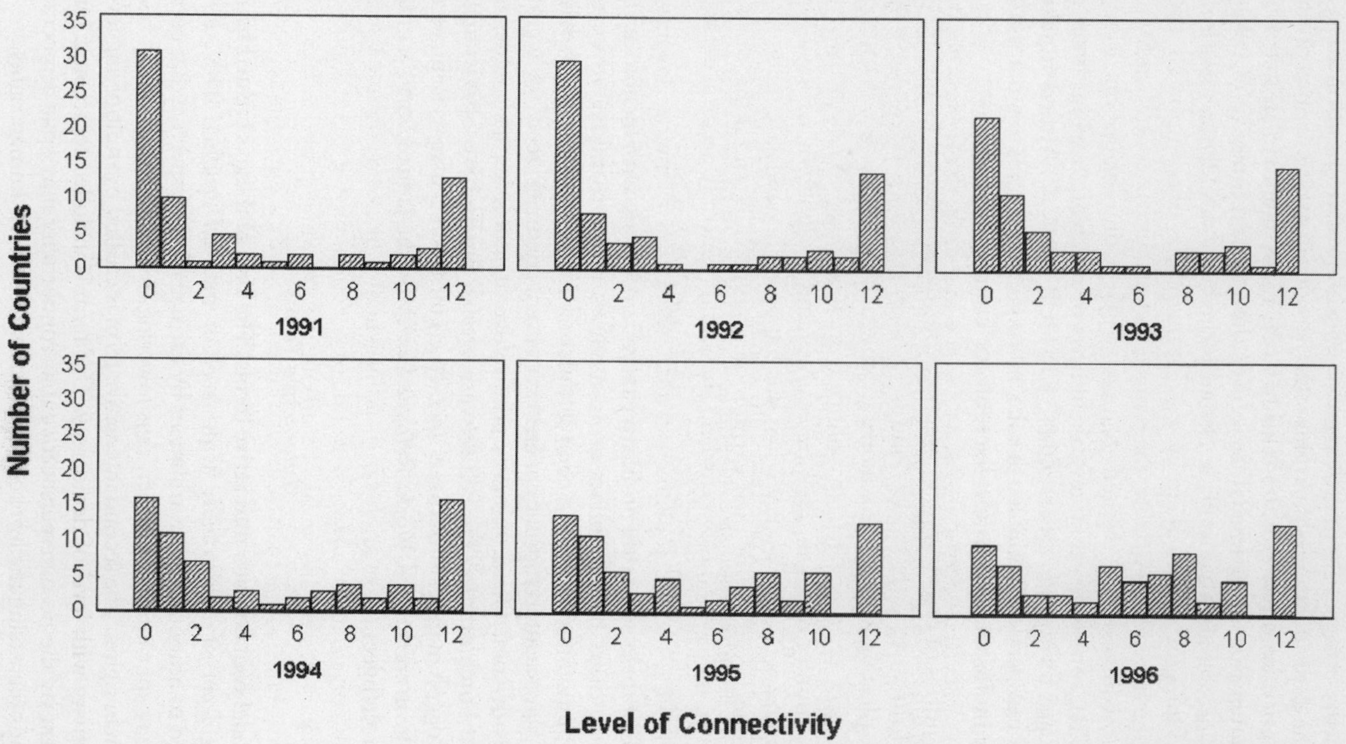

Figure 7.1. Distribution of Level of Connectivity by Year, 1991–1996

instruments, refugees are outside regular political protections afforded to citizens. The dependent variable in this study, governmental violations of physical integrity, does not indicate who has had their rights violated. It is also well-known that governments do violate the physical integrity of refugees. Thus, since refugees are outside citizen protections, and since violations of physical integrity against them by a government may show up in an estimation of the dependent variable, the refugee factor must be controlled for.

According to the United Nations High Commission on Refugees (UNHCR), sometimes in large-scale inflows of refugees, "asylum states may feel obliged to restrict certain rights" (UNHCR 1997, 2). Armed attacks on refugee camps by asylum-states take in response to raids on the asylum-country by forces from within the refugees' country of origin:

> countries of origin have, in practice, considered refugees as a potential threat to their security and have harbored suspicions that they are plotting against the country from which they have fled. Because refugees often come from politically active opposition elements in the country of origin, they are easily blamed—rightly or wrongly—for any acts of sabotage. When this happens, demands are made to the host country for their extradition or expulsion, and if this does occur, punitive raids are carried. These raids generally occur in areas where refugees are sheltered. . . . (Mtango 1989, 92)

Because of these and other problems that refugees bring with them to asylum-countries, these host-countries are sometimes prone to taking revenge on refugee populations in the name of self-preservation or self-defense. Persistent and/or significant refugee populations within countries tend to aggravate these tendencies. Often, refugees take refuge in countries with widespread abuse of human rights. The refugee indicator in this study is operationalized as the logged number of refugees in each country in each year. Refugee data comes from the annual *World Refugee Survey* by the United States Commission on Refugees.

Interactive Terms

The model contains two interactive terms. The first of these is created by multiplying *level of connectivity* with *level of internal conflict*. This term is included to account for the argument by the negative perspective that connectivity may spur internal conflict, thus lowering the level of government respect for human rights. The second interactive term is created by multiplying level of connectivity with level of democracy. This term is included to account for the argument by the positive perspective that connectivity may spur democratization, thus increasing the level of government respect for human rights.

Findings

Figure 7.2 shows the distribution of physical integrity scores at each level of connectivity.[9] In effect, Figure 7.2 illustrates a zero-order relationship between connectivity and government respect for human rights. We see that despite having no connectivity, there are many cases where there is a moderate to high level of government respect for physical integrity. At the same time, countries with no connectivity are more likely than those in any other category to have little to no government respect for physical integrity. Countries at connectivity level one, the second lowest category, are more likely to have moderate to high levels of government respect for physical integrity than to have little to no respect. At the other extreme, we see that at the highest level of connectivity, countries are more likely than not to have moderate to high levels of government respect for physical integrity. However, even at this high level of connectivity, there are many countries with less than perfect government respect for human rights.

Table 7.1 shows the ordered-logit analysis results for the model described in the preceding section. Unlike figure 7.2, this model examines the relationship between connectivity and government respect for human rights controlling for the influence of other factors. The chi-squared statistic returned assures us that we can confidently reject the null hypothesis that the slopes of all the independent variables are simultaneously zero. Likewise, the log-likelihood of this model is an improvement over that of the null model. Liao (1994) points out that one of the first things we can do when interpreting a probability model such as an ordered logit model, is to look at the direction of the signs of coefficients and their statistical significance. If a coefficient is statistically significant, then we can interpret the signs. A statistically significant positive sign for a coefficient would indicate that the probability of increased government respect for physical integrity increases along with the level of the phenomenon (independent variable) that coefficient represents. Likewise, a statistically significant negative sign for a coefficient would indicate that the probability of increased government respect for physical integrity decreases along with the level of the phenomenon (independent variable) that coefficient represents.

Looking at Table 7.1, we see that level of connectivity is not a statistically significant predictor of government respect for physical integrity rights. That is, this simple test finds no statistically reliable direct association between a country's level of connectivity, and its level of government respect for human rights. Table 7.1 does show us, however, that the democracy/connectivity interactive term is a statistically significant predictor of government respect for human rights. The ordered logit coefficient tells us that connectivity has an extremely modest, but statistically reliable effect,

Figure 7.2. Level of Government Respect for Physical Integrity Rights Categorized by Level of Connectivity

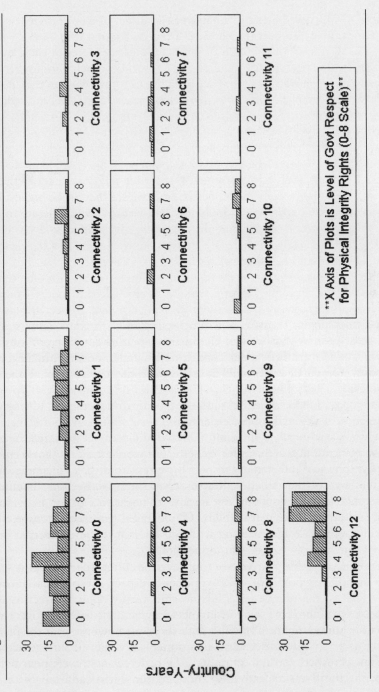

Table 7.1. Ordered Logit Estimates of the Effect of Connectivity on
Government Respect for Physical Integrity Rights, 1991–1996

Variable	Ordered Logit Coefficient	z	P > z
Economic Development	.322*	3.05	0.002
Refugees	.015	0.67	0.504
Level of Connectivity	−.039	−0.67	0.505
Level of Internal Conflict	−.276*	−4.87	0.000
Presence of External Conflict	−.502*	−2.53	0.012
Level of Democracy	.138	3.31	0.001
Population Size	−.431*	−2.94	0.003
(Internal Conflict * Connectivity)	−.008	−1.03	0.301
(Democracy * Connectivity)	.012	1.98	0.048

N = 413
Log Likelihood = −747
Prob. > x^2 = 0.000
* $p < .05$

helping democracy to increase government respect for human rights.[10] This supports the positive perspective. The internal conflict/connectivity interactive term is not statistically significant, offering no support for the negative hypothesis that connectivity will interact with internal conflict, lowering government respect for human rights. The sign for this term is in the hypothesized direction, but because the coefficient is not statistically significant we should not put too much stock in that fact.[11]

Finally, we also see from table 7.1 that the number of refugees in a given country is not a statistically significant predictor of government respect for physical integrity rights. Of the predictors that are statistically significant, we see that all their effects are in the hypothesized directions, and they perform as previous research would predict. External conflict, internal conflict, and population all bode poorly for government respect for physical integrity, while democracy and economic development hold promise for increasing government respect for these rights.

Conclusion

This chapter examined the relationship between a country's level of information globalization (connectivity) and its level government respect for physical integrity rights, a subset of internationally recognized human rights. First, three perspectives were set out from which this relationship might be viewed. The positive perspective advanced reasons why connectivity might increase government respect for human rights. The negative perspective proposed some reasons why connectivity might decrease government respect for human rights. The null perspective held that connectivity may have no effect at all on this relationship.

A simple empirical test found that although there is no statistically significant direct relationship between a country's level of connectivity and its level of government respect for human rights (support for the null perspective), connectivity may have a very modest indirect role in improving government respect for human rights by aiding democratization (support for the positive perspective). This finding that connectivity may have some indirect effect on respect for human rights augments Kedzie's findings (1996, and in this volume) that connectivity is associated with democratization, as it says that this connectivity/democratization relationship helps (in a minor fashion) to increase government respect for human rights.

For policymakers, the empirical findings here give some reason for optimism. First, it was not found that connectivity worsens government respect for human rights. The march of connectivity shown in figure 7.1 is so evident that were this true, it would be rather disturbing. Second, it appears that government respect for human rights may be affected, however slightly, by the electronic diffusion of democratic ideals. The scientific literature on government respect for human rights is not exactly rife with reliable indicators that are manipulable in any real sense. We know from this literature, for instance, that a country's population size and its level of economic development affect its level of government respect for human rights—but that is not to say that these things are easily, or at all, manipulated. The electronic diffusion of democratic ideals, however, can be done, and cheaply.

One important question at hand is, Why is there no direct relationship between connectivity and government respect for human rights? The first reason might have to do with globalization's assumption that states become weaker actors as the forces of globalization grow stronger. Jack Donnelly would argue that "'state-centric conceptions of human rights obligations are likely to persist,' in the absence of the development of a cosmopolitan moral community" (Clark 1999, 130). Clark adds that Donnelly "sees no evidence of this taking place" and that "human rights, in practice, do not correspond to globalization, in theory" (Clark 1999, 130). The negative perspective, which posited that connectivity may worsen government respect for human rights, gave numerous examples of how states can assert power over the external influences that the positive perspective discussed. The finding in support of the null hypothesis that connectivity has no direct effect on government respect for human rights may be evidence that states are alive and well as the primary actors on the world stage and that international nongovernmental actors are still relatively weak in comparison.

A second reason for the lack of a direct relationship between connectivity and government respect for human rights is simple, but powerful. That is, those who are the most at risk of human rights abuse are those with the least access to connectivity. If those most at risk are those least likely to be exposed to external communication, then the positive perspective's direct argument is significantly weakened. A third reason may be that the time-frame of analysis is too short. As figure 7.1 showed, the distribution of connectivity across states is rapidly changing from a "have and have-not" scenario to a "have-a-lot and have-some" scenario. We saw that the number of countries with no connectivity plummeted by two-thirds between 1991 and 1996. Surely, economic and political elites are the first in any society to have access to new technologies, but as the rate of technological advancement increases, so should the trickle down of older technology to nonelites, giving them perhaps basic connectivity potential. This may take significant time, however.

Fourth, there is much work to be done in improving the relatively crude existing measures of connectivity. Future indicators should be able to tell private from government or corporate connections. This way, we may be able to get a grasp of the distribution of connectivity in a given society. One way to do this might be to use a measure of the number of functioning IP addresses in a given country. An IP address is a numeric identifier given to a computer hooked to the GII. Two advantages of using the number of IP addresses in a country as an indicator of connectivity would be that such a measure would be ratio-level rather than ordinal-level and that it would get to the heart of the "getting information out" thesis by counting the actual number of computers connected to the GII rather than just connected that are hosting information (as they are typically counted). There are also disadvantages, however. Typically, IP addresses for those connected at home or through a remote hookup are temporary addresses. Thus, the number of these that are on at any given time would fluctuate, and the time and day of the IP address count would bias the count estimate somewhat. In addition, such IP address records do not exist for most countries and for very few time points for those on which there exists information.

In conclusion, the findings that connectivity does not seem to decrease government respect for human rights, and that it may, in fact, indirectly increase respect by aiding democratization are encouraging. This relationship is also well-worth revisiting, as with better connectivity data and more time behind us we will be able to render a sharper image of this important aspect of globalization in the future.

Notes

1. The terms *human rights* and *physical integrity* will be used interchangeably in this chapter.

2. Pages referenced for Moore (1998) refer to the printout pages from a preformatted .pdf file made available by the publisher, The Gale Group. The reference section references the original page numbers.

3. A host is any computer that is on-line, hosting information that may be pinged, FTP'd, telneted, or reachable through any other interactive application.

4. Mokken Scaling is a probabilistic version of Guttman's cumulative scaling technique. For an informative explanation of Mokken scaling, see Jacoby (1994, 1995).

5. The raw data used to construct the connectivity scale used in this study is © 1991–1996 Lawrence H. Landweber and the Internet Society. It may be found via anonymous ftp to ftp.cs.wisc.edu in the connectivity table directory.

6. BITNET falls out of Landweber's compilation for the year 1996 because it ceased to exist. To compensate, 1996 is assigned the 1995 level of BITNET access.

7. The citation for the Cross-Polity data is 1971, as that is the latest edition of the authoritative data manifest for those data. The data themselves, however, have been continuously updated by Arthur Banks through the year 1995, and by the author, among others, for 1996.

8. This indicator was brought up-to-date by the author, among others, using the same country files used to compile *The Political Handbook of the World*. Militarized Interstate Dispute data can be acquired via the Peace Science Society home-page at http://pss.la.psu.edu.

9. The distribution of the connectivity scores did not have an effect on the results of the ordered-logit analysis.

10. The ordinal marginal effect of this coefficient (.012) would be 1.01. For more information on ordinal marginal effects, see Richards, Gelleny, and Sacko (2001).

11. Estimation of the model without the interactive terms did not affect the statistical significance of any of the additive terms. Consequently, we can assume that multicolinearity, which often accompanies interactive terms, is not responsible for the insignificance of the additive connectivity indicator.

References

Ambah, Faiza S. 1995. "Dissidents Tap the 'Net' to Nettle Arab Sheikdom." *Christian Science Monitor,* 1 and 18 August.

Amnesty International. Annual. International Report. New York. Amnesty International Publications.

Banks, Arthur S. 1971. *Cross-Polity Time Series Data*. Cambridge: Massachussetts Institute of Technology Press.

Beck, Nathaniel and Jonathan N. Katz. 1995. "What to Do (And Not to Do) with Time-Series Cross-Section Data." *American Political Science Review* 89, no. 3: 634–647.

Bollen, Kenneth. 1992. "Political Rights and Political Liberties in Nations: An Evaluation of Human Rights Measures, 1950–1984." *Human Rights and Statistics: Getting the Record Straight.* Eds. Thomas B. Jabine and Richard P. Claude. Philadelphia: University of Pennsylvania Press.

Brown, Michael E. 1996. Introduction to *The International Dimensions of Internal Conflict.* Ed. Michael E. Brown. Cambridge: Massachussetts Institute of Technology Press.

Cherry, Colin. 1978. *World Communication: Threat or Promise?* New York: Wiley.

Cingranelli, David L. and David L. Richards. 1999(a). "Measuring the Level, Pattern, and Sequence of Government Respect for Physical Integrity Rights." *International Studies Quarterly* 43, no. 2: 407–417.

Cingranelli, David L., and David L. Richards. 1999(b). "Respect for Human Rights after the End of the Cold War." *Journal of Peace Research* 36, no. 5: 511–534.

Clark, Ian. 1999. Globalization and International Relations Theory. Oxford: Oxford University Press.

Couch, Carl J. 1996. *Information Technologies and Social Orders.* New York: Aldine De Gruyter.

Davis, Dennis and Michael D. Ward. 1990. "They Dance Alone: Deaths and the Disappeared in Contemporary Chile." *Journal of Conflict Resolution* 34: 449–475.

Donnelly, Jack. 1989. *Universal Human Rights in Theory and Practice.* Ithaca, New York: Cornell University Press.

Global Reach. 2000. "Global Internet Statistics by Language." URL: http://www.glreach.com/globstats/index.php3.

Gourevitch, Philip. 1999. *We Wish to Inform You that Tomorrow We Will Be Killed with Our Families: Stories from Rwanda.* New York: Farrar.

Gurr, Ted Robert. 1970. *Why Men Rebel.* Princeton: Princeton University Press.

Gurr, Ted Robert. 1986. "The Political Origins of State Violence and Terror: A Theoretical Analysis." *Government Violence and Repression: An Agenda for Research.* Eds. Michael Stohl and George Lopez. Westport: Greenwood.

Hegener, Michiel. 1999. "The Internet, Satellites, and Human Rights" *On The Internet.* URL: http://www.isoc.org/oti/articles/0399/hegener.html

Henderson, Conway. 1991. "Conditions Affecting the Use of Political Repression." *Journal of Conflict Resolution* 35: 120–142.

Henderson, Conway. 1993. "Population Pressures and Political Repression." *Social Science Quarterly* 74: 322–333.

Hofferbert, Richard I. and David L. Cingranelli. 1996. "Democratic Institutions and Respect for Human Rights." *Human Rights and Developing Countries.* Ed. David L. Cingranelli. Greenwich, CT: JAI Press.

Human Rights Watch. 1996. "Silencing the Net: The Threat to Freedom of Expression On-Line." Human Rights Watch.

Human Rights Watch. 1999. "Freedom of Expression on the Internet." URL: http://www.hrw.org/worldreport99/special/internet.html

Human Rights Watch. 2000. "Government-Imposed Filtering Schemes Violate the Right to Free Expression." URL: http://www.hrw.org/advocacy/internet/ mena/filters.htm

Huntington, Samuel. 1993. *The Third Wave.* University of Oklahoma Press.

Internet Society. 2000. URL: http://www.isoc.org/isoc/publications/oti/tocs/africa.shtml

Internet Software Consortium. 2000. "Internet Domain Survey." URL: http://www.isc.org/ ds/hosts.html

Jacoby, William G. 1994. "Public Attitudes toward Government Spending." *American Journal of Political Science* 38: 336–361.

Jacoby, William G. 1995. "The Structure of Ideological Thinking in the American Electorate." *American Journal of Political Science* 39: 314–335.

Jaggers, Keith and Ted Robert Gurr. 1996. *Polity III: Regime Change and Political Authority, 1800–1994.* [Computer File]. Boulder: Keith Jaggers/College.

Park, M.D.: Ted Robert Gurr [producers]. 1995. Ann Arbor, MI: Inter-university Consortium for Political and Social Research [distributor].1996.

Kedzie, Christopher. 1996. "International Implications for Global Democratization." *Universal Access to E-Mail: Feasibility and Societal Implications.* Eds. Robert H. Anderson, Tora K. Bikson, Sally Ann Law, and Bridger M. Mitchell. RAND.

Liao, Tim Futing. 1994. "Interpreting Probability Models." Thousand Oaks, CA: SAGE Publications.

Lustig, Myron W. and Jolene Koester. 1996. *Intercultural Competence.* New York: HarperCollins College Publishers.

Lyall, Sarah. 2000. "British Authorities May Get Wide Power to Decode E-Mail." *New York Times,* 19 July.

Metzl, Jamie F. 1996. "Information Technology and Human Rights." *Human Rights Quarterly* 18, no. 4: 705–746.

Mitchell, Neil J. and James M. McCormick. 1988. "Economic and Political Explanations of Human Rights Violations." *World Politics* 40: 476–498.

Moore, Rebecca R. 1998. "Globalization and the Future of US Human Rights Policy." *Washington Quarterly* 21, no. 4: 193–213.

Mtango, Elly-Elikunda. 1989. "Military and Armed Attacks on Refugee Camps." *Refugees and International Relations*. Eds. Gil Loescher and Laila Monahan. New York: Oxford University Press.

Muller, Edward N. 1972. "A Test of a Partial Theory of Potential for Political Violence." *American Political Science Review* 66, no. 3: 928–949.

Poe, Steven and Neal Tate. 1994. "Repression of Human Rights to Personal Integrity in the 1980s: A Global Analysis." *American Political Science Review* 88, no. 4: 853–872.

Poe, Steven C., C. Neal Tate, and Linda Camp-Keith. 1999. "Repression of the Human Right to Personal Integrity Revisited: A Global Cross-national study Covering the Years 1976-1993." *International Studies Quarterly* 43, no. 2: 291–313.

Richards, David L. 1999(a). "Death Takes a Holiday" National Elections, Political Parties and Government Respect for Human Rights." Ph.D. diss.: State University of New York, Binghamton.

———. 1999(b). "Perilous Proxy: Human Rights and the Presence of National Elections." *Social Science Quarterly* 80, no. 4: 648–665.

Richards, David L., Ronald Gelleny, and David Sacko. 2001. "Money with a Mean Streak? Foreign Economic Penetration and Government Respect for Human Rights in Developing Countries." *International Studies Quarterly.* 45, no. 2: 219–239.

Smith, Erika. 1997. "Mexican Women's Movement Makes the Internet Work for Many Women." URL: http://www.isoc.org/oti/articles/1197/smith.html

Stonier, Tom. 1983. "Microelectronics' Effects on East/West Relations." *Political Quarterly* 54, no. 2: 137–151.

Stover, William James. 1984. *Information Technology in the Third World: Can I.T. Lead to Humane National Development?* Boulder: Westview Press.

Tilly, Charles. 1978. *From Mobilization to Revolution*. Reading, MA: Addison-Wesley.

U.S. State Department. Annual. Country Reports on Human Rights Practices. Washington, D.C. U.S. Gov't Printing Office.

United Nations High Commission of Refugees (UNHCR). 1996. "Who Is a Refugee?" URL: http://www.unchr.ch/un&ref/who/whois.htm

Wresch, William. 1996. *Disconnected*. New Brunswick, NJ: Rutgers University Press.

CHAPTER EIGHT

Gender, Women's Organizing, and the Internet

DEBORAH STIENSTRA

Critics of, and apologists for, information and communications technologies (ICTs) are agreed that the advent of electronic mail and the Internet has made significant changes to the world in which we live. These technologies have made it possible for some to access easily information about government policies and services, examine United Nations documents, make friends, meet future lovers, discuss cooking or education, and do their banking. Some have argued that these technologies fundamentally affect how international politics is done. Greater access to information, the possibility of an electronic global civil society, the mobilization of citizens for action, and the possibility of increased accountability of governments all have the potential of creating greater citizen involvement in international politics. This supports many liberal arguments about the decreasing role of the state in an increasingly global international system.

But underlying the changes surrounding the Internet are substantial inequalities based especially upon gender, "race" class, and ability. Their continuing presence and the direction-setting for the Internet by transnational telecommunications enterprises illustrate that the Internet is reflective of the way our current world order is and of the dominant power relations that support that order. Numerous activists argue that the Internet has the potential to substantially change this world order. I will explore how social movements, and especially the women's movements, use the Internet to challenge these values and to create potential sources for change both on the Internet and in the broader world order. Specifically in this chapter, I will examine the ways in which the Internet is gendered, how it reflects similar power relations in international relations and further intensifies the potential for conflict along these lines, and the ways in which women are organizing to resist the directions of the world order and to take advantage of the new information technologies.

International Relations and the Internet

It is almost a truism to say that ICTs and international relations rely on each other. They both are global in scope and shape our lives as we know them. Yet there is little literature on the intersections between these two areas. Existing approaches to international relations, such as free trade liberalism, transnationalism, and critical theory, help to clarify the interactions and their significance. These are not exhaustive of approaches either to international relations nor ICTs, but are the most appropriate for this analysis. I argue that free trade liberalism highlights the motivating forces for many of those giving existing direction to the Internet; transnationalism offers an optimistic and naive account of the possibilities of the Internet for citizens; and critical theory reflects the underlying power relations of both the Internet and international relations, the ways in which the Internet maintains these, and how women are resisting and challenging these power relations.

The Internet is often touted as the most democratic community on earth—able to break down barriers of gender, race, and sexual orientation—open to all with minimal rules and obstructions. While the flexibility of the Internet may enable some people to "change" or to camouflage their gender, race, or class while on-line, the mainstream Internet is unable to address these unequal power relations off-line. As well the Internet is not open to all, and remains unavailable to most, of the world's population. For those who can access it, the Internet has opened the possibility for greater and faster communications. Despite these limitations, some argue that the greater possibility of global communications reduces the possibility for conflict at the global level because with greater knowledge and access to information, there is potential for greater understanding of differences and thus greater potential for cooperation.

The community of the Internet has grown rapidly from the military ARPANET (Advanced Research Projects Agency Network) born in 1969. It is impossible to say how many Internet users there are across the world, but the community of users has grown exponentially since its inception. The Internet is larger than many other international forum. Yet the development of technology for the Internet is dominated by transnational telecommunications corporations. There are many, especially those who are part of the private sector, who argue that the intersections between the public and the private around information technologies should be minimal. Their arguments are very similar to those used to expound increasing global free trade. They suggest that the international "trade" in information should remain "free" of government intervention and regulation. The private sector should lead the way in developing information technologies. This will, in turn, enhance the possibilities of communications and possibly even cooperation. Greater communications and information will ensure the spread of democratic values and ensure access to the global market. Some academics might suggest that this is evidence of a specific international regime or set of norms emerging related to ICTs.[1]

While this approach is the de facto approach of many who develop international policies related to ICTs, it has some significant weaknesses as a way to understand international relations. First, it assumes that there is and/or could be universal or at least significant access by those across the world. This simply is not the case, nor is it likely to be in the near future as we shall in see in forthcoming sections. But it also argues that increased information can lead to greater understanding and possibly fewer conflicts. This is a classic argument and one that has classic problems. Put simply, just because we have information about each other's position, it does not mean that we agree. As well, information or access alone will not necessarily change the poverty, lack of education, or other ills that many people live with. Indeed many of those within the private sector recognize that their goal is not to help the poor or to create a better life for all rather it is to strengthen markets. It is not just nice or humanitarian. The facts of the matter are that the developing world will become the markets of tomorrow. Newly industrialized economies are already the markets of today." This argument illustrates that for free trade liberals, the purpose of the information technologies is not to undermine or alter the system of global capitalism; rather it is to strengthen it and increase its reach. The implicit argument would likely be that with greater access to the technologies and greater markets, we will likely have greater cooperation across the world. Yet the technologies and markets do little to address some of the fundamental disparities across the world. While they may increase cooperation between those who benefit from them, they will do little to benefit those who receive little from them.

International relations theorists who use transnationalism to explain the world around them are also optimistic that the new technologies will enable greater "democracy" around the world, while focusing on different communities who will benefit. Some transnationalists, such as Risse-Kappen (1995) or Kedzie (in this volume), argue that international and domestic structures shape the effects that transnational actors such as transnational corporations and international nongovernmental organizations can have.

This suggests that in the area of ICTs, we would do well to explore how strong or weak both individual states, like the United States, and international organizations like the International Telecommunications Union (ITU) and the Organization for Economic Cooperation and Development (OECD) are in order to see how much influence nonstate actors can and will have. Yet, it could be argued that the development of ICTs and especially the Internet, is a substantially different type of interaction than other areas of international relations because it has less obvious and less significant state involvements.

Frederick (1993) makes a similar argument in relation to the emergence of a global civil society and movements by nongovernmental organizations (NGOs) facilitated especially through ICTs and through the work of the Association for Progressive Communications (APC). He suggests that for the first time in history NGOs have access to the same technologies as governments and transnational corporations, thus ensuring more "democratic" and decentralized information flows. The APC has helped to bridge the gap between rich and poor by developing low-cost infrastructure and access for people across the world. NGOs have used these technologies to share information about struggles around the world, especially when other networks were blocked by official "censorship," facilitate citizen participation in global summits, and take action to assist in struggles against violations of human rights, poverty, and for peace.

While this approach highlights some positive developments as a result of ICTs, especially the strengthening of the capacities of NGOs, it looks less at the disparities between what NGOs have access to and what states and corporations control. This is a significant inequality and substantially affects the direction of the development of ICTs. NGO networks, like the APC, provide a crucial alternative voice. But they remain marginal in the whole scheme of the Internet. Any analysis of the relations between the Internet and international relations will have to take these disparities into account.

Critical international relations theory attempts to look specifically at the inequalities in international relations to identify why institutions and practices are developed and for whose benefit.[2] While little has been written to address ICTs, the argument that will be made from a critical theory perspective is similar to that made in relation to international relations generally. First, we need to recognize that the development of any form of international relations must be understood in a broad historical context. It is also something that has been created or constructed in response to the underlying power relations at work. We need to examine how it relates to the existing world order, the hegemonic power within that order, and any counterhegemonic movements.[3] We should examine the underlying power relations at work that reinforce or sustain the existing world order. This will enable us to identify where there are potential areas for transformation of the order or potential conflicts.

This chapter will examine the Internet and ICTs from a critical theory perspective. First, I will explore the construction of the Internet in terms of who is part of it and who is not. I will look briefly at the development of the Internet and its dominance by transnational telecommunications corporations. I will argue that the Internet has been used to support and maintain the existing hegemonic world order. I will also explore in greater detail the ways in which the Internet is gendered and maintains unequal gender relations. Finally I will explore how the Internet has been used to develop counterhegemonic movements, especially through women's organizing.

Casting the Net

The Internet began as a systems of communications for the U.S. military in 1969 and has been used to promote and sustain world order values throughout its life. Developed at the height of the Cold War, the ARPANET provided a more global system of communications to the U.S. military. Initially, at least, the creation of this system of communication was directly linked to the perceived need of the United States to maintain hegemony in the world. Many would argue that it has come a long way since those early years. While the ARPANET was initially only open to those who had funding from the U.S. Department of Defense, a separate, almost underground, network called USENET was established in 1979 for those without access. USENET is a world-wide distributed discussion system URL: http://www.faqs.org/faqs/usenet/what-is/part1/ USENET has been called "the poor man's Arpanet" (Hauber & Hauben 1997, chapter 3). Both ARPANET and USENET were developed without commercial interventions although both relied on AT&T's technology and computer systems. By 1983 when the military withdrew from ARPANET, it became more of a research network, primarily linking academics especially in the sciences throughout the United States and Europe (Vissing Laursen 1996). The network expanded when more commercial links were made after 1986 and has grown significantly with the introduction of each new technology (Zakon 1993).

This widening of the audience provided an opening for nongovernmental organizations to begin to use the new technology as well. In 1984, PeaceNet, the first wing of what was to become known as the "Association for Progressive Communications" was born as the "world's first computer network dedicated exclusively to serving the needs of the movement for peace, human rights and social justice" (Frederick 1993, 288–289). This was paralleled by the establishment of the EcoNet by the Farallones Institute also in 1984. Together with ConflictNet, established in 1990, these three networks became part of the largest computer network dedicated to the aims of peace, social justice, ecological sustainability, and human rights. While these three were initially based in the United States, a similar network, Green Net was established in 1987 in Britain. The transnational links were further developed with the establishment of five more networks in Sweden, Canada, Brazil, Nicaragua, and Australia (Frederick 1993, 289). The Association for Progressive Communications was born in 1990 and provided global coordination for these different networks. The APC has become an Internet service provider for many groups in regions of the world where commercial service providers do not think there is a sufficient market. Currently the APC has 25 partner networks across the globe, providing service to over 50,000 NGOs, activists, educators, policymakers, and community leaders in 133 countries (APC Mission statement). The APC provides a unique set of relationships on the Internet, providing support for numerous justice-related groups including those involved in the environment, labor, criminal justice, women, and economics.

While the day-to-day direction on the Internet is given by the Internet service providers, common protocols and cooperation are maintained by the World Wide Web Consortium (comprised of over 200 industry members) and by the Internet Society (a more technical organization). More globally, transnational telecommunications corporations are attempting to influence the direction of public policy. One of the most striking attempts is the Global Information Infrastructure (GII) initiative instigated at the International Telecommunications Union meeting in 1994. While the GII began at a meeting of states, it has been transformed to a private sector initiative. The Global Information Infrastructure Commission (GIIC), based out of the Center for Strategic and International Studies in Washington, D.C., has a three-year mandate to foster private sector leadership and private-public sector cooperation in the development of information networks and services to advance global economic growth, education and quality of life (URL: http://giic.org). The commission is comprised of representatives (primarily presidents and CEOs) of forty-five transnational telecommunications corporations that have a significant stake in the development of these technologies. For example, Electronic Data Systems (EDS), Mitsubishi Corporation, Siemens AG, Texas Instruments, NEC Corporation, and AT&T are all participants in the GIIC. However, some of the larger corporations have been working independently of the GIIC. IBM, for example, has pursued the development of the GII through its ongoing connections with public policymakers especially in the OECD and Asia-Pacific Economic Cooperation (APEC) (IBM GII page URL: http://IBM.com/ibm/publicaffairs/cryptolindex.html).

When ARPANET was established, it was clearly designed to be a tool to maintain U.S. hegemony. Much has changed throughout the world since the 1960s, including the type of world order that currently exists. Some argue that we are still in an order maintained by the United States, while others, notably Cox (1996) insists that the world order has shifted, although still primarily built on the norms and values of a liberal economic order. These norms provide a framework for understanding the development of the Internet as well. As Cox (1996) suggests, norms and values in a hegemonic world order are stable and often appear to be the natural way of doing things. The central norm relevant to ICTs is the call for minimal state intervention in the transmission of information and the development of information technologies. This is often linked to libertarian cries for democracy and against free speech. As noted earlier, this is critical to industry leaders and to those involved in the GII. It is also important to the many users of the Internet. Some would argue that the role of states is to act or intervene only when self-regulation fails. They would also argue that the role of international organizations, such as the International Telecommunications Union, is to facilitate the workings of the transnational telecommunications corporations. These corporations are working as capitalists and their bottom line is making money. These values are boldly proclaimed by industry spokespeople and government representatives alike. There are few who challenge these values and they remain much more marginal actors, like the APC, having few of the resources or technological capacities of the transnational corporations. They are the counterhegemonic voice within this order.

One of the indications of the significance of this norm was the 1996 debate in the United States and on the Internet concerning passage of the Communications Decency Act, which was intended to prevent the distribution of indecent materials over the Internet.[9] It was ruled unconstitutional by the U.S. Supreme Court in 1997. But across the Internet, many organized to prevent what they saw as censorship or the restriction of free speech. Internet users have continually identified privacy and censorship as the two most important issues for the Internet (Graphic Visualizations Unsability Center, 1997).

These values of free speech and minimal regulation are integrally tied to the broader values of the international liberal economic order. In the existing world order, free trade, a global economy, and the reduction of barriers to trade, financial goods and services have provided the basis for the increased involvement of the Bretton Woods institutions (the International Monetary Fund and the World Bank) in setting the direction of the global political economy. They have been the driving force for the establishment of the World Trade Organization and are now providing the foundation for the Multilateral Agreement on Investment. The push by transnational telecommunications corporations, as well as by many Internet users (for differing reasons), for similar freedoms related to ICTs is a direct outgrowth of the dominance of these values within the existing world order. The GII and similar initiatives will be institutions created to embody these values and to maintain the dominance of transnational telecommunications corporations in these endeavors. These norms or values related to ICTs have provided the direction for many practices related to the Internet. The Internet has become primarily a market-driven, commercial set of enterprises. These practices maintain existing unequal power relations around the world.

The Internet is often touted as a global system of communications. An increasing number of people can obtain access to it, especially in North America and Europe. Yet there remain distressing inequalities between countries of the industrial North and developing South, and within countries of the North America, especially in terms of rural access and access for poorer people. One of the key indicators of pervasiveness of the new information revolution is the access to telephone lines. Across the world, the "teledensity" is 11.57/100 inhabitants. Yet for rich countries of North America, the density is 52/100 inhabitants while those in poor countries average 1.48/100 inhabitants. "Excluding China and India, the 57 low-income countries, which together account for one-fifth of the world's population have one-hundredth of the global telephone main lines" (ITU, "Inter-Agency Report"). More than one-half of the world's population does not have access to a telephone, and some estimates claim that 80 percent do not have a telephone. This unequal access is compounded when we consider computer hardware. About 84% of the world's personal computers are found in the rich countries of the North. As well, 97% of Internet users are in these rich countries. (ITU, "Inter-Agency Report"). The markets for telecommunications services and technology are also concentrated in countries of the North. For example, roughly 75% of the global market for services is found in the Americas and Europe with an additional 20% in Asia. The market for information technology shows similar levels of concentration with 90% concentrated in the United States (39%), Western Europe (34.5%), and Japan (19%) (ITU, "Inter-Agency Report").

Within both the South and the North there are significant disparities between access for those in urban and rural areas. This is especially true in the South where in rural areas teledensity is often only one telephone per 1,000 inhabitants. For example, nearly 58,000 villages in Indonesia, 535,000 villages in India, and 150,000 villages in Africa have no telephone connection (ITU, "Inter-Agency Report"). Reliable electricity often prevents access as well. Even in countries of the South that have some access to the infrastructure, there are problems with limited training or access to on-line resources. Access in languages other than English is a serious deterrent around the world.

The users of the Internet reflect those in dominant power relations within the global society: the vast majority are white, able-bodied, heterosexual males in North America and Europe. Recent surveys suggest that almost 90.0% of users identify themselves as white/Caucasian, almost 93.0% identify themselves as heterosexuals, almost 92.0% identify English as their primary language, and just over 92.0% consider themselves without physical impairment (GVU 1997). The Internet is also very much a gendered community. Just over 60% of Internet users are men, although the number of women is increasing, especially in North America. According to the GVU's Eighth World Wide Web User Study, while the gender ratio in North America is 40.5% female and 59.5% male, in Europe users are still primarily male (78.0%).[5]

Some have suggested that these differences are not as significant on the Internet as they may be off-line because on the Internet users can change or hide their gender, race, or other characteristics. While this potential indicates that the Internet may provide a unique forum for discussion, it fails to recognize that once users go off-line they are faced again with their "realities," nor that Web sites, advertising, and marketing are targeted to specific groups of people, not to their on-line personae. For example, while some women may take on the persona of a man in a chat group, once off the computer they are again faced with the evidence of their unequal location in gender relations, including for many the double burden of childcare, housework, and their paid jobs. Since the Internet is at this time primarily a tool for the global elite, most of the world's population do not have the luxury of playing with their gender or "race" on-line. Whether they will be able to in the future remains dependent upon their access to, and use of, the technologies. For these reasons, the issues of representation on the Internet are less important than the impact of gender inequalities on participation and organizing on the Internet. In the next section, we examine these gender relations in greater detail, exploring why a gender gap exists and how it is maintained through the use and development of ICTs.

The Gendered Internet

Across the globe, the Internet remains a highly gendered community. Many more men than women use the Internet, more computer scientists and programmers are men, and more decision makers on ICTs are men. As well, there are different impacts of ICTs on women and men. Some have even argued that the very technology of computers and computer-mediated communications is more masculine than feminine (Balka 1996). Why is this so? In answering this question, I will consider three different streams of argument: the gendered gap in ICT usage, gendered disparities in ICT development and maintenance especially as evident in computer and science education and careers, and the gendered impacts of ICTs. In making these arguments I recognize that the reasons for why more men than women use computers and ICTs may be different than the reasons for fewer programmers or direction-setters. As well,

examining the gendered impacts of technology could be substantially different than either of the other two. While these arguments are framed in gender
terms, they are much more complicated and reflect the power relations
related to urban/rural, South/North and race.

More men than women use the Internet and computers (GVU 1997).
As well, we can note that the number of women users, particularly young
women in North America and Europe, is increasing. But to state these as
"facts" does little to explain why this gender gap exists. Some have argued,
stereotypically, that women simply do not like this sort of technology, or
that it is too hard for them, or the converse, that men are just better at it and
therefore more interested in it. While both stereotypes appear to contain
some truth, neither recognizes the complexities of why these differences occur.
More succinctly, the positions of women and men in society often shapes their
ability and willingness to interact with computers. Many women are more
often than not responsible for childcare and domestic responsibilities within
their families. They often have lower levels of education and training, lower
pay, less autonomy, and less time. For these women, their other responsibilities may mean less time to learn about how to use a computer and less
money with which to buy one or pay for Internet access. This is true for many
women in the North and South. As Huyer suggests, women in Africa face all
of these problems:

> The economic hardships in our countries make it impossible for
> women, who have to pay school fees for children and to cater for
> other basic needs, to save money to buy computer hardware, for
> example. That is why after attending computer courses, if one does
> not have a computer in the office to practice, then one will lapse
> back into illiteracy because she cannot afford to buy a computer
> for herself . . . many men are already computer literate because
> they have more time to themselves, access to ICTs and a supportive
> environment for them to acquire whatever new skill comes up.
> (Huyer 1997)

Yet even this picture is distorted. Middle- and upper-class women of the
North often have as much interest, time, and money for getting involved
with ICTs as men. For an increasing number of women, using computers is
part of their paid work, although most are primarily involved in data entry
rather than programming (Global Knowledge '97, "Focus Piece #2").

Some have argued that these technologies are primarily masculine and
oriented toward men in our society, which helps to explain why men are the
primary users. Balka (1993) suggests that early computing technology was
not able to provide the type of networking in which women were interested.
While it is difficult (although not impossible) to argue that any technology is

inherently gendered, it is important to recognize that there are highly gendered environments and uses to technology. In many ways, the culture of computer technology is masculine. Early on, many boys are drawn to video and computer games that are not as interesting to many girls. The high numbers of men who are the teachers, students, users, and designers ensures that the computer environment will appear to be more masculine. But Spender suggests, quoting research by Lynda Davies, that the culture goes well beyond just having more men than women. Indeed, many male students, teachers, and support staff see computers as an extension of their bodies and thus provide an environment that excludes women:

> The linkage of hardware to the penis is often made in jokes shared by computing students. This is witnessed in face-to-face interactions. "Ah, my machine's got more megabyte extensions than your machine" (thrusting of the pelvis and hand placed upon the groin); and in electronic interactions over the network. "What do you call a supercomputer? A memory with balls." (Spender 1995, 183)

These analogies are reminiscent of the work done by Cohn on the masculine language of defense intellectuals (Cohn 1987). The masculinity of the culture is reinforced by the disparity in participation between women and men and we continue to see a gender gap in ICTs.

If we want to understand why there is a gender gap in Internet and computer usage, we will have to recognize that people's life circumstances affect and shape their abilities to use these technologies. This is true of women and men. Class, location, education, family circumstances, sexuality, and ability all assist in making someone "info-rich" or "info-poor." Access to the Internet is not something determined by biology or whether one is female or male. However, more women are info-poor than men and therefore we can see that there is a disparity of information power based in gender.

Once we see that there is a gender inequality, we must ask, How are those who set directions in the area of ICTs addressing the disparity? The short answer is that they are not. While there have been calls by some states and international organizations for greater measures to address the gender inequality, and industry women have attempted to develop their own networks, little is being done to ensure access for men and women. The United Nations Division for the Advancement of Women together with the UN Development Fund for Women have created a website for information about women called "WomenWatch." The Gender Working Group of the UN Commission on Science and Technology published a report on the gender dimension with many recommendations. The 1995 Beijing World Conference on Women adopted recommendations for nation-states to ensure better access for women. Yet, in the public and private sectors, little has been done.

Few transnational telecommunications corporations or other parts of the ICT industry have made this an area for priority (or any sort of) action. Women, however, have become an increasing focus for marketing as companies realize that women are the fastest-growing segment on the Internet. In 1997, American On-Line launched a separate women's site called "Electra." The contents of this site reflect the pages of many women's magazines found in North American supermarket shelves, on relationships, food, entertainment, and the like. Women already in the industry have organized to assist in bringing other women in through Women in Technology International. International WebGrrls is another network providing support for women who want to be part of the new technologies. Despite these efforts, the gender gap in ICT usage remains.

The gender disparities in computer education, science, programming, and decision making are even more significant and will have much broader effects. Across the globe, girls and women have less access to education than do men. Women are more frequently illiterate than men; rural and older women are even more disadvantaged (Peterson and Runyan, 1993 (UN). These statistics become even more disturbing when we consider access to scientific and technological education. For example, in the United States, the number of women graduating with advanced computer science degrees is dropping. In 1994 and 1995, 17 percent of computer science Ph.D.'s were awarded to women; in 1996, there were only 12 percent (DeMocker 1997). While education in science and technology is not essential to using computers, it is crucial to getting a career in computing fields and helping to shape the directions and content of these new technologies. "A 1996 report by the Gender Working Group of the UN Commission on Science and Technology for Development argues that the barriers for women and girls, especially those in the South, to science and technological education extend beyond those faced by boys and men, [and] prevent women from fully contributing to scientific and technological advances, including ones that could better meet women's basic needs and support their hopes and aspirations for the future" (GWG 1996, chapter 2). Some of these barriers are gender stereotyping, lack of sufficient resources for the education of girls as opposed to boys, parental preferences for the education of boys over girls and

> the misleading perception of parents, some teachers and guidance counselors that science and mathematics are "difficult subjects" and not as suitable for girls as for boys, curricula and textbooks that do not relate science to everyday experiences of both boys and girls, contain gender-biased language, fail to give due recognition

to the contributions to women scientists, and do not promote women role models for girls, and in some countries, lack of sufficient equipment for girls classes and schools in comparison with boys. (Spertus 1991; GWG 1996, chapter 2)

These experiences are echoed by girls and women across the globe. Spender writes of watching the exclusion of girls from computer classes by the teacher and by the boys in an Australian classroom:

> In more than one school that I have visited, there were sufficient computers in the room for everyone to be working at their own terminal. But the girls could be found huddled in a group away from the computers while the boys sometimes kept two terminals going! In one such classroom I asked the teacher, whose manner was visibly hostile to the girls, why it was that the female students stayed together and made [no] use of the computers. I was informed that this was the girls' choice. That there was only trouble when the girls got to a keyboard. And the reason they wouldn't "learn" was because they were out of their depth, and didn't want to appear stupid. . . . [When she visited the classroom and the girls tried to have a turn at the computers, the following occurred.] Some boys physically pushed [the girls] away from the computers and insisted that they needed two terminals for the purposes of their project. They verbally abused the girls ("slut" and "slag" being among the most printable) and generally engaged in loud and bullying behavior. Far from being embarrassed by this appalling display, the teacher felt vindicated. "I told you girls were trouble," he said. "They stop everyone from working." (Spender 1995: 178–179)

As a result of the barriers for girls and women to science and technological education as well as to what many have referred to as a "chilly climate" or hostility in these fields for women, there are fewer women than men engaged in science and technology careers. This severely hampers women's abilities to provide technical support, and to participate in setting the directions for and to decide the contents of information technologies. As a result, most of the decision making is done by men. Of the forty-three GIIC commissioners, most of whom are presidents and CEOs in significant ICT corporations, only one is a woman and she is part of a research center, not a corporation. The impacts of this have been seen in the different impact that ICTs have had on women and men.

The gendered impacts of ICTs have affected employment and income generation. They are also evident in the types of technology developed and in the level of harassment and privacy issues for users. We shall look at each of these in greater detail.

There have been mixed benefits in the employment sector as a result of the new technologies. Some have gained jobs, while others have lost them. The new technologies have made many manufacturing jobs redundant or obsolete, affecting both women and men. These changes have affected men and women differently, but overall more female labor has been displaced than male labor (GWG 1996). Many of the jobs created have been relatively low skilled (and low paid), in the banking or financial services sectors. Others have been "telework," more flexible work done out of the home. Consistently, however, women have failed to get access to the jobs that are higher skilled and higher paid because they lack the necessary training.[6] One of the questions to be raised is, How can women take advantage of the higher-paid, more highly skilled information jobs when they have difficulty getting access to the necessary training? (Shade 1997).

The ICTs also have different and gendered impacts on income generation. It is widely accepted that poverty on a global scale wears a feminine face. Many agencies, states, and international organizations provide support for income-generating projects for women, recognizing that these are means whereby poverty can be reduced and self-sufficiency enhanced. Support for microenterprises and microcredit has grown dramatically over the 1990s, especially with the Microcredit Summit in February 1997. While many recognize that women's needs for income generation are different than men's because of their different life circumstances (and microcredit is one of the best examples of a gendered strategy), there have been few attempts to use ICTs to assist women in income-generation. The Gender Working Group suggests that this is a result of gendered assumptions about women's use of technology. They argue that it would be extremely beneficial for women to receive access to training related to information technologies and management in order to ensure their increased income generation:

> Computer-aided small-scale management and accounting systems have been found to improve business efficiency of women working as street vendors, garment pickers and tailors in the informal sector. Self-Employed Women's Association in India is an example of an active NGO that works with women to make modern technologies accessible for business efficiency to those groups that are normally excluded from the benefits of modern science and technology. (GWG 1996)

The development of ICTs is also gendered. While few women participate in the work related to the development, there are also assumptions made about what knowledge is important for this development. For example, little effort is made to ensure that the unique knowledge of rural or indigenous women related to their lives is essential to the development of ICTs, yet in order to ensure universal access, it will be crucial to know what these women know.

The final area in which we see the gendered impacts of ICTs is related to on-line conduct. The GVU User Survey noted that more women than men place issues related to privacy as the most important for the future development of the Internet. This is hardly surprising. Many women face on- and off-line harassment as a result of electronic discussions. These are often abusive and sexual in tone. Numerous studies have been undertaken that illustrate that while both women and men flame, men's flames are often more abusive and personal in tone (Herring 1994; We 1993). Others illustrate the level of sexual harassment that women have to face (Bell and de La Rue; Spender 1995).

In my own experience as a electronic discussion list manager for four years, harassment was common. I managed a feminist list and was naive about the extent and scope of hostility to women and feminism on-line. When the first announcement across the Internet about our list opening appeared, I received some significant misogynist hate mail. Throughout my tenure as list manager and eventually comoderator, the most virulent discussions were those dominated by antifeminist men, who took the opportunity to call the women in the discussions "cunt" and other derogatory names and to undermine their credibility by harassing them publicly and in private messages. There is little recognition of this climate of harassment by the Internet service providers and little recourse for women who have been harassed (WHOA). Yet as we will see in the following sections, women have created very successful alternative spaces that provide for greater security on-line and in many cases challenge the hegemonic values that dominate ICTs.

Widening the Net

For those who are "info-poor" and without access to ICTs, there is an accompanying sense of being less powerful in the "new information society" and already existing inequalities are reinforced:

> For those in possession of information technology, power, influence, privileged status and domination are further enhanced and assured. The reverse is true for those without access to informatics. But it has also great chances of contributing to equity, development and progress, permitting those lagging behind to leap-frog to more advanced stages of development. Informatics has enormous potential to redress the disparities and material inequalities of our

world the cheapest and fastest way. But in it are also great possibilities of accentuating our material inequalities, the powerlessness of
the have-nots and the misery of millions bypassed by the information superhighway. (Diseko 1996)

The lack of access to the Internet and its accompanying sense of powerlessness for many people around the world cannot be solved simply by more
telephone lines or more computers, which has been the primary strategy
pursued by most states, international organizations, and transnational telecommunications enterprises. Counterhegemonic movements must challenge
the dominant values supported by the Internet. By examining who develops
sites and lists, for what purpose, and for what audience, their global reach,
their attempts to bring about transformation or change to the situation of
the powerlessness and to the structure or technology of the Internet, and
their connections to other transformative networks, we will be able to identify places on the Internet with counterhegemonic potential. We will examine how existing women's organizing on the Internet addresses these and
whether they are creating a counterhegemonic presence on the Internet.

There are thousands, if not millions, of resources and activities related
to women to be found on the Internet. It is impossible to give any survey
evaluation of their content without lapsing into vague generalizations. The
sites and lists are so varied that many aspects of women's diversities are
reflected and if they are not yet, just wait, someone will create a site or list to
respond to the gap. As well, within different sites and at different times there
can be significant differences. What can be said meaningfully about women's
global organizing on the Internet? In this section, I will argue that the Internet has two very different streams of sites/lists related to women: those that
are commercial and support the status quo, and those nonprofit, commu-
nity-based networks that seek transformation of the existing order. The
increasing feminist transformative presence on the Internet is, in large part,
supported and directed by the Association for Progressive Communications
Women's Program and those involved in these sites and lists are creating an
effective alternative presence that could become part of a sustained counterhegemonic movement.

Despite my disclaimer about not wanting to overly generalize about
sites, I would like to briefly look at two large commercial sites related to
women, sites that I consider to be status quo. Women.com and Electra.com
are large and diverse sites, which provide a multitude of resources, including
links related to feminism, health, parenting, employment, entertainment, and
the arts. Several indicators, however, illustrate that their goals are not to
change the position of women within society, but to "capitalize" upon and

use women's situations to make more profit. The creators of the sites are quite open about their goals. They identify women as the fastest-growing segment on the Internet and hope to get access to their money (Kornblum 1997). As one advertiser noted, "Women mean business." Therefore, they need to have sites that appeal to women's interests. How they identify women's interests reflects the fact that women have the most significant purchasing power in the North American markets. They are primarily white, middle- or upper-class, professional women, and it is these women who the companies are targeting. The sites attempt to make their spaces as inviting as possible and as easy to navigate, but they fail to reach beyond their target audiences. These sites take the Internet as a given, using the existing technology very well, but remaining focused on the Internet primarily as a medium to interact with individuals on personal or business computers for their personal or business interests. There are very few attempts to reach outside of North America, or to issues of concern to women who are poor or without significant education. There is no suggestion that any attempts are being made to bring more women outside the target groups onto the Internet and none that any other means for access are needed. These sites do provide opportunities for women to organize around issues of concern through chat rooms and the like, but there is no attempt to look critically at the situation of women in the world or to promote change in their situations.

Other sites, like the women's net at the APC, and aviva.org, provide a significant contrast to the status quo groups. The sites that they maintain provide significantly different information for women than do the commercial sites; those who manage the sites work to promote women's participation on the Internet, especially through women's organizations; they have a broad global reach and they facilitate strategies for action by women that promote change in women's lives. Primarily through their mission to ensure access for many women around the world, they also challenge the technological and structural limits of the Internet and begin to develop technological alternatives to the current individualized focus of ICTs.

There are many different locations for information and resources related to women's global organizations. Many, such as the global resources link at feminist.com, are simply a listing of sites and electronic discussion lists promoting feminist and women's organizing. One of the best of these is Joan Korenman's list of Gender-related Electronic forums. Even a quick search for women using standard navigators on an international scale such as Yahoo or Lycos will provide a substantial result. But probably more useful for women's organizing are the news items that provide critical evaluations of women's lives and situations around the world that are posted on some sites. These are rarely part of mainstream news sources, which are reflected as well on the Internet. For example, the Institute for Global Communication Women's Net (the U.S. partner of the APC) posts weekly news stories about women on its home page. Aviva.org is a relatively recent global news source about women. Its monthly magazine provides regional and international stories, events, and action alerts. Other unique news sources include the Women's International Net and the Women's Feature Service. The Women's Cybrary is a source for women's writing on-line. Many women's groups across the world also have their own web sites with information about their work, or are part of the APC network in their region.

But women's organizing on-line is significantly more than the sharing of information; it also includes the gaining of new skills. One of the most significant activities for organizing on-line has been to ensure access for women who are illiterate. On one electronic discussion list, a member asked why people who do not have access to water or electricity or are illiterate want (or need) to have access to electronic mail. For many, striving for universal access may seem to be imposing inappropriate technology on those who are not yet ready for this level of technology. Literacy may seem to be a prerequisite for electronic communications. But those who live in Africa and in other regions of the world where illiteracy is high argue that ICTs will facilitate literacy. Huyer gives two specific examples of how women have used ICTs to combat illiteracy and encourage employment:

The Center for Communications and Women's Self-Employment, in Quakchott, Mauritania, like many successful literacy projects, ties literacy training to a package of skills and services provided to support women's entrepreneurial activities. The Center provides classes aimed at self-employment, such as sewing, cleaning and drying of fish, rug weaving and reading lessons. The reading lessons are intended to allow women to more efficiently manage their day-to-day entrepreneurial activities, but also pertain to the recognition that "for women, the biggest problem is information." For this reason, lessons in computer technology and typing are also offered. A similar approach was taken by the Community of Living Water in South Africa who worked with the "Masizakhe" group of women in Kayamandi, South Africa. The purpose of the project was to support women's organic gardening activities. ICTs were used in two ways: to deliver information on organic gardening techniques and resources, and to teach English language skills via CD-ROM. Two web sites in particular were used by the group, one at Ohio University, and the Life magazine Gardening Encyclopedia. Reading skills, initially developed by use of CD-ROMs, were supplemented by adult education information found over the Internet. This use in fact sparked a community initiative to donate used clothing to finance the women's enrollment in additional adult education courses available on the local network, SANGOnet. (Huyer 1997)

These are examples of how women's organizing can ensure that more women are able to use these technologies and to use them to better their own situations. But they also indicate areas for the transformation of ICTs. They focus attention on technologies that facilitate collective learning and knowledge. In doing this they challenge the values upon which the Internet exists and provide the potential for groups to organize to challenge the hegemonic values of the current world order.

Both the APC and the International Women's Tribune Centre worked hard in preparation for the 1995 Beijing Conference on Women and NGO Forum, during and after to ensure access to ICTs for women all over the world. The APC has made access for women one of its priority areas for action and is working to bring women's groups on-line through its regional partner networks (APC Global Action Plan). This work, together with some innovative Internet projects such as the Acacia Initiative funded through the International Development Research Centre, the UN Economic Commission for Africa's African Information Society Initiative, and the Food and Agriculture Organization of the UN's initiative on developing a rural Internet approach for rural agricultural communities, is pioneering alternative ICTs such as telecenters. These initiatives pick up where most commercial Internet providers leave off. They take on service provisions that are not necessarily profitable to rural Africa and identify them as a means of promoting sustainable development. This work challenges, as well, understandings of development and of the responsibilities of the international community.

Once groups are on-line, the APC Women's Program has trained local women to provide support and training. The APC Women's Program, in a recent survey on networking, found that training was a critical issue for all women around the world. Most argued that women were not getting adequate training because of availability (especially in some regions), cost, time restrictions, and lack of gender and/or culturally sensitive approaches. The most effective training was that which was women-specific, free, and linked with ongoing user support and mentoring in the communities where women live. Women called for training that was action-oriented and developed with the women's movements in their communities. They also supported the APC Women's Program approach of developing a global network of technical women to serve local needs as a training model to build on (APC Women's Program 1997).

As a result of this level of support, women's groups across the world have been able to participate in the development of alternative policy documents related to health, human rights, or economic justice, especially through the Women's Caucus process facilitated by WEDO (Women's Environment and Development Organization), in preparation for the Beijing Conference (Stienstra 1998). Groups have also been able to develop greater connections with other groups, and thus strengthen women's organizing globally.

Another initiative using ICTs that has strengthened women's global organizing has been the Global Faxnet organized and distributed through the International Women's Tribune Centre (IWTC). In preparation for, and following, the Beijing Conference, the Faxnet (which has since become an Internet network) provided information to women's groups across the world (Frankson 1996). At the NGO Forum, the IWTC also organized the Once and Future Network Pavilion that included a computer corner along with introductions to other communications technologies. This has blossomed into the Once and Future Action Network (Gittler 1996, 92). In some ways this initiative illustrates how the Internet is simply an extension of existing technologies. As the means of communications have changed from the telephone to fax to electronic mail, women's movements have adopted each form of communications technology and increased the ease and scope of their organizing.

Women have been using the Internet in more traditional ways to lobby and ensure that their perspectives are included in policy making at the international and national levels and to develop common strategies for action across the world. The catalyst and focus for much of this activity was the 1995 Beijing World Conference on Women. Both intergovernmental and nongovernmental communities used ICTs to ensure access to conference documents and information. The UN Division for the Advancement of Women established a World Wide Web site for the conference and became an Internet service provider at the official conference site. There was significant public interest in this site: a total of 158,722 requests for files under the conference site were received from 68 different countries (DAW 1996). At the NGO Forum, there was considerable access for participants, facilitated by APC Women's Net. At least 1,700 women opened E-mail accounts, almost half were using E-mail for the first time, and over 30,000 participants visited the Forum/Conference Web site (Gittler 1996, 88).

ICTs have also been used effectively to ensure that women's voices were heard in the discussions surrounding the Global Knowledge conference in Toronto in 1997. Led again by the APC Women's Program, participants made recommendations to the conference about ways in which gender needs to be addressed in areas such as access, training, support, and networking. With over 300 participants, it was a highly successful discussion group and in the end was able to modify and endorse the declaration on gender, partnerships, and information technologies developed by the Independent Committee on Women and Global Knowledge. The concerns and examples raised illustrated how women have successfully used the ICTs to strengthen their own networking, share information, and form strategies around common goals.

Women's On-line Organizing: Counterhegemonic Activities?

Throughout this chapter, I have argued that there are hegemonic values that are found on the Internet and that perpetuate unequal gender relations. These are maintained by those who provide direction to the development of the Internet, especially the transnational telecommunications enterprises. Yet there is a substantial voice of opposition to these values as well. Women have organized on-line to promote changing the status quo and challenging these values. The Association for Progressive Communications Women's Program has been one of the most significant vehicles for ensuring access for many women and for addressing gender inequalities. The question that remains is whether or not these transformative actions have become or are becoming part of a counterhegemonic movement.

While women's global on-line organizing has many of the aspects of a growing counterhegemonic movement, it remains nascent. The organizing is increasingly global in scope, but there are still many, many women (and men) who do not have access. There is considerable information on the Internet, yet much less strategic thinking is evident. Much of what is available are lists of resources. This is a significant improvement from the limited information available earlier, but there is still much more that needs to be made available. There are connections between different transformative movements, especially through the APC. Yet there is little coalition work evident on the Internet. The first steps seem to have been taken in the Global Knowledge conference, but much more needs to be done. While women are an increasingly important part of the decision-making and technical support for networks like the APC, these networks remain marginal in the grand scheme of the Internet. In general, the Internet has provided technology whereby individuals and groups can gain greater information and knowledge. Yet access is so unequal and those who are attempting to address the balance remain on the margins, that this inequality will take considerable time to be redressed. As one Peruvian respondent to the APC Women's Program Networking Survey replied, "Personally, I believe we can talk about the democratization of communication, but I believe that what is occurring is an increased communication elite, and this is the case with women. . . . Information is power, and only a small amount of women and organizations have access to this power." Information and knowledge are essential, but they do not ensure that a strong counterhegemonic presence will develop on the Internet. This will require movements recognizing and addressing the ways in which the Internet maintains and supports world order values.

Notes

1. I am not aware of any published work that undertakes such an analysis, but it would be a fruitful area of study, well beyond the limits of this chapter.

2. See for example, Cox (1996); Stienstra (1994); and Whitworth (1994).

3. Hegemony is not used here simply to refer to dominance. Rather I agree with Cox who suggests that hegemony is

> a structure of values and understandings about the nature of order that permeates a whole system of states and non-state entities. In a hegemonic order these values and understandings are relatively stable and unquestioned. They appear to most actors as the natural order. Such a structure of meanings is underpinned by a structure of power, in which most probably one state is dominant but that state's dominance in itself is not sufficient to create hegemony. Hegemony derives from the ways of doing and thinking of the dominant social strata of the dominant state or states insofar as these ways of doing and thinking have acquired the acquiescence of the dominant social strata of other states. These social practices and the ideologies that explain and legitimize them constitute the foundation of hegemonic order. (Cox 1996, 151)

4. While this debate has centered around the United States, several other countries have already instituted restrictions on the Internet. For example, in China users and Internet service providers are required to register with the police; in Germany, some newsgroups carried on Compuserve have had their access removed; in Saudi Arabia, Internet access is restricted to universities and hospitals; in Singapore, those who provide political and religious content are required to register with the state; and in New Zealand, computer disks are classified as publications that can be seized or censored (Zakon 1993).

5. The number of female users increased 7 percent in the Eighth Survey in comparison to the previous three surveys, where the percentages had remained stable. Whether this increase will be sustained remains to be seen.

6. See Mitter (1995) for a general discussion of these issues, Pearson (1996) for a discussion of the situation of women's employment in Great Britain, and Ng (1996) for a similar discussion on women's employment in Malaysia.

References

Association for Progressive Communications (APC). 1997. "Global Action Plan." URL: http://www.apc.org/global.html.

Association for Progressive Communications. 1997. "Mission Statement." URL: http://www.apc.org/english/about/mission/index.html.

Association for Progressive Communications Women's Program. 1997. "Global Networking for Change: Experiences from the APC Women's Program." URL: http://community.web.net/womensweb/apcwomen/detailed.htm. May.

Balka, Ellen. 1993. "Women's Access to On-line Discussions about Feminism." *Electronic Journal of Communication* 3, no. 1.

———. 1996. "Communicating Feminism and Feminist Communication: Women and Computer Access in Six Countries." *Journal of International Communication* 3 (July): 66–84.

Bell, Vicki and Denise de La Rue. 1995. "Gender Harassment on the Internet." URL: http://www.gsu.edu/~lawppw/lawand.papers/harass.html.

Cohn, Carol. 1987. "Sex and Death in the Rational World of Defense Intellectuals." *Signs* 12: 687–718.

Cox, Robert W. 1996. *Approaches to World Order.* Cambridge: Cambridge University Press.

DeMocker, Judy. 1997. "Women Use Web to Crack the Glass Ceiling." *Web Week*, 10 November.

Diseko, Mathe. 1996. "Statement to the Economic and Social Council," New York, 16 July.

Division for the Advancement of Women (DAW). 1996. "Women and the Information Revolution" *Women 2000* 1 (October). URL: http://www.un.org/womenwatch/daw/public/w2cont.htm.

Frankson, Joan Ross. 1996. "Women's Global Faxnet: Charting the Way." *Journal of International Communication* 3 (July): 102–110.

Frederick, Howard. 1993. "Computer Networks and the Emergence of Global Civil Society." *Global Network: Computers and International Communication.* Ed. Linda M. Harasim. Cambridge: Massachussetts Institute of Technology Press.

Gender Working Group (GWG), United Nations Commission on Science and Technology for Development. 1996. *Science and Technology for Sustainable Human Development: The Gender Dimension.* Ottawa: International Development Resource Centre. URL: http://www.idrc.ca/sip/gender/scitech/

Gittler, Alice Mastrangelo. 1996. "Taking Hold of Electronic Communications: Women Making a Difference." *Journal of International Communication* 3 (July): 85–101.

Global Information Infrastructure Commission (GIIC) homepage URL:http://www.gii.org/index.html.

Global Knowledge '97. "Focus Piece #2: Why Should Women Bother?" URL: http://community.web.net/gk97/focus2.htm.

Graphic, Visualization and Usability Center's (GVU). 1997. *Eighth WWW Users Survey*. Atlanta: Georgia Institute of Technology. URL: http://www.gvu .gatech.edu/user_surveys/survey-1997–10.

Hauben, Michael and Ronda Hauben. 1997. *Netizens: On the History and Impact of Usenet and the Internet*. Los Alamitos, CA: IEEE Computer Society Press.

Herring, Susan. 1994. "Gender Differences in Computer-mediated Communication: Bringing Familiar Baggage to the New Frontier." URL: http://www.inform.umd.edu/EdRes/Topic/WomensStudies/Computing/Articles+ResearchPapers/gender-differences-communication.

Huyer, Sophia. 1997. "Supporting Women's Use of Information Technologies for Sustainable Development." URL: http://www.idrc.ca/acacia/outputs/womenicts.html.

IBM Global Information Infrastructure homepage, URL: http://www.ibm.com/IBM/publicaffairs/crypto/index.html.

International Telecommunications Union (ITU). Office of the Secretary General. "Inter-Agency Project on Universal Access to Basic Communication and Information Services," URL: http://www.itu.int/acc/rtc/itu_paper/task1r.htm.

Kornblum, Janet. 1997. "AOL Joins Women's Site Trend." CNET News.com, 8 December. URL: http://www.news.com/News/Item/0,4,17042,00.html.

Mitter, Swasti. 1995. "Information Technology and Working Women's Demands." *Women Encountering Technology*. Eds. S. Mitter and S. Rowbotham. London: Routledge.

Ng, Cecelia. 1996. "The Economic Position of Women in the Information Era." Paper presented at the International Conference on Empowering Women in an Information Era, Center for Korean Women and Politics, Seoul, Korea, 18–20 November.

Pearson, Ruth. 1996. "Informationalisation and Employment in the U.K.: Implications for Women." Paper presented at the International Conference on Empowering Women in an Information Era, Center for Korean Women and Politics, Seoul, Korea. 18–20 November.

Peterson, V. Spike and Anne Sisson Runyan. 1993. *Global Gender Issues*. Boulder, CO: Westview Press.

Risse-Kappen, Thomas, ed. 1995. *Bringing Transnational Relations Back In: Non-state Actors, Domestic Structures and International Institutions*. Cambridge: Cambridge University Press.

Shade, Leslie Regan. 1997. "Post-Beijing and Beyond: Gendered Perspectives on Access." *Women in Computing*. Eds. Rachel Lander and Alison Adam. Exeter, Great Britain: Intellect Books. URL: www.intellect-net .com.

Spertus, Ellen. 1991. "Why Are There so Few Female Computer Scientists?" URL: http://www.inform.umd.edu/EdRes/Topic/WomensStudies/Computing/Articles+ResearchPapers/WhySoFewWomen/.

Spertus, Ellen. 1996. "Social and Technical Means for Fighting On-Line Harassment." Paper presented at Virtue and Virtuality: Gender, Law and Cyberspace, Cambridge, MA, 20–21 April. URL: http://www.ai.mit.edu/people/ellens/Gender/glc/.

Stienstra, Deborah. 1998. "Dancing Resistance from Rio to Beijing: Transnational Women's Organizing and United Nations Conferences, 1992–1996." *Gender and Global Restructuring*. Eds. Marianne Marchand and Anne Sisson Runyan. New York: Routledge.

Stienstra, Deborah. 1994. *Women's Movements and International Organizations*. London: Macmillan.

Troung, Hoai-An. 1993. "Gender Issues in Online Communications." URL: http://www.inform.umd.edu/EdRes/Topic/WomensStudies/Computing/Articles+ResearchPapers/gender-issues-online.

Vissing Laursen, Jesper. 1996. "The Internet: Past, Present and Future: Internet & WWW History." *American Studies in Scandinavia* 28: 101–112.

We, Gladys. 1993. "Cross-Gender Communications in Cyber-Space." URL: http://www.inform.umd.edu/EdRes/Topic/WomensStudies/Computing/Articles+ResearchPapers/cross-gender-communication.

Whitworth, Sandra. 1994. *Feminism and International Relations*. London: Macmillan. Women Halting Online Abuse (WHOA). URL: http://whoa.femail.com/index.html.

Zakon, Robert H. 1993, "Hobbes' Internet Timeline," v3.1. URL: http://haltabuse.org

Appendix

Significant events related to gender and ICTs

12–17 February 1994 Women Empowering Communication Conference, Bangkok, Thailand

4–15 September 1995 Fourth World Conference on Women, Beijing, China

26–29 June 1996 United Nations Expert Workshop on Global Information through Computer Networking Technology in the Follow-up to the Fourth World Conference on Women (FWCW), New York.

18–20 November 1996 International Conference on Empowering Women in an Information Era, Center for Korean Women and Politics, Seoul, Korea

8–11 February 1997 Association for Progressive Communications (APC) Africa Strategy Meeting, Johannesburg.

22–25 June 1997 Global Knowledge '97: Knowledge for Development in the Information Age, World Bank and the Government of Canada, Toronto

Sites related to global women's organizing

- Association for Progressive Communications (APC) Women's Net, URL: http://www.gn.apc.org/gn/women/index.html
- Aviva.org, URL:http://www.aviva.org/index.html
- Global Knowledge '97 - Gender, URL: http://www.igc.apc.org/gk97/gk97.gender/
- IGC Women's Net, URL: http://www.igc.org/igc/womensnet/ International Women's Tribune Centre, URL: http://www.igc.org/beijing/ngo/iwtc.html
- List of Gender-related Electronic Forums, URL: http://www.umbc.edu/wmst/forums.html
- Women's Cybrary, URL: http://www.womenbooks.com/
- Women's Feature Service, URL: http://www.igc.org/wfs/
- Women's International Net, URL: http://winmagazine.base.org
- Women Watch of the United Nations Gateway on the Advancement and Empowerment of Women, URL: http://www.un.org/womenwatch/

CHAPTER NINE

Technology Transfer
in the Computer Age

The African Experience

ALI A. MAZRUI AND ROBERT L. OSTERGARD JR.

The significance of the computer in Africa has to be seen in relation to three processes with much wider implications: modernization, development, and alien penetration. Much of the literature on modernization conceives it as a process of change in the direction of narrowing the technical, scientific, and normative gap between industrialized Western countries and the Third World. Partly because the industrial revolution first took place in the West, modernization until now has largely been equated with Westernization, in spite of rhetorical assertions to the contrary.[1]

Because modernization has connoted a constant struggle to narrow the technical, scientific, and normative gap between Westerners and others, development has often been seen as a subsection of modernization. Most economists in the West and in the Third World itself have analyzed economic development in terms of narrowing the economic gap between those two parts of the world both in methods of production and in output. Most political scientists have evaluated political development as a process of acquiring Western skills of government, Western restraints in political behavior, and Western institutions for resolving conflict.

If both modernization and development are seen as a struggle to "catch up with the West," the twin processes carry considerable risks of imitation and dependency for the Third World. That is, imitation may engender vulnerability to continued manipulation by Western economic and political interests.

While we have chosen the computer as an example of technology with tremendous potential benefits to Africa, we see the computer in a broader sense

213

as representative of information technology that has consequences for modernization and dependency. The computer in the Third World has to be seen in this wider context. In using the computer, is Africa enhancing its capacity for development? Is it facilitating the modernization of management, planning, analysis and administration? Or is Africa instead adopting a technology that is inappropriate to its current needs, expensive in relation to other priorities, detrimental to job creation, and vulnerable to external exploitation?

The answers to these questions are mixed. We see great potential for the computer to play a larger role in Africa; however, the current development status of many nations there leads us to conclude that the haphazard introduction of the computer can be the source of many ills suggested by our final question, particularly as the world has moved toward a more globalized economy.

Framing the Debate

The debate has been underway in parts of Africa for decades now. Indeed, as early as 1976 the leading intellectual weekly journal in East Africa, *The Weekly Review*, carried an article that tried to balance the then present costs of computers to a country such as Kenya with the potentialities and presumed benefits in the days ahead. Although computers have probably adversely affected Kenya's economy in the fields of job creation and outflow of foreign exchange, it is obvious that their potential has not been exploited to the fullest extent for the benefit of society.

But even this relatively guarded statement was soon taken up by another writer as being excessively optimistic about the utility of computers for a country such as Kenya:

> One understands . . . that over 100 such [mini] machines have been bought in Kenya: fifty million shillings [shs.] for the mini-computers alone. Add to this the cost of the 40 or 50 larger computers, and one must reach a figure of at least Shs. 100 million. Much of the greater part of the work done by these machines could be carried out by human beings. There are large numbers of adequately educated people who with a little instruction could do most of this work, and to whom a job at over a thousand shillings a month is a dream. Think how many of these could be employed with a fraction of Shs. 100,000,000![2]

The debate has not changed over two decades. Put another way:

> Scarce foreign currency has been spent on equipment which is not used. The dependency on multinational corporations and expatriate

personnel has increased, and sociocultural conflicts introduced. Moreover, what Africa has experienced for the most part so far is not IT [information technology] transfer but transplantation, the dumping of boxes without the necessary know-how . . . (Odedra et al. 1993, 26)

Stripped of the rhetoric, the authors' analyses charge that computers are, first, a waste of scarce resources; secondly, it aggravates balance-of-payments problems; and thirdly, it is detrimental to the struggle to reduce unemployment and underemployment.

The first author carries the attack further. He sees the type of technology symbolized by the computer as one that perpetuates the neglect of the countryside, versus the city, while aggravating the status of African countries themselves as peripheral appendages to developed industrial states. Inappropriate technology, when introduced into a Third World country, both maintains the peripheral, rural status of the country as a whole in its dependent relationship with the northern metropolis, and deepens the neglect of the domestic countryside as against the new urban "civilization." There is indeed a case against the computer when it attempts to invade an economically poor and technologically underdeveloped country. In its most compelling form, that case centers around the problem of Third World, and particularly African, dependency, which means that the computer, and information technology in general, must once again be examined in relation to those wider processes mentioned earlier: modernization, development and alien penetration. But these in turn have to be redefined if Africa is not to be misled into the dark alleyways of technological robbery.

Development in the Third World

We define development in the Third World to mean modernization minus dependency. In this sense, we expand the traditional concept "development" from one of a strictly internal process, to one with an international dimension. Conceptually, the internationalization of development has been hastened along within the process of globalization, with significant consequences for Africa and the rest of the Third World. Information technology exerts tremendous influence over the globalization process, and in turn over the patterns of winners and losers that globalization can induce (James 1999, 2). Indeed, some of the gaps between the West and the Third World must be narrowed—but this narrowing must include the gap in sheer power. To narrow the gap in, say, per capita income in a manner that widens the gap in power is to pursue affluence at the expense of autonomy. To narrow the gap in the use of computers while increasing Western technological control over the Third World is to prefer gadgetry to independence. The chasm between North and South cannot be filled with the latest technological fads that produce a sensation of matching the North American device for device while increasing the reliance on North America for those products. The implications of this differentiation are wide-reaching.

Somehow each African society must strike a balance between the pursuit of modernization and the pursuit of self-reliance. Some African countries have and will continue to promote one of these goals more successfully than the other. It may well be that Tanzania under Julius Nyerere, for example, realized greater self-reliance than modernization in the first thirty years of independence (1961–1991). However, Tanzania is still falling short of an adequate developmental balance. Alternatively, Kenya arguably achieved greater success in promoting modernization than in realizing self-reliance. Yet Kenya, too, currently falls short of genuine development. In other words, just as self-reliance on its own can never give Tanzania development, neither can modern techniques on their own give Kenya an adequate progressive thrust. The formula for development in Africa is both modernization and decolonization.

But what is modernization? And how do the two processes relate to the technology symbolized by the computer? For our purposes in this chapter, the three most important aspects of modernization are

- secularization, or a shifting balance in the science of explanation and in the ethic of behavior away from the supernatural to the temporal;
- technicalization, or a shifting balance in technique from custom and intuition to innovation and measurement;
- future-orientation, or a shifting balance between a preoccupation with ancestry and tradition to a concern for anticipation and planning.

With respect to these three processes, the role of the computer is to some extent related to the role of transnational corporations generally. But here an important distinction needs to be drawn between the technology of production and the technology of information. The technology of production ranges from the manufacture of shoes to the processing of petroleum. Most transnational corporations are primarily involved in the technology of production. The technology of information, however, ranges from radio and television to computers and the Internet. If modernization consists of the three subprocesses of secularization, technicalization, and future-orientation, then the two technologies of production and information relate differently to each.

Historically in Africa it was transnational corporations concerned with the technology of production that helped to facilitate the process of secularization. But it may well be those transnational corporations that have specialized in the technology of information that have gone furthest in promoting the third aspect of modernization—that is, future—orientation. Here radio, television, and computers are involved. Between these two—secularization and future-orientation—lies the intermediate subprocess of technicalization as part of the modernizing process. Technicalization involves both production as well as information technologies. And transnational corporations become intimately involved in these aspects of modernization, with all the risks of dependency.

Modernization: Secularization and the Transnationals

Positive contributions of Western firms to the process of secularization in the Third World include their role in the two subprocesses—secularization of education, in the sense of reducing a religious focus, and practicalization of education, in the sense of promoting greater relevance to concrete social needs. In most societies, education was initially closely connected to religion. This process was no different in Africa, especially with the introduction of colonial rule. In Africa during the European colonial period, Christian missionaries took the lead in establishing schools. Education and salvation were closely allied under the imperial umbrella. But when transnationals arrived, education was pushed in a different direction. The impact of transnationals on colonial schools was in the direction of both reducing schools' focus on religion (secularization), and increasing their interest in teaching practical skills (practicalization). More specifically, multinationals contributed to these two trends in the following ways:

- They helped to create a labor market in which practical skills were needed.
- They operated like a secular lobby, influencing colonial policymakers, and counterbalancing the influence of the missionaries.
- They demonstrated the impact of some of their own training programs, especially those designed to educate lower-level workers.
- They promoted a "consumer culture" in the colonies, one that characteristically emphasizes materialist tastes as opposed to religious preoccupations.
- They fostered urbanization and general labor migration.

As a result, tensions between economic forces and the missionaries in the colonial territories were sometimes inevitable. Those colonies that had extractive (mining) industries experienced special types of tensions. There were times when the missionaries favored alternative forms of practical-orientation in education, especially the development of those skills that would help to keep young Africans in their own villages. From the missionaries' point of view, it seemed that the African who remained in his farming community was more likely to remain faithful to spiritual values than the migrant in search of work with multinational mining industries.

The transnationals have indeed substantially contributed to industrialization and commercialization; in the process they have also contributed to the secularization of education and to the trend toward giving education a greater practical component. But the precise nature of the industrialization and commercialization has itself distorted certain directions of both cultural and educational change. The need for a new adjustment is becoming more urgent.

Modernization: Technicalization and Technology Transfer

At the center of that part of modernization that technicalizes society is the process of technological transfer. Again, transnational firms have in fact become the major media of technology transfer outside the military field. The transfer takes place mainly in four forms. The technology is embodied in, first, physical goods and equipment; secondly, skilled labor; thirdly, know-how that is legally recognized in patents and trademarks; and fourthly, knowledge that is either not patented or not patentable. Computers are themselves physical goods needing skilled labor, embodying knowledge and designed to generate further knowledge.

Helleiner (1975) sees a consensus emerging among analysts and some planners that the unpatentable know-how with respect to most forms of technology is of greater significance than the patented knowledge:

> Technology payments in licensing and collaboration agreements in which patent rights are not involved typically exceed those in agreements in which they are. Knowledge embodied in the patent is, in any case, normally insufficient by itself to permit its efficient working. [As Harry G. Johnson has put it], "In contemporary conditions, public tolerance and legal protection of commercial secrecy has become more important than the patent system."[3]

Helleiner regards the effect of patents on technology as being restrictive, but a good deal depends upon the options available in a given situation. There are certainly occasions when commercial secrecy is an inescapable de facto alternative to patented knowledge—and the secrecy can be a worse constraint on technology transfer than the patent. But as technology has advanced in the information age, so too have the institutional structures needed to protect it. Globalization, fueled by information technology, has brought the issue of intellectual property rights protection to the center of international trade and investment decisions.

With the establishment of the controversial World Trade Organization, uniform standards for the minimal protection of intellectual property rights were established for all member countries. The idea behind such protection was to protect innovation from illicit duplication by those seeking a quick profit. But in doing so, the door has been left open to widening the chasm between the "knowledge-rich" countries and the "knowledge-poor" countries. Some have even decried the enforcement of intellectual property rights as "Western-style imperialism" (Hamilton 1997, 257). While this is debatable, it does raise an important question of access to technology and the ability of Third World countries to provide basic services to their people.[4] But where the knowledge is indeed made available for local use, an educational process may be under way.

Another substantial part of the debate about technology transfer has concerned the issue of appropriateness. And within this issue, the distinction between labor-intensive and capital-intensive technology has loomed large. Computers are once again a good illustration of that debate. The bias in technology transfer by transnationals has generally been towards capital intensity. There have been a number of reasons for this bias. Helleiner has drawn our attention to the following, with special reference to the technology of production:

- Transnational firms have access to relatively cheap capital.
- Unskilled labor is frequently of very low productivity. The wage rate may seem low, "but it is not cheap in terms of efficiency wages."
- The heavy protection, which the transnationals enjoy, reduces the incentive to change to the really efficient labor-intensive techniques.
- The transnational firms have tended to operate in industries (e.g., minerals processing) in which technology is both capital-intensive and fixed.
- In the manufacturing sector their products—originally designed for richer markets—are standardized and subjected to strict quality control. These controls over standards "imply relatively capital-intensive and inflexible techniques of production for these particular products, although it might have been possible to meet consumer demand for the same basic characteristics through the provision of an alternative product with a more appropriate production technology and/or more flexible quality controls."
- Labor-intensive technologies tend to be associated with smaller scale production—whereas the multinationals have, on the whole, preferred to produce on a large scale.
- Shortages of skills in less-developed countries make capital a more efficient functional alternative.
- Labor relations in less-developed countries are at least as uncertain as in the developed states. Labor-intensive techniques increase the risks of disruptions and interruptions.

- Capital-intensive techniques sometimes provide better insurance against unexpected fluctuations in demand than do labor-intensive ones.
- Governments and private purchasers of technology in less-developed countries often prefer "the latest" in technological development as conferring a status of modernity, even if the latest technique is less appropriate for the particular developing country than an older method or older model of equipment. (Helleiner 1975, 169–171).

From the transnational's point of view, what we should keep in mind is that capital-intensive techniques also tend to be skill-intensive. Initially, the skilled personnel are imported into the developing country from outside, sometimes in response to demands for "streamlining" that are generated by computer vendors. The quest for this streamlining in administration can succeed in reducing inefficiency, but this is sometimes in exchange for increasing the importation of skilled manpower.

In such enterprises, which are capital-intensive, and in which the technology is complex, the training required for the indigenization of personnel may be substantial. This has implications for the whole problem of the brain drain, especially in situations where a country first adopts capital intensity and then shifts from capital-intensive to labor-intensive techniques. Both India and Gamal Abdel Nasser's Egypt had personnel who were well-trained for certain highly technical roles and who then left their own countries when those skilled roles were no longer adequately used at home. A relatively sudden contraction of skill-intensive roles in the country—either because of the consequences of a change in ideology or a change in techniques of management—may result in the transfer of technology in the reverse direction as well-trained engineers, technicians, and accountants from the Third World seek the kind of employment in the industrial countries that is more appropriate to their new skills:

> As soon as it is granted that some technology is embodied in human capital, and that it can therefore be transferred internationally through the movement of engineers, scientists and managers, it follows that the "brain drain" can also be viewed as part of the international technology transfer question. While it is quite customary to consider the role of the multinational firms in transferring technology through human capital from rich countries to poor, it has been less usual, though no less logical, to analyze their role in transferring it in the reverse direction. Their employment of indigenous talent for the pursuit of their own particular interests may deflect it from more socially profitable research and development activity, even if it does not physically leave the country. (Helleiner 1975, 165)

One of the worst damages inflicted on the African people by both slavery and colonialism is the undermining of their capacity to help themselves economically and technologically. Colonialism did build schools and universities in Africa, but these institutions often produced skills of dependency rather than of self-reliance. The group of seven or eight industrial nations have embarked on a program of helping poorer countries to "digitize" themselves. But for the time being, there is at least as much skill-transfer from Africa to the West as there is from the West to Africa.

Nigerian analysts have started examining their country's skill-transfer to countries like the United States. The best-educated ethnic group in the United States, according to the U.S. Census Bureau, is the population of Nigerians living in the United States. It is estimated that 64 percent of Nigerians over the age of eighteen living in the United States have one or more university degrees. When you compare the Nigerian presence in the United States in the year 2001 with what it was when Nnamdi Azikiwe, the first president of Nigeria, came to the United States in the 1920s, the contrast is stark. As the end of the twentieth century approached, the number of Nigerians in the United States had risen by a quarter of a million (Otutola 2000).

Philip Emeagwali, a computer analyst from Lagos, Nigeria, may have been overstating the case, but even his hyperbole is at least worth considering. Emeagwali says "One in three African university graduates live and work outside Africa. In effect, we are operating one third of African universities to satisfy the manpower needs of Western nations. One third of [the] African education budget is a supplement for the American education budget. In effect, Africa is giving developmental assistance to the United States" (Emeagwali 2000). Yes, there is indeed a skill transfer, but it seems to be going in the wrong direction. Former victims are paying knowledge-reparations to their former victimizers. While this has been happening, what technology is received from the West can be of further benefit than the receipt of the technology.

There are occasions when the training and education imparted go beyond the particular job with a computer and could make the recipient an innovator in his own right. In the words of Baranson

> more important than the imparting of technical knowledge and manufacturing capabilities is the ability and willingness to implant indigenous engineering and design capability for continued technological transformation. (Baranson 1970, 362)

This is what Boulding would presumably describe as "knowledge which has the capacity of generating more knowledge in a single head" (Boulding 1966, 3).[5]

Where the training transmitted in engineering or computer science promotes such self-generating knowledge in a single head, it could indeed contribute to the innovative capacity of a particular sector of a developing economy. But what should continue to be borne in mind is that such a level of knowledge may as likely be diverted toward the brain drain. This particular dilemma of skill-intensity continues to pose problems for the policymaker. Does it therefore provide an additional argument for shifting from mechanized efficiency to labor-intensive techniques that require lower levels of expertise? As indicated earlier, labor-intensive techniques that follow a period of sustained capital intensity could in any case worsen the brain drain by aggravating the problem of skilled redundancy following the shift.

Under the technology of production, a distinction does need to be made between modifying factor proportions in an industry already established and selecting new industries or new products on the basis of their being more labor-intensive. Whether labor can be substituted for capital in a particular manufacturing process depends substantially on the product:

> In continuous process industries (chemicals, pharmaceuticals, metal refining, oil refining) and in the production of many consumers' goods and intermediate goods on an assembly line the scope for such substitution is quite limited, except in certain ancillary operations, particularly materials handling and packaging. The main types of activity in which gain (measured in terms of social costs) may be achieved by the substitution of labor for capital are in road-building, irrigation, housing and construction generally and in the production of woven fabrics, clothing, woodworking, leather, some foodstuffs (including foodstuffs for local consumption in local areas), bricks, tiles, and some of the simpler metal products. (Collings 1972, 13)

The level of training needed for the second category of employment is usually less complex than for the first category. Moreover, the less complex skills lend themselves better to in-service or in-plant training than the advanced technical skills. This is a gain if one agrees with the United Nations Economic Commission for Africa that "in-plant training is more effective than formal technical training in an academic atmosphere" (Collings 1972, 19). There are times when an existing industry that is capital-intensive can be scaled down and in the process made more labor-intensive, or research could be undertaken to develop unconventional indigenous raw materials. The development or use of new raw materials could itself create new skills in the society. The scaling down of an industry to adjust to the smallness of the market may alter factor-proportions in favor of labor.

One example of scaling down was the plant once specially designed by Philips N.V. of the Netherlands for the assembly of radios in certain less-developed countries:

The main object of this design was to develop a low cost production unit for smaller volume of output than is typical in Europe; in the process the unit also turned out to be somewhat more labor-intensive. The firm also developed simpler types of equipment which can more readily be repaired or replaced from local stocks. (Collings 1972, 15)

From an educational point of view, the following propositions have therefore emerged from this analysis so far:

- Capital-intensive technological processes tend to be skill-intensive. The computer is a preeminent example.
- The education required for capital-intensive projects is likely to be at least partly formal, acquired in an academic atmosphere.
- Individuals trained for capital-intensive projects is subject to the temptations of the brain drain, in part because the technical skills involved have a market in the advanced economies.
- Labor-intensive processes lend themselves more easily to informal training and education, in-service or in-plant.
- Labor-intensive processes, almost by definition, spread skills more widely in the society and help to democratize education by broadening its distribution.

To the extent that computers have had a bias in favor of capital-intensity, they have been a constraint on educational democratization. The skill-intensity required will tend to aggravate the elitist tendencies inherited from the patterns of education under colonial rule.

Modernization: The Science of Anticipation and the Computer

The third aspect of modernization relevant to this analysis is, as we indicated, a reorientation toward the future and away from excessive deference to the past and to ancestral ways. Sensitivity to the future includes an interest in identifying trends, both positive and negative. Positive trends may need to be facilitated, and negative ones arrested. A science of anticipation, therefore, must be developed. The ability to harness information for future planning is critical in this regard.

A major obstacle to efficient planning in a new state may well be the very fact that the country is still undermodernized. Planning needs data on which to base estimates. Yet even basic data such as census figures are notoriously unreliable or imprecise in most new states. Planning under modern conditions needs the help of the technology of information, including the computer. Such a technology requires expertise, and African states have a dearth of this expertise.

Reliance on foreign experts has serious inadequacies and sometimes hazards for the host country (Odedra et al. 1993, 26). Planning needs a certain local competence in implementation. The administrators, as well as their political superiors, have yet to accumulate adequate experience for the tasks that planning might impose upon them. But planning works best in an already developed economic system with reliable data, efficient managerial expertise, and general technical and technological competence. An undermodernized society may well need planning most, but precisely because it is undermodernized it has a low planning capability.

Can the computer help? As a major instrument of the technology of information, can it improve the databasis of African planning? Can it facilitate that aspect of modernization that is concerned with the future? Strictly speaking, data for African planning cannot be processed by a computer unless those data exist in the first place. The problem of planning without adequate data will not be solved simply by installing additional computers in Mali, Zambia, or the Congo.

There is little doubt that the computer can assist in the data problem in other ways. Analyzing the information that exists can itself yield further information to the planner. Data analysis typically yields inferences, conclusions, and findings. Such analyses, in turn, augment the body of knowledge available. Two pieces of information analyzed in relation to each other often result in additional pieces of information. Processing data is frequently an exercise in augmenting knowledge. It seems reasonable, therefore, to suggest that the computer should be conscripted in the war against poverty, ignorance, and disease in African countries. The computer's role as a storage system of information can also be critical for the African planner. Data can be retrieved at relevant moments for measured and well-defined purposes. The computer could facilitate efficient consultation of existing information as well as efficient processing and analysis of what is newly obtained. A computer might also aid that aspect of modernization that is concerned with identifying trends, both positive and negative. The computer may thus strengthen the science of anticipation.

But the computer's evolution, particularly in the developed countries, also makes it a valuable tool in the production and transmission of information. No longer are computers relegated to the simple tasks of processing existing information. Instead, computers have become a primary instrument in producing, controlling, managing, and disseminating information. The centrality of the computer now makes it an even more attractive planning instrument than in its early days, a fact that is not overlooked by developing nations.

But a basic question arises, Does the computer help planning while simultaneously harming development? Is the science of drawing up a rational and well-informed blueprint of planning strengthened by the computer, but at the cost of the actual substance of development? There is certainly evidence to support this paradox. Because of a number of factors, most computers in Africa are unavoidably and grossly underused. Spending a large amount of foreign exchange to buy a single piece of expensive equipment is one cost. Incapacity to use that piece of equipment adequately is an additional one. It implies waste in a situation of scarce resources. As Hayman (1993) points out, there are numerous cases of large sums of money spent on computers and related systems without attention to issues of compatibility, rendering unsatisfactory results. Yet the incapacity to use computers fully is due to wider problems of underdevelopment that probably need to be solved *before* proficiency in using computers attains adequate levels.

One example where the underdevelopment issue has become more relevant in recent years has been in the area of telecommunications and computer technology. The UN's International Telecommunications Union reported in 1998 that approximately one-quarter of the world's population live in countries with insufficient basic telephone service. Sixty-two percent of all telephone lines are installed in just twenty-three industrialized countries, which also have only 15 percent of the world's population. As developed countries continue to push computers as a major tool in communications, the basic format by which computers communicate—telephone lines—is insufficient to realize the computer's full potential. While computers either by themselves or centralized can be useful, the inability of computers to communicate decreases their potential effectiveness.

Beyond the single issue of the telecommunications and computer, the relationship between these two technologies illustrates a more widespread issue in Africa: the lack of a proper infrastructure. A major factor in Africans' inability to fully utilize information technology is the lack of an adequate infrastructure. Reliable sources of energy, telecommunications infrastructure, and regulatory and procedural policies are all needed, in both rural and urban areas, in order to take full advantage of the benefits that the computer and information technology in general can bring (Lall et al. 1994, 193; Mansell and Wehn 1998, 25–31; Metzl 1996, 716–717; Ngwainmbi 1995, 3; Odedra et al. 1993, 26). In this sense, the underdevelopment of basic, reliable infrastructure services places developing countries in the position of putting the cart before the horse, buying computers before they have the capacity to use them efficiently and sufficiently.

Related to this problem is the whole issue of high vulnerability to exploitation in an industry of high technical know-how. The relatively nontechnical buyer is often at the mercy of the highly specialized salesman (Odedra et al. 1993, 26–27). Discussing the Kenya situation, Ouma observed;

More often than not, the idea of installing a computer originates from computer manufacturers, who are intent on increasing their sales, rather than from company executives. This has meant that feasibility studies on the equipment which are put before firms' boards are more often than not prepared by the computer salesmen themselves. The firms' executives probably do not understand technical computer jargon, leave alone have the ability to translate it into everyday language. [The resulting] excess capacity in expensive equipment can have serious consequences on the economy of a developing country (Ouma 1976, 23).

This vulnerability to exploitation has a number of antidevelopmental consequences. The foreign exchange is depleted not only with the purchase of the equipment but also with the continuing costs of its use and maintenance. The expatriate specialists who are imported command high salaries, large portions of which are paid in hard currency. It is true that developing countries need to import certain types of skilled manpower for a while. But are computer specialists the most relevant expatriate engineers needed for the time being?

Also antidevelopmental in its implications is the economic stratification that takes place between expatriates and locals. In the case of computer specialists, this stratification can be particularly glaring. The employers in a developing country are faced with interrelated dilemmas. On the one hand, if the local specialist earns much less than the expatriate for the same job, the foreigner appears privileged and the citizen seems to be a victim of discrimination. On the other hand, if the local's pay is raised to something approximating what the foreigner earns, a new form of stratification is formed among the local people themselves. Again, if the local computer specialist is paid a much lower salary than her expatriate counterpart, a morale problem is created. As a result, the local may leave to seek a "less discriminatory" appointment elsewhere in another field. The expatriate preponderance in skilled computer jobs thus becomes aggravated. Then, if scales for locals are based on international rates, and this attracts better local intellects to such jobs, would this genuinely stabilize the Africanization of personnel? Or would it increase the international mobility of the African personnel—and potentially contribute to the brain drain?

Some of these dilemmas are more real than others. What is clear is that a certain number of antidevelopmental cleavages open up as computers enter technologically underdeveloped societies. As Ouma puts it with regard to some of these dilemmas of personnel in Kenya;

Expatriates installed the first systems, often with the understanding that they would train local people to take over. But two things happened. First, because most users were government or quasi-government bodies, there was an attempt to fix salary scales for local computer personnel on a level with the then existing salary scales without regard to world scales. While paying expatriate personnel more or less what they asked for, computer users did not seek any independent advice on the remuneration of local computer personnel. The result has been that a local programmer is often paid half the salary of a less qualified expatriate programmer, to take an example of imbalance in the salary structure prevalent in the industry (Ouma 1976, 25).

Ouma describes the effect as "disastrous." The very low salaries paid to local staff have failed either to attract or to retain "the right calibre of local people" in the computer industry. One consequence is that "while most of the junior posts—junior programmers, operators and key-punch operators—are held by Africans, there are very few senior local people in the industry" (Ouma 1976, 25).

Another antidevelopmental consequence of the computer takes us to another dilemma. Does the computer in Africa have real, "automatic" consequences? Does it reduce significantly the number of employees needed for specific tasks? If so, the computer complicates the problem of job creation, as we indicated earlier.

Wallace refers to evidence obtained in interviews in Nigeria and Uganda, which suggests that computers there have no employment impact. But if there is no automatic result, is the computer in such nations a case of wasteful duplication? In the words of Wallace;

Computers are used in these developing countries almost exclusively on tasks for which clerical workers are the next best substitute. If, as the interviewees claimed, there is no employment impact, it is likely that computers are duplicating rather than substituting for clerical resources and that the countries are paying foreign exchange for no benefit, at least in the short run. (Wallace 1977, 13)

Little has changed over twenty years, with computers relegated to routine data-processing rather than to better decision making (Odedra et al. 1993, 26).

Another antidevelopmental consequence of the computer overlaps with some of the other considerations mentioned before. The computer does aggravate structures of technological dependency between developing countries and the industrial states that produce them. Considering the continent as a whole, in 1972 there were an estimated 1,000 computers in Africa. Half of these were in the Republic of South Africa. Obudho and Taylor (1977) relate this estimate to the original arrival of the computer in Africa in the late 1950s. African independence has indeed witnessed speedy computerization, but the absolute number is still modest. Obudho and Taylor's estimate for 1975 was 1,200 computers in Africa. On the other hand, by 1972 the campuses of the University of California alone were using over 200 computers (Obudho and Taylor 1977; see also El-Hadi 1975 and Bussel 1972). The disparity between the developed and developing countries in terms of computers can also be seen in the most recent figures released by the World Bank. In 1995, high-income or developed countries possess about 201 computers for every one thousand people while that figure for low- and middle-income countries or developing countries dropped to approximately 6 computers for every one thousand people.

Although the speed of computerization is modest in absolute terms, and countries such as Tanzania have even attempted decomputerization, the new culture that is coming to Africa with computers cannot but strengthen or aggravate technological dependency. The science of anticipation still has its most elaborate expertise outside Africa. The initial phases of the computerization of Africa carry the risk of a new form of colonialism. Africa could be duly "programmed." The "machine man's burden" looms ominously on the horizon as a new technological crusade to modernize Africa.

The arrival of the computer may well be contributing to modernization, but it is also adding dependency. The computer is probably helping to make planning more efficient, but is simultaneously making development more difficult. The science of anticipation is, for the time being, caught up in the contradictions of premature technological change.

Toward Decolonizing Modernity

If development in the Third World equals modernization, minus dependency, and decolonization, how can the contradictions of premature technological change be resolved, and in what way does the computer illustrate these wider issues? Our answer to this lies in the process of decolonization and in the careful use of the computer in this process.

The process of decolonization involves five subprocesses: (1) indigenization, (2) domestication, (3) diversification, (4) horizontal inter-penetration, and (5) vertical counterpenetration. The strategy of indigenization involves increasing the use of indigenous resources, ranging from native personnel to aspects of traditional local technology. But in applying this to the computer we have to relate it to the strategy of domestication as well. While indigenization means using local resources and making them more relevant to the modern age, domestication involves making imported versions of modernity more relevant to the local society. For example, the English language in East Africa is an alien medium. To domesticate it is to make it respond to local imagery, figures of speech, sound patterns, and to the general cultural milieu of the region. The promotion of Swahili as against English in Tanzania is, alternatively, a process of indigenization. It involves promoting a local linguistic resource, rather than making an alien resource more locally relevant.

With regard to Western institutions in Africa, domestication is the process by which they are, in part, Africanized or traditionalized in local terms. But with local institutions, the task is partly to modernize them. Thus English in East Africa needs to be Africanized, while Swahili needs to be modernized in the sense of enabling it to cope with modern life and modern knowledge.

Clearly the two strategies of domestication and indigenization are closely related and are sometimes impossible to disentangle. This is particularly so when we apply these strategies of decolonization to computers. The computer is of course more like the English language in Africa than like Swahili. The computer is a piece of alien culture. Can it be domesticated?

We believe it can, but the introduction or expansion of this piece of technology in an African country must be much more carefully planned than it has been so far. The domestication of the computer would first and foremost require a substantial indigenization of personnel. This would necessitate, first, greater commitment by African governments to promote relevant training at different levels for Africans; second, readiness on the part of both governments and employers to create a structure of incentives that would attract Africans of the right caliber; third, greater political pressure on computer suppliers to facilitate training and to cooperate in related tasks; and fourth, stricter control by African governments of the foreign exchange allowed for the importation of computers.

The indigenization of high-level personnel in the local computer industry should in time help to indigenize the uses to which the computer is put and the tasks that are assigned to it. When the most skilled roles in the computer industry in an African country are in the hands of Africans themselves, new types of problems will in turn be put to computers. The cultural and political milieu of the new personnel should affect and perhaps modify problem-definition. This Africanization of computer personnel should also facilitate, over time, the further Africanization of the users of computer services. What should be borne in mind is that the efficient indigenization and domestication of the computer requires a gradual and planned approach.

The difficulty of this task is compounded, particularly in recent years, as Africa braces for its second partition by transnational corporations and their respective governments. The move to conquer the world's last great untapped consumer market in Africa has brought concerted efforts to modernize Africa. One such effort is on the part of the United States Agency for International Development's (USAID) Leland Initiative. The goal of the initiative is to bring full Internet connectivity to approximately twenty African countries over a five-year period in order to promote sustainable development (USAID Bureau for Africa 1998).

The trend toward greater computer technological sophistication in the underdeveloped countries of Africa carries the risk of a commercial colonization of the continent. The evolution of the computer industry has led to increasingly rapid change in computer technology. As these changes occur, the chance to domesticate and indigenize the new technology may dissipate, given that many African countries will find it difficult to keep pace technologically and economically. The rapid pace of technological change will make a gradualist and planned approach to domestication and indigenization of the computer in Africa a difficult task. The resources needed to sustain these new technologies may promote additional problems. As technology levels increase in these countries, the dependence of these countries on transnational corporations may likewise increase in order to maintain them.

Diversification, at the broader level of society, means the diversification of production, sources of expertise, techniques of analysis, types of goods produced, markets for these products, and general trading partners, aid donors, and other benefactors. This approach—though often inefficient—should help an African country to diversify with respect to its dependence on other countries. Excessive reliance on only one country is more dangerous for a weak state than reliance on half a dozen countries.

But even if an African country has to deal primarily with the West when it comes to computers, it makes sense to exploit competitive tendencies between Western corporations. What this implies is a trade-off between African countries and transnational corporations: access to large consumer markets in Africa could be contingent upon the transfer of knowledge and diversification of the transnational's workforce. The result of such cooperation would yield a greater diversification in production techniques and skills for Africans, leading to some self-sufficiency while also diversifying their nations' external dependence. Just as international business monopolies once facilitated Western imperialism, so too could international business facilitate decolonization, if the victims of imperialism can learn how to exploit the opportunities presented to them.

At least as important an element in the strategy of diversification is to find the right balance between the older manual techniques and the new computer techniques. Computerization should not be allowed to proceed too fast. Wherever possible, manual alternatives should consciously be encouraged alongside computers. Yet it would be wasteful if the computer only duplicated manual clerical work, for example. Between the hypothetical extremity of complete mechanization and the wasteful extremity of complete duplication there must lie a more viable diversified mixture of functions.

The computer is underutilized in Africa, not merely in terms of capacity or in terms of hours per day, but also in terms of the range of tasks assigned to it. Even in economic planning the computer in Africa is still greatly underutilized. We argued in the previous section that the computer can help planning, while simultaneously harming development. If the computers have already been purchased, and are being used in ways that already harm development, should they not at least be made to perform their more positive functions in planning as well? Once again, diversification of usage—if handled with care— could extract certain benefits from the computer, while sustaining its developmental costs.

The next strategy of decolonization is horizontal interpenetration among Third World countries. In the field of trade this could mean promoting greater exchange among African countries themselves. In the field of investment it could, for example, mean allowing Arab or Malaysian money to compete with Western and Japanese money in establishing new industries or promoting new projects in Africa. In the field of aid it must also mean that oil-rich Third World countries should increase their contribution towards the economic and social development of their resource-poor sister countries. In the field of technical assistance, it might mean that Third World countries with an apparent excess of skilled manpower in relation to their absorption capacity should not only be prepared, but also be encouraged, to facilitate temporary or permanent migration to other Third World countries. This last process is what might be called the horizontal brain drain—the transfer of skilled manpower from, say, Egypt to Abu Dhabi, United Arab Emirates, or from the Indian subcontinent to Nigeria.

In the field of computers, skill transfers among Third World countries are particularly promising in the short run as part of the process of decolonization. If an African country wants a computer, for now it has to buy it from Europe, North America, or from a small number of Asian countries. But an African country does not have to import highly skilled computer personnel from those same industrialized states. As part of horizontal interpenetration, Third World countries must learn to poach on each other's skilled manpower, at least as a short-term strategy. President Idi Amin of Uganda learned after awhile to distinguish between Indians with strong economic and historic roots in Uganda and Indians on contract for a specified period. He expelled almost all of those who had strong local roots—and then went to the Indian subcontinent to recruit skilled professional teachers, engineers and doctors on contract terms. The wholesale expulsion of Asians with roots was basically an irrational act. But the recruitment of skilled Indians on contract was sound. Today, African nations should turn increasingly to the Indian subcontinent, instead of to Western Europe, for some of their temporary needs for skilled personnel, including the need for computer personnel, pending adequate indigenization.

The final strategy of decolonization is that of vertical counterpenetration. It is not enough to facilitate greater interpenetration among Third World countries. It is not enough to contain or reduce penetration by northern industrialized states into southern underdeveloped economies. An additional strategy is needed, one that would increasingly enable southern countries to counter-penetrate the citadels of power in the north.

The Middle Eastern oil producers have already started the process of counterpenetrating Western Europe and North America. This vertical counter-penetration by the Middle East ranges from manipulating the money market in Western Europe to buying shares in West German industry, from purchasing banks and real estate in the United States to obtaining shares in other trans-national corporations. Even the southern capacity to impose clear political conditions on Western firms is a case of vertical counterpenetration. The Arabs' success in forcing many Western firms to stop trading with Israel if they wish to retain their Arab markets was a clear illustration of a southern market dictating certain conditions to northern transnational corporations instead of the older reverse flow of power.

The possibilities of southern counterpenetration into the computer industry are modest, given the decline of Organization of Petroleum Exporting Countries' (OPEC) financial power and the economic problems of Southeast Asia. Recent events in the oil markets have brought a semblance of life back to a once moribund OPEC. Whether an increase again in OPEC financial power could make any difference is, for the time being, hypothetical.

Another question is how far the African computer market, as it expands and acquires greater sophistication, would be able to exert greater counter-influence on the computer industry. This would depend at least in part upon the extent to which each domestic African market is internally organized and to what extent African countries using computers consult with each other and possibly with other Third World users on application of the computer and related issues. Obudho and Taylor (1977) tell us that there is greater aware-ness and organization on computer-related matters in Francophone Africa than in Anglophone Africa. Gabon, Madagascar, Côte d'Ivoire, Morocco, Algeria, and Burundi have all been experimenting with domestic institutions to coordi-nate information sciences. Such consultations on computer applications should still be encouraged as part of horizontal interpenetration among African systems of informatics. But the greater sophistication that will in time be acquired should increase the influence of the African market on the computer industry itself.

Yet another element in the strategy of counterpenetration is the northward brain drain itself. Third World countries generally cannot afford to lose their skilled manpower. But it would be a mistake to assume that the northward brain drain is completely disadvantageous to the south. Indian doctors in British hospitals are indeed recruited to some extent at the expense of the sick in India. But those emigrant Indian doctors are becoming an important sub-lobby in British society to increase British responsiveness to the health and nutritional needs of India itself. The American Jews who are not prepared to settle in Israel are not merely a case of depriving Israel of skills and possessions that they would have taken there. They also constitute a counterinfluence on the American system to balance the influence of the United States on the Israeli system. The presence of Irish Americans in the United States is indeed partly a case of agonizing economic disadvantage for the Irish Republic. But Irish Americans are also, conversely, an existing economic and political resource for the benefit of the Irish Republic and Catholics in Northern Ireland. This is also true of Greek Americans, Polish Canadians, and Algerians in France. Migration from one country to another is never purely a blessing nor purely a curse to either the donor country or the receiving country. The costs and benefits vary from case to case.

As more and more Africans become highly skilled in computer technology and usage, some of them will migrate to developed states. As matters now stand, the costs of this kind of brain drain are greater than the benefits for African countries. It is essential to understand that the intellectual penetration of the south by northern industrial states must one day be balanced with reverse intellectual penetration by the south of the think tanks of the north. Given the realities of an increasingly interdependent world, decolonization will never be complete unless penetration is reciprocal and more balanced. Part of the cost may well be the loss of highly skilled African computer workers.

Conclusion

We have attempted in this chapter to place the computer in the context of the much wider issues raised by it. In a technological sense, the computer is a piece of modernity. Its functions in a society have identifiable modernizing consequences. The computer helps to secularize the science of explanation, to technicalize analytical approaches to data, and to promote a capacity for estimating the future and planning for it.

But modernization is not development. In the northern industrialized states, development should now mean rationalization plus social justice. The rationalization should include a proper balance between social needs and ecological conditions, a proper relationship not only between the individual and society but also between society and nature. Resource depletion and ecological damage have to be moderated by an adequate sensitivity to the future. As a consequence of its waste and pollution, the West has revealed that it has not yet modernized enough in the sense of adequately responding to the future by making allowances for it. By falling short of standards of justice between classes, races, cultural subgroups, and sexes, the industrial states have not attained adequate standards of development either. But while development in the north equals rationalization plus social justice, development in the Third World must for the time being mean modernization minus dependency.

The computer in Africa probably helps to promote modernization, but it also aggravates Africa's technological and intellectual dependency on Western Europe and North America. The computer, were it used more efficiently, would greatly aid the process of African planning. But its consequences are anti-developmental in such tasks as job creation, reducing dependency, conservation of foreign exchange, definition of priorities as between town and country, and devising optimal salary structures for both locals and expatriates.

Africa cannot escape the computer age indefinitely. So long as the computer is an instrument for modernization, but not for development, can it be made to contribute to both processes? How is the dependency factor to be subtracted from modernization in order to give us a true effect on development?

We enumerated the five strategies of decolonization. The computer has to respond to the imperatives of indigenization, domestication, diversification, horizontal interpenetration among Third World countries, and vertical counterpenetration from the south into the sites of technological and economic power in the north.

But, in the final analysis, the computer is merely a symbol of much wider forces, ranging from technology transfer to job creation, from the impact of transnational corporations to the process of national planning, from race relations in South Africa or Uganda to the quest for an international economic justice.

When adequately domesticated and stripped of its colonial appendages, the computer in Africa could become a mediator between the ancestral world of collective wisdom and personal intuition on one side and the new world of quantified data and scientific analysis on the other. The sociology of knowledge is undergoing a change in Africa. And the computer is part of the process of change.

Notes

1. For background on modernization theory see Parson (1952) and Huntington (1968).

2. "Computers: Benefit or Detriment?" (1976, 25). Approximately eight Kenya shillings amount to one American dollar at the time of the article; today the exchange rate is approximately seventy-nine Kenya shillings to the dollar.

3. Helleiner (1975). We would like to thank Helleiner for simulation and bibliographical guidance on this point.

4. On this point, see Ostergard (1999a) for a discussion on the relationship between strong intellectual property rights protection and a nation's ability to provide for basic human needs. Additionally, see Ostergard (1999b) for a clear example of how international patent protection has been hindering attempts to curb the AIDS epidemic in South Africa.

5. It has also been pointed out that the introduction of technological knowledge is not enough to make a difference; entrepreneurs must have an active role in advancing the new technology; In some cases, the inventor and the entrepreneur are the same people, in other cases, they are different. But even the introduction of new technologies can spawn new ideas for different kinds of new businesses that have what economists call "effective demand" (Volti 1995, 35–45).

References

Baranson, Jack. 1970. Comment. to *The Technology Factor in International Trade*. Ed. Raymond Vernon, p. 362. New York: National Bureau of Economic Research.

Bartkelt, Vernon. 1953. *Struggle for Africa*. New York: Praeger.

Boulding, Kenneth E. 1966. "The Economics of Knowledge and the Knowledge of Economics." *American Economic Review* 56 (May): 1–13.

Bussel, C., ed. 1972. *Computer Education for Development*. Proceedings based on the Rio Symposium on Computer Education for Developing Countries, August, Guambara, Brazil.

Collings, Rex. 1972. *The Multinational Corporations in Africa*. New York: United Nations Economic Commission for Africa.

"Computers: Benefit or Detriment?" 1976. *Weekly Review* (Nairobi), 7 June.

Davis, Merle J. 1933. Modern Industry and the African, Report of Commission of Inquiry Set Up by the Department of Social and Industrial Research of International Missionary Council. New York: Macmillan, 1933.

de Vleeschauwer, M. A. 1943. "Belgian Colonial Policy." *Crown Colonist* 13 (August): 549.

El-Hadi, Mohamed M. 1975. The Status of Informatics in the African Administrative Environment, Doc. 75–1. Tangier: Center Africain de Formation et de Recherche Administratives pour de Dévelopment.

Emeagwali, Philip. 2000. "Why Nigerians Are Not Returning Home." *News* (Lagos).

Hamilton, Marci A. 1997. "The TRIPS Agreement: Imperialistic, Outdated and Overprotective." *Intellectual Property: Moral, Legal and International Dilemmas*. Ed. Adam D. Moore. Lanham, MD: Rowman & Littlefield Publishers.

Hayman, John 1993. "Bridging Higher Education's Technology Gap in Africa." *Technological Horizons in Education Journal*. 20, no. 6 (January 1993): 63–69.

Helleiner, G. K. 1975. "The Role of Multinational Corporations in the Less Developed Countries' Trade in Technology." *World Development* 3 (April): 161–190.

Huntington, Samuel P. 1968. *Political Order in Changing Societies*. New Haven: Yale University Press.

James, Jeffrey 1999. *Globalization, Information Technology and Development*. New York: St. Martin's.

Lall, Sanjaya, Giorgio Barba Navaretti, Simon Teitel, and Ganeshan Wgnaraja 1994. *Technology and Enterprise Development: Ghana under Structural Adjustment*. New York: St. Martin's.

Mansell, Robin and Uta When, eds. 1998. *Knowledge Societies: Information Technology for Sustainable Development*. For the United Nations Commission on Science and Technology for Development. Oxford: Oxford University Press.

Metzl, Jamie F. 1996. "Information Technology and Human Rights." *Human Rights Quarterly* 18, no. 4: 705–746.

Ngwainmbi, Emmanuel K. 1995. *Communication Efficiency and Rural Development in Africa: The Case of Cameroon*. Lanham: University Press of America.

Obudho, R. A. and D. R. F. Taylor, eds. 1977. *The Computer in Africa*. New York: Praeger.

Odedra, M., M. Lawrie, M. Bennet, and S. Goodman 1993. "Sub-Saharan Africa: A Technological Desert." Communication of the ACM. 36, no. 2: 25–29.

Ostergard, Robert L. 1999a. "The Political Economy of the South African-US Patent Conflict." *Journal of World Intellectual Property* 2, no. 4: 875–888.

Ostergard, Robert L. 1999b. "Intellectual Property Rights: A Universal Human Right?" *Human Rights Quarterly* 21, no. 1: 156–178.

Otutola, Banjo 2000. "Letters and Viewpoints: Atlanta Presidential Diaologue." *Nigerian World:* September.

Ouma, Hilary. 1976. "The Changing World of Computers in Kenya." *Weekly Review* (Nairobi), 17 May.

Parson, Talcott. 1952. *The Social System*. London: Lavistock Press. *Weekly Review* (Nairobi). 1976. 17 May.

United Nations Educational Scientific and Cultural Organization (UNESCO). 1959. *Chronicle* (Paris) 12 (December): 395.

United States Agency for International Development (USAID) Bureau for Africa. 1998. URL: http://www.info.usaid.gov/regions/afr/leland/project.htm.

Volti, Rudi 1995. *Society and Technological Change, 3rd ed*. New York: St. Martin's.

Wallace, John B. Jr. 1977. "Computer Use in Independent Africa: Problem and Solution Statements." *The Computer in Africa*. Eds. R. A. Obudho and D. R. F. Taylor, 13–41. New York: Praeger.

Contributors

Juliann Emmons Allison is Assistant Professor in Political Science at the University of California, Riverside, where she is Director of the department's Honors Program and teaches international political economy and environmental politics. She earned her Ph.D. in Political Science from the University of California, Los Angeles in 1995. Her central research projects employ a range of methods to describe and explain the process and outcomes of international negotiations, particularly those devoted to resolving disputes over the natural environment, the role of domestic political processes in shaping international cooperative arrangements, and women's contributions to the world's political economy. Her most recent work has appeared in *Flashpoints in Environmental Policymaking Controversies in Achieving Sustainability,* Sheldon Kamieniecki, George A. Gonzalez, and Robert O. Vos; Eds., *Policy Studies Journal, Shades of Green, Peace & Change*, and the *Journal of Conflict Resolution*.

Janni Aragon is currently writing a doctoral dissertation examining the second-wave feminist movement at the University of California, Riverside. Her ongoing research is in the area of feminist theory and women in politics.

Matthew A. Baum is Assistant Professor of Political Science and Communications at the University of California, Los Angeles. His research addresses the influence of the mass media and public opinion on foreign policy decision making. His most recent articles have appeared in the *American Political Science Review* and *Comparative Political Studies*.

David Johnson is pursuing his Ph.D. in International Relations and Comparative Politics at George Washington University. He holds MAs in Science, Technology, and Public Policy from George Washington University and in Mechanical Engineering from the University of Colorado, Boulder. He worked as an engineer on the F–16 *Fighting Falcon* fighter aircraft, the YF-22

Raptor stealth fighter prototype, the international Space Station, and the first Shuttle-*Mir* mission.

Christopher R. Kedzie, a distinguished graduate from the Air Force Academy who also earned graduate degrees form Massachussetts Intitute of Technology and Harvard University, is the Program Officer in the Ford Foundation's Moscow office concerned with Russian democratic reform. Earlier, as a researcher at RAND, he analyzed the effects of information revolution technologies in international affairs, particularly on global democratization. Before joining RAND, he lived overseas acquiring substantial field experience on the use of information and communication technologies to influence societal change. He is published widely in English, Russian, and Ukrainian on topics related to information technology to societies in transition.

Ali A. Mazrui D.Phil is Albert Schweitzer Professor in the Humanities and Director of the Institute of Global Cultural Studies, Binghamton University; Albert Luthuli Professor-at-Large, University of Jos, Jos, Nigeria; Ibn Khaldun Professor-at-Large, School of Islamic and Social Studies, Leesburg, Virginia; Andrew D. White Professor-at-Large Emeritus and Senior Scholar in Africana Studies, Cornell University; and Walter Rodney Professor, University of Guyana, Georgetown, Guyana. He is the author of the BBC/PBS television series, *The Africans: A Triple Heritage* (1986). Mazrui has also written over twenty books, including a novel, *The Trial of Christopher Okigbo, Cultural Forces in World Politics,* and, most recently with Alamin Mazrui, *The Power of Babel: Language and Governance in the African Experience.*

Robert L. Ostergard Jr. is a Postdoctoral Research Fellow and Visiting Lecturer at the Institute of Global Cultural Studies, Binghamton, New York. His articles have appeared in *Human Rights Quarterly* and in the *Journal of International Business Studies*. His recent dissertation, "The Making of a Regime: Intellectual Property Rights in the International System," is a detailed examination of the evolution of global intellectual property rights and their impact on national technical development and economic growth.

David L. Richards is Assistant Professor of Political Science at Missouri Southern State College. His research interests include political violence, democratic institutions, measurement, and globalization within the context of government respect for human rights. His most recent publications appear in the *Journal of Peace Research, International Studies Quarterly,* and *Social Science Quarterly*.

James N. Rosenau is University Professor of International Affairs at the George Washington University; he was previously on the faculties of Rutgers

University, Ohio State University, and the University of Southern California. He held a Guggenheim Foundation Fellowship (1987–1988) and is a former president of the International Studies Association (1984–1985). His most recent publications include *Turbulence in World Politics: A Theory of Change and Continuity, Along the Domestic-Foreign Frontier: Exploring Governance in a Turbulent World, Thinking Theory Thoroughly: Coherent Approaches to an Incoherent World,* and *Global Voices: Dialogues in International Relations.*

Cherie Steele is Assistant Professor of Political Science at the University of Vermont. A graduate of Harvard University, she received her Ph.D. from the University of California, Los Angeles.

Arthur Stein is Professor of Political Science at the University of California, Los Angeles. A graduate of Cornell University, he received his Ph.D. from Yale University. He is best known as the author of *The Nation at War* and *Why Nations Cooperate.*

Deborah Stienstra is Professor of Politics at the University of Winnipeg and is active in global women's campaigns. In addition to two books: *Women's Movements and International Organizations* and, with Barbara Roberts, *Strategies for the Year 2000: A Woman's Handbook,* she has published numerous articles on prostitution and international law, gender and social movements, and gender and foreign policy. She may also be credited with initiating the electronic mail list FEMISA, a discussion list exploring the links between gender and international politics, in 1993.

Frank Webster is Professor of Sociology and Head of the Department of Cultural Studies and Sociology at the University of Birmingham, Great Britain. Educated at the University of Durham and at the London School of Economics, he was Professor of Sociology, Oxford Brookes University from 1990 to 1998. He is the author and editor of several books, including: *The New Photography: Responsibility in Visual Communication,* with Kevin Robins, *Information Technology: A Luddite Analysis; The Technical Fix: Computers, Industry and Education; Theories of the Information Society,* with Anthony Smith; *The Postmodern University?* with Kevin Robins; *Times of the Technoculture: From the Information Society to the Virtual Life,* with Gary Browning; *Understanding Contemporary Societies: Theory and Society;* and *A New Politics? Politics and Culture in the Information Age,* with Abigail Halcli. He and Robins are currently collaborating on *The Virtual University?*

Index

SUNY series in Global Politics
James N. Rosenau, editor

List of Titles

American Patriotism in a Global Society—Betty Jean Craige

The Political Discourse of Anarchy: A Disciplinary History of International Relations—Brian C. Schmidt

From Pirates to Drug Lords: The Post—Cold War Caribbean Security Environment—Michael C. Desch, Jorge I. Dominquez, and Andres Serbin (eds.)

Collective Conflict Management and Changing World Politics—Joseph Lepgold and Thomas G. Weiss (eds.)

Zones of Peace in the Third World: South America and West Africa in Comparative Perspective—Arie M. Kacowicz

Private Authority and International Affairs—A. Claire Cutler, Virginia Haufler, and Tony Porter (eds.)

Harmonizing Europe: Nation-States within the Common Market—Francesco G. Duina

Economic Interdependence in Ukrainian-Russian Relations—Paul J. D'Anieri

Leapfrogging Development? The Political Economy of Telecommunications Restructuring—J. P. Singh

States, Firms, and Power: Successful Sanctions in United States Foreign Policy—George E. Shambaugh

Approaches to Global Governance Theory—Martin Hewson and Timothy J. Sinclair (eds.)

After Authority: War, Peace, and Global Politics in the Twenty-First Century—Ronnie D. Lipschutz

Pondering Postinternationalism: A Paradigm for the Twenty-First Century?—Heidi H. Hobbs (ed.)

Beyond Boundaries? Disciplines, Paradigms, and Theoretical Integration in International Studies—Rudra Sil and Eileen M. Doherty (eds.)

Why Movements Matter: The West German Peace Movement and U.S. Arms Control Policy—Steve Breyman